TIGER MEN

An Australian Soldier's
Secret War in Vietnam

TIGER
MEN

Barry Petersen
with John Cribbin

SIDGWICK & JACKSON

LONDON

First published in Great Britain in 1988 by Sidgwick & Jackson Ltd

Originally published in Australia in 1988 by
The Macmillan Company of Australia Pty Ltd
107 Moray Street, South Melbourne 3205
6 Clarke Street, Crows Nest 2065

ISBN 0 283 99816 4

Set in 11/13 pt. Sabon by Graphicraft Typesetters Ltd
Printed by The Book Printer, Victoria, Australia
for Sidgwick & Jackson Ltd
1 Tavistock Chambers, Bloomsbury Way
London WC1A 2SG

Contents

Acknowledgements

Grateful acknowledgements are due to Y-Jut Buon To, Colonel Le Van Thanh, Bevan Stokes and John Roy for their assistance in verifying much of the detail in this book.

I greatly appreciate the considerate attitude shown by General Hoang Phuong of the People's Army of Vietnam towards his former enemies and I am indebted to him for his remarks on the fighting qualities of the Australian soldier.

Thanks go to John Cribbin for his patient help in the reshaping of the original manuscript, and to Janet Bunny for her editorial assistance.

Foreword

by Lieutenant General Sir Thomas Daly, KBE, CB, DSO

Some twenty years ago, I invited a young man just returned from an extended tour of duty in Vietnam to share a pot of tea with me in my office at Victoria Barracks in Sydney. Having coaxed from him a somewhat reluctant account of his extraordinary experiences in the Vietnamese central highlands, I suggested that perhaps one day he should settle down to writing a book about this remarkable episode in the history of the Vietnam conflict.

The Australian Army Training Team was an outstanding group of skilled, brave and dedicated Australians, and by any standards, Barry Petersen was a worthy member of this élite unit. To be set down in a strange provincial town in a completely foreign environment, armed with only a vague directive and a bagful of Vietnamese piastres, with no knowledge of the language and — to make matters worse — an injunction as far as possible to avoid contact with the only English speaking group in the area, would be enough to daunt the stoutest heart. Yet with remarkable skill and initiative, reinforced no doubt by an adventurous streak inherited from his Danish ancestors, this young Australian officer in less than two years built up a formidable Montagnard force of more than a thousand well-armed troops, with a sound command and administrative structure. This force succeeded in denying to the Viet Cong control of much of the high plateau which dominates central Vietnam and guards the northern approaches to Saigon.

He was assisted in this task by two able Australian warrant officers; first, the happy-go-lucky Danny Neville, an old friend of mine from Korean days, who sadly left this life much before his time, and subsequently the redoubtable Bevan Stokes. He was also well supported in his material needs by his CIA superiors in distant Saigon, but his was the ultimate responsibility for success or failure. His task was made no easier by his need to find a safe passage through a tortuous maze of often conflicting authorities, an exercise which might well have defeated one far more experienced in diplomacy or, indeed, in intrigue.

His second tour of duty in Vietnam as a member of the 2nd Battalion, Royal Australian Regiment, provides an interesting insight into the problems and responsibilities facing that vital cog in the military machine, the infantry company commander.

This story is a mine of information about a little known episode in the war in Vietnam. It is also a tale of high adventure which might have emerged from the pages of the *Boys' Own* paper. Perhaps, more importantly, it is a record of the courage and resourcefulness of a young Australian officer and his loyal assistants and of the brave peoples of the central highlands fighting in the defence of their families and their homes.

Thomas Daly

Author's note

In a few instances I have used pseudonyms in my story to protect those in danger (or their families) from persecution, embarrassment or anguish. For similar reasons I have not revealed, or fully revealed some of my sources of information. Although in my work in the highlands of South Vietnam I had a number of interpreters and offsiders, I have attributed the activities of those persons to just two of our principal helpers — Y-Jut Buon To and Y-Tin Hwing. This was to avoid the confusion of too many Montagnard names.

Barry Petersen.

To my loyal, trusted and courageous friends, the Montagnard of the southern highlands of Vietnam

1

A Taste of the Depths

It was a small room — dank and stinking and quite evil. There were no windows, but bright light totally surrounded me, shining fierce and penetrating like the desert sun. Normally the room would be cold, but the lights purged all chill and burned a path deep into the soul.

A broomstick lay flat on the floor and I was kneeling on it. How simple are the means of torture — how ingenious the methods with which man can inflict pain upon his fellows. For the broomstick, nestling just below both kneecaps, had become a living thing — a carnivore gnawing at joints and thighs and threatening to devour my whole body. I knelt motionless; back straight, both arms stretched out like some demented amputee perched ready to dive from the high tower.

The questions were about to begin.

'Name?'

'Petersen.'

'Rank?'

'Captain.'

'Number?'

'13668.'

'Unit?'

I recited my protective litany.

'13668 Captain Arthur Barry Petersen.'

There would have been three, maybe four interrogators in the room. It was never easy to tell for they stood behind the lights, they were shadows with harsh voices and batons that prodded and punched and hurt.

The voice of the First Interrogator was precise, without emotion.

'Today Petersen, you'll tell us more.'

'— The others have told us,' a second voice said.

'The others have *told* us, Petersen,' the First Interrogator intoned.

I said nothing. My knees were on fire and the pain was as though bayonets were thrusting up my thighs, but my back was still straight, my arms steadfastly thrust forward, and most importantly, my mouth was shut. 'Number, Rank and Name' was the only safe communication with the world. It was dangerous to say more: folly even to seek refuge in a lie. Just one hint of information and their wedge would find a hold, then it would be driven in, bit by bit, until the crack became a crevasse and all would be lost.

For a week I had been undergoing this. A series of dark rooms then glaring lights and activities which made day and night lose their meaning; where time had gone weirdly awry and nothing was rational. I was filthy. In all this I had not bathed, nor shaved, nor slept between sheets or even on a mattress. My clothing — all that there was to sustain human warmth in this eerie, bitterly cold place — was an old battledress jacket, too small by far to draw closed, and ludicrously over-large pants. Neither jacket nor trousers had buttons or fastenings of any kind. The trousers had to be held by hand, or bunched or knotted to stop them falling to my ankles. I had committed a 'crime' not yet discovered — I had contrived to steal wire from a disused light fitting, just enough to encircle my waist, and thus to experience the joy of walking with my trousers up. With the waist-band of the trousers rolled over the wire belt, my crime was concealed.

On this day, kneeling on the broomstick with my trousers held in place, I had at least a vestige of dignity. But the pain in the knees and thighs was becoming intolerable and I could see my outstretched fingers trembling with the strain. I was drenched with sweat.

'He stinks!' one of the interrogators said, and his tone carried such scorn it hurt.

'I can smell him,' another said.

'He's foul,' added a third.

The First Interrogator turned on me and spoke, almost as though I had injured him.

'Have you no *pride* Petersen?'

13668, Captain Arthur Barry Petersen. The good soldier, the conscientious officer, the fastidious man. Yes, I had pride.

I said nothing.

The First Interrogator spoke again: 'Have you no sense of decency, you dirty, filthy man?'

Yes, I had a great sense of decency. My appearance was important to me. Throughout my army career, my seniors, in their reports, had commended my soldierly bearing and scrupulous attention to personal appearance. The 'dirty filthy man' could hardly remember showering less than twice a day.

I said nothing, but my shoulders and arms were like lead weights and my hands were beginning to drop.

'Get them up!'

A baton jabbed my back, just above the kidneys. It was a sharp, positive blow, not enough to damage, but sufficient to bruise. My body jolted upright and the arms went out again, ramrod straight. Yet the movement was enough to loosen my trousers, so illicitly held.

'He's got wire!' the Second Interrogator said.

I looked down and saw that the waist-band of the trousers had slipped and the wire was exposed.

The First Interrogator was calling —

'Get it off him! Get it off him!'

Hands were grabbing at my waist and the frail wire toggle I had so carefully contrived when I first obtained this treasure broke apart. The trousers slumped to my knees and I was kneeling, bare-bummed, penis flapping, miserably exposed.

'Where did the wire come from, Petersen?' the First Interrogator said, leaving no doubt that I had been judged guilty of a heinous crime.

I said nothing.

'Where did you get the wire?'

I said nothing.

'You have been vandalizing this prison, Petersen!'

I wanted to say something. To tell them how desperately I needed to hold up my trousers so that I could move with dignity. I wanted to explain and obtain understanding and forgiveness. But then too, I was suspicious, obstinate.

I said nothing.

The First Interrogator spoke to me more quietly then.

'Why do you do it Petersen?' he said. 'Why do you keep leaving yourself open to punishment? The *others* are far more sensible.'

The others? I hardly knew them. I had caught glimpses of some of them, dressed like me, shuffling about this strange place. Occasionally I had heard their voices in the various interrogation rooms. But they remained anonymous, sharing neither companionship nor affinity.

* * *

I had met them when we first arrived. We had gathered as strangers at the Australian Army Intelligence Centre at Middle Head in Sydney. There were fourteen of us — all young officers, most in our twenties. Some, like me, were destined for service overseas in South-east Asia. We had volunteered for the Code of Conduct Course, a euphemistic title which the media, perhaps too sensationally, had dubbed as the 'School of Torture'. Many countries, including the United States and Britain, conduct counterparts to the School of Torture. Quite simply, it is designed to familiarize selected personnel with the propaganda and interrogation techniques used on prisoners of war by Communist countries. To learn what it's like to be a prisoner we had to become prisoners, and for approximately twelve days we experienced the privations, indignities, confusion and humiliation that this wretched circumstance entails.

It was early in 1963. I was twenty-eight, a one-time National Serviceman, then a graduate of the Officer Cadet School at Portsea in Victoria and now a reasonably seasoned soldier. For two years I had commanded an infantry platoon on anti-Communist terrorist operations in the jungles of Malaya. I was very fit, enormously enthusiastic and confident of my growing abilities as an officer of the Australian Army. Already that year I had undertaken a series of courses, some quite arduous — a jungle warfare course at Canungra in southern Queensland, an intelligence briefing course on South Vietnam at the School of Military Intelligence, and a special operations course involving the training of a few selected officers for liaison duties with guerilla forces behind enemy lines. I was soon to be posted to South Vietnam, to work in an area that could be difficult and sometimes dangerous. There was a chance that I might be captured. What would it be like? What were the pressures that would be put on me? How would I behave in such circumstances? Would I crack?

The School of Torture offered a minor simulation of what can in reality be a profoundly dreadful experience. A taste of the depths of despair.

* * *

We were an awkward lot that first day. Fourteen fit but unusually reserved young men, gathered in the main lecture room of a building overlooking Sydney Harbour. The view from Middle Head can be beautiful but there was no inclination amongst any of us to spend time observing that. We knew this was to be a tough course — perhaps the toughest any of us had experienced. Most were nervous and uncertain. There was also an element of suspicion. I had been warned by those in the know to beware of everyone — even fellow volunteers. They could be spies. Say nothing, I had been told, trust nobody, give them only your regimental number, rank and name.

The commandant of the school addressed us. It was a brief, not very informative address, with little hint of welcome about it. Yet he ended with one ominous remark: 'Remember,' he said, 'you are volunteers. Any man who wishes to withdraw from the course may say so, and he will be released instantly without prejudice.'

We looked at each other then. Who would be strong? Who would get through?

Suddenly the doors burst open. There were shouts and the milling about of many soldiers dressed in indeterminate khaki with red stars on their caps. Each of us was seized then manhandled from the main lecture room to a series of underground tunnels and cells. Middle Head has been a military fortification for almost a century. The area is a maze of tunnels and underground cells and command posts. We were taken to what must have been the oldest part, where the water dripped incessantly and the walls were discoloured by age and slime. We were unceremoniously stripped, and amid shouted orders and jostling we were issued with the outrageously inappropriate prison uniform. Nothing fitted, nothing buttoned or fastened in any way — it was clothing that even the most wretched would hardly covet. What use is a pair of trousers that have to be held by hand to prevent a man being shackled at every step? Indeed, that was the very purpose of the clothing. It was representative of one of the basic rudiments of torture: humiliation.

There was no individual, or even group cell in the prison. Rather a series of cells through which we were rotated like restless itinerants at any time, day or night. Each had its singularly offensive characteristic. There was one I dubbed the 'Music Room', where a loudspeaker in the ceiling blared the 'Internationale' or 'The East is Red', interspersed with fanatical voices haranguing the listener with the 'Principles of Communism'; the 'Whistlestop' had another loudspeaker out of reach. It emitted a series of high shrieks so penetrating that it was virtually impossible to sleep or think clearly. The 'Conversation Suite' was a place where the really bad interrogations were conducted; the 'Pit' was a cellar with ankle-deep water and the variation of relative quiet, total darkness — and time to reflect on past and future punishments.

After possibly eight days, I had experienced all these places time and again. As punishment for the wire incident I was taken to the Pit — where I had been many times before. The procedure was the same for every move from cell to cell. First a calico bag was placed over the head, then guards pushed you through the corridors. It was never easy to tell the destination, because the routine was always changing — all part of the process of disorientation.

The Pit was quite deep and entered from the top by a trapdoor. There was a ladder to climb down, then it was removed and the trapdoor shut. It was very dark. The water level varied from ankle-depth to somewhere above the shins. Water was always dripping somewhere and it was bitterly cold.

There were rats in the Pit. Quite a number. Perhaps our jailors had put them there for our company. I don't like rats — but if I have to tolerate them I can. In the jungles of Malaya on my first tour of duty there, there had been lots of rats. I've had them run across my body while I slept. It wasn't pleasant, but they didn't eat me. I learned afterwards that some men stood for hours in the Pit for fear of the rats. I found a stray plank, left floating in the water. There were a few bricks there, too. Perhaps there was a reason for them. I used to stack the bricks to just above the waterline and bridge them with the plank. As a bed, it was quite superior to the awful corrugated wooden bunks in some of the cells, with their selected (it seemed) missing slats. I managed some sleep on that plank. I don't think my friends the rats slept at all.

From the Pit, I would be hooded beneath the calico bag and herded to one of the other cells, perhaps the Music Room. There I would wait to be fed while the martial music played, and the frenzied voices blared out:

'Comrades! Have you learned your Principles of Communism? We *all* must learn the Principles of Communism!'

Sooner or later — but never at any regular hour — my food would arrive. I would stand at attention, but with hands cupped so that the guard could ladle a ball of glutinous rice into them. The rice was unpleasant initially, but after a time, real hunger made it bearable. At first I used to eat it all, directly from hands to mouth. But later I learned to save some, rolling it into a ball and placing it in my jacket pocket. This was a punishable offence. But it was a necessary insurance against the vagaries of the kitchen, for very early on I experienced the oddities of feeding time. On several occasions a guard had returned within fifteen minutes with a second offering of rice.

Once I made one of my few unsolicited comments.

'You fed me fifteen minutes ago,' I said.

The guard responded indignantly.

'Are you going mad?' he said. 'That was four hours ago!'

After that, he didn't return for a long time. I learned it was wiser to have something set aside in my pocket. After all, if it ever proved that I had too much, I could always use it to while away the time in the Pit, feeding the rats.

*   *   *

I was losing all sense of time. There was no night or day, no measure of the hours, nor any clear routine to give life an intelligible pattern. I was in a constant state of apprehension about unpleasant experiences that were always imminent. It was almost a relief to find I had something concrete to do: I was to see the 'Counsellor'.

He was in an office I had not previously seen. It was a clean and relatively warm place where there was a chair for me to sit, and a desk behind which sat the Counsellor, an affable man in his mid-thirties.

'Sit down, Petersen,' he said, quite brightly.

'Thank you.'

'Cigarette?'

I did not smoke. Even if I had, I would not have taken it. It might have compromised me.

'No thank you.'

'Well,' he said, 'how about a cup of coffee?'

I would have loved a cup of coffee. I would have given an arm for a cup of coffee!

'No thank you.'

He looked a little troubled.

'You can have water if you like.'

I could have water. I did not feel I would be compromised by accepting water.

'Yes please.'

The Counsellor looked pleased. There was a guard who got a tin mug of water while the Counsellor studied a little piece of paper before him.

'Now,' he said as I drank the water and he eyed the paper, 'Arthur Barry Petersen ... a captain! What do I call you, Arthur or Barry?'

I do not like the name Arthur. Never have. I've always been known as Barry.

But beware, the wedge!

'Captain Petersen, will do,' I said.

'Come on now. It's not necessary to be that formal,' he said, and he was laughing a little.

I said nothing.

'Well, let's start somewhere else,' he said. 'Can I ask you how you're feeling?'

'I'm well, thank you.'

'The cold worry you?'

I said nothing.

He was smiling at me. Almost as though I were a child, frightened of the bogeyman.

'I'm only asking you because I know how miserable this place can be,' he said. 'All right for us cold-blooded southerners, but no place for a Queenslander.'

I said nothing, but I must have blinked, for he had startled me.

How did he know I was a Queenslander?

The Counsellor was watching me.

He said, 'Petersen, there's no need to be so sensitive. I'm not asking you for military information.'

I said nothing.

'. . . I don't need military information. I have it all here.'

He was holding up the piece of paper, but it was blank side towards me. He was lying! The rules of the game were that only information I had given could be used against me. In all these long days my only revelation had been regimental number, rank and name.

I said nothing.

The Counsellor was smiling.

'You're aware that the Australian Army Staff Corps list is freely available and anyone can look it up?'

No response.

'You know I can refer to that and find, as I've got here, your date of birth, your qualifications, when you were promoted, the units you served with? I have all that.'

He was waving the paper. He was a liar!

He changed tack.

'Let's try another way: tell me about your parents. Are they still alive?'

Yes, they were. I would love to talk about them; to say normal things. But I could not, and would not.

He persisted.

'Still living in Queensland?'

There it was again! Queensland! How did he know?
Even if he did have, as he claimed, the Army Staff Corps
List, that carried nothing about state of origin. Where
had I slipped up?

He was learning forward. There was a glint in his eye. His question had remained unanswered.

'Well?' he asked.

He knew and I knew he had found the place for the wedge. I shut the door. The response was rapid-fire.

'13668, Captain A.B. Petersen.'

'I'll leave you to the others, Captain,' he said.

I was taken to the Music Room, to squat on the damp

floor and think about Queensland. Such a small thing, yet so important. I searched every corner of my memory to try and remember a moment when I might have slipped. I could think of nothing. I remembered the time on the first day when we had been seized by our captors. Perhaps some item I carried then, had been taken and examined and had proved tell-tale. But no! I had foreseen such an incident and had been at great pains to carry nothing that would tell a tale. On the first day my only possessions had been a few banknotes, a watch and a pen. All anonymous.

✳ ✳ ✳

I slept even worse than usual that night. I thought about Northern Queensland and growing up in Sarina and Innisfail — the tropical north where the air was always warm and the vegetation deepest green and where the rain in the Wet would descend in buckets. I have always loved the tropics, and hated the cold of places further removed from the Equator.

My father had a small radio repair business before going off to war. He had become a staff-sergeant, but for years I saw little of him. My mother raised me through that time.

My great companion was my grandfather — Hans Christian Petersen, a first-generation Australian of Danish descent. He listened to my stories and taught me the responsibilities of being a man. He had no time for the faint-hearted. He made nets for fishing off the shallow waters of Sarina Beach, south of Mackay. They were long drag-nets, a pole on either end, with cork floats along the top length of the net and lead weights along the bottom. 'Pop' Petersen insisted that I drag the lead end of the net out into deep water, then around in an arc back towards the shore. I feared the sharks. There were hammerhead and flathead and often young grey nurse sharks in the area. I know now they were not so dangerous really. But I was terribly frightened of them.

'In you go,' Pop would say. 'The sharks won't touch you while you are dragging the net.'

'No!'

'In you go!'

And reluctantly I would enter the water dragging the twenty-metre net out into the deep, feet scrabbling on the sandy bottom, heart pounding, water up to my chin, terrified of the unseen lurking in the sea.

'Come on you young bugger,' Pop would shout from the shore. 'Further out! Faster!'

I would drag the net as directed then return to Pop to receive his approval for courage confirmed and a frailty overcome. I needed to please, to prove I was a man. But I never overcame that fear of the sharks.

* * *

I must have been closer to giving in than I had realized. Soon I was moved from the Music Room to the Whistlestop. Although the routine was never really predictable, there was a pattern to this. The sessions in the Conversation Suite — the bad sessions — were generally prefaced by time in the Whistlestop. The awful shrieking tore at the nerves in just the right manner to soften candidates for interrogation, and perhaps revelation.

I sat on the bunk and waited for the call. The shrieking tuned the nerves so tightly it was as though they were about to snap like overstretched piano wires. I *wanted* the interrogation. I had prepared for it in my mind and had my every response prepared. If they talked about Queensland, I would be totally mute. They would get nothing from me, no matter what the pressure of the discomfort. I was ready!

But nobody came. I waited and waited. Nothing happened. The shrieking was turned off. There was silence. Then my whole body was shaking, out of control. I was drenched with sweat as though overtaken by a profound fever. I was Pavlov's dog. I'd been salivating for the test, but it had not come.

Then, at the lowest moment, I saw the answer to the Counsellor's information about Queensland.

Regimental number 13668, Captain Arthur Barry Petersen.

That was it! That number! It was prefaced by the number one. And the one signified Queensland. The initial numbers two, three and so on, represented other states, and so indicated the point of recruitment and possibly birth. I had been broadcasting my origin ten or twelve times a day and had been too stupid or confused to realise it.

I had not slipped up. I had not revealed a secret.

Soon after — perhaps it was just as well — I was taken from my cell, hooded. Then, for the first time since we were 'captured', I found myself among fellow prisoners, or at least it seemed so. I could hear guards shouting orders at others apparently in a similar condition to me. We were prodded, shoved and pushed around until we were jostling one another like blind sheep. The guards were evidently trying to herd us into some sort of formation.

Suddenly, my hood was ripped off. It was a stunning moment. We stood around a table laden with food.

'It's all over,' the guards said. 'You're through!'

It's another one of their tricks, I thought. Be careful.

I looked at my fellow prisoners, all but one had survived the test. They were as dirty and dishevelled as I. And many were in tears — half-laughing, half-crying with relief. So was I, and when I remember that moment, even now I feel like crying still.

* * *

I do not condemn the School of Torture. I praise it. I was a volunteer who wanted to arm himself against the possibility of capture and persecution in enemy hands. I learned a lesson, I learned about myself. I am grateful for the assurance it gave me — that I could at least summon the strength and capacity to resist such a trial.

I have known instances of captives who have undergone terrible inhumanities — men who were incarcerated underground, or imprisoned in fuel drums, or bestially mutilated and carried in cages like animals on show. It never did happen to me, I am profoundly thankful for that. But if it *had* been me, I at least had achieved the knowledge to hope, and perhaps to survive.

Soon after, I was flying to South Vietnam. I had been trained as comprehensively as anyone could have expected at that time. Theoretically I was an expert, in practice I knew little about that country and that war. But then, this was 1963. Neither did most people in the world outside.

2 Last Days of Innocence

The Saigon I first saw in August 1963 was a city soon to fade away. In a sense, these were the last days of its innocence. Here, at least, there was no clear manifestation of war or conflict. President Diem and his family were in the eighth year of their autocratic rule of South Vietnam. John F. Kennedy was President of the United States of America and Sir Robert Menzies was Prime Minister of Australia. And the French and their influence, Dien Bien Phu notwithstanding, were still in evidence.

I loved Saigon. I still feel a nostalgia for the city of that time. It was Asia textured with the finest French-colonial influence. Seated in a rattan chair on the wide verandah of the Hotel Continental Palace on the Rue Catinat and sipping iced *citron*, the tart juice made from lemons or limes, I found the boulevards fascinating to behold. Such a pleasant and gentle atmosphere: bicycle-powered rickshas — *cyclos* — ambling by, motor scooters scuttling on their way, French-made cars — Citroëns, Renaults, Simcas — interspersed with the occasional larger Chevrolet or Buick. For the Americans were already there and beginning to proclaim it in their own inimitable way. Yet for the South Vietnamese there was no haste, no frenzy and seemingly no fear.

Whatever the sins of the French in Indo-China, their best influences contributed much to the beauty and character of

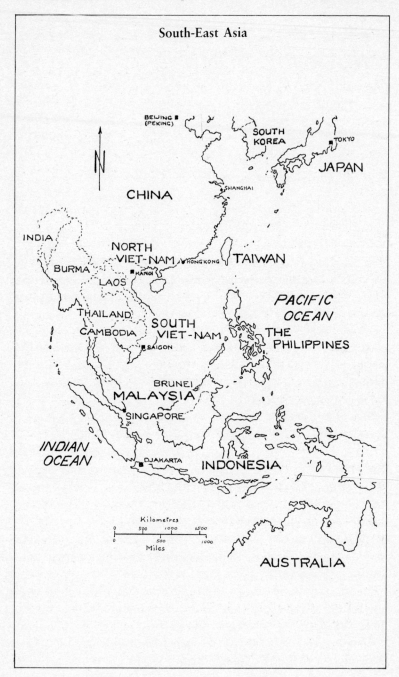

South-East Asia

the cities. They saw the value of trees and encouraged their growth. Old Saigon was alive with trees and brilliant poincianas, mangoes, palms, and rubber trees framed the boulevards, their leaves brushing the facades of the old colonial buildings. Some streets were enclosed by such an umbrella of trees that even on the hottest of days it was possible to walk for long periods and not really feel the heat. The cycle-powered rickshas would sidle up as you walked.

'Cyclo! Cyclo!' the riders would pester. But it was so often more pleasant to continue strolling beneath the shade of the trees.

At the time, there was an avenue of poincianas, or flame trees, lining the thoroughfare from the airport to the centre of the city. In spring when they were in bloom, the trees provided one of the loveliest sights I have seen. Soon after, the American planes leaking defoliants would gradually kill some and the rest were torn out to make way for the growing stampede of military traffic.

By contrast with what was to come later, Saigon in 1963 was a prim city, too. The girls with their beautiful, honey-coloured skins glided by, shrouded by pastel-coloured parasols, or wearing conical hats. Their graceful *aodais*, the ankle-length dresses worn over equally graceful pantaloons, were always high to the neck. Madame Nhu, 'The Dragon Lady' and powerful sister-in-law of President Diem, wielded her own version of Catholic morality in a largely Buddhist community. She ruled that it was brazen for girls to wear a dress with anything less than a mandarin collar. It was also a punishable offence for women to dance, and prostitution was banned. Even in the bars, the girls refused requests to dance for fear of arrest by the police. All that would soon change.

And in those first few days I too was an innocent.

* * *

I had been sent to South Vietnam as a member of the thirty-man Australian Army Training Team Vietnam. Although officially an Australian Army adviser, I was to be one of two officers of that team, working with the American Central

Intelligence Agency (CIA). The Australian team was tiny compared with the sixteen thousand-strong American military advisory effort at that time.

Because of Australia's early involvement in counter-terrorist and counter-insurgency operations in Malaya, the Americans seemed to think that we were experts in that field. I assumed that the two positions with the CIA had been arranged by our own Australian Secret Intelligence Service (ASIS) which had sponsored our special operations training.

I was not a secret service officer, but a simple soldier with that special operations training. Now I was to become a CIA man, without understanding what the term meant, or what it entailed.

I had met Colonel Ted Serong the previous year back in Australia. He was a quiet man, did not smile much, and perhaps enjoyed the aura of mystery around him. I also thought him very experienced.

'I have arranged for you to go to Ban-Me-Thuot — do you know where it is?' he asked.

'Yes sir.'

I knew it was the capital of Darlac Province in the central highlands of South Vietnam, but I didn't know much more.

'You will be working with the Montagnard.'

The prospect excited me. I knew of the Montagnard, the mountain people, who made up the thirty-odd tribal groups in the highlands.

The colonel continued:

'I've managed to get the CIA to agree to let an Australian officer run his own field program. You're the first one. I want others to get the chance, so make a good job of it.'

I was more than pleased. This was what I had always wanted — to be given my own responsibilities.

'I'll be up to see you from time to time Barry,' he said. 'Remember, you'll be working for the Americans and reporting directly to them.'

Captain John Healy, the officer I was to replace on the team, was at this meeting. He took me to meet my new American masters in the CIA's Covert Action Branch.

It says something about the relative calm of Saigon then that the Covert Action Branch was located in a pleasant, but unremarkable villa within walking distance of central Saigon. It was the home of Cliff Strathern, head of the branch, and his family. A path leading between the villa and its garage led to an additional windowless building at the rear. Its walls were bare save for the protruding rear ends of a number of purring air conditioners.

John Healy knocked on a locked door and, after a minute or so, we were admitted to a different world. Acoustic tiles covered most of the walls and the ceiling. There were maps on the walls, office furniture, and a disproportionate number of large combination safes. Here and there on desks were used coffee cups — to become a familiar sight on my later visits to American offices. In a corner, on a table, sat a coffee percolator stewing away mercilessly.

There were half a dozen Americans in the main room, some in suits, jackets discarded. Others wore khaki drill trousers and a short-sleeved shirt worn outside the trousers. This served to conceal the hand-gun and holster belted to most waists. This was the unofficial uniform of the CIA field officers in South Vietnam.

John introduced me to Cliff Strathern, the branch chief, and Bryan Mills who was to be my future 'agent handler'. Bryan was in his early-thirties, slimly built, clean-cut, probably a product of one of the better American universities. He had spent twelve years in Thailand and Indo-China.

He was a particularly quiet man — especially reserved towards me. I was an army officer reporting for a new job and expected to be briefed about my tasks. But neither Mills nor Strathern seemed interested in discussing anything other than pleasantries.

Bryan said finally:

'We'll be going up to Ban-Me-Thuot together. I'll collect you from where you're staying on my way to Ton-Son-Nhut Airport.'

'Am I to be briefed?' I asked.

'There's plenty of time,' he said.

With Bryan there was always plenty of time.

*   *   *

We boarded an Air America aircraft for the 265 kilometre flight to Ban-Me-Thuot. First we flew over a patchwork of villages, canals and paddy fields, and vast areas of jungle. Then we reached the mountains — rugged, jungle-covered terrain, up to 1500 metres above sea level, with mountain streams and sometimes large rivers which became rapids and cascaded over waterfalls. We could see the cleared areas of the Montagnard villages — clusters of long-houses with high-peaked, thatched roofs, laid out in neat rows.

The sprawling town of Ban-Me-Thuot was set on the high plateau of the central highlands, 500 metres above sea level. Almost 45 000 people lived in Ban-Me-Thuot. It was a town gone wrong. The centre, the older sector, was laid out in French-colonial style — and graced with the wide, shady, tree-lined streets so familiar in Saigon. But, from the air, it was possible to see how the new town had been added with little regard for the niceties of town planning or for aesthetic care. The new, more haphazard sectors had been built only in recent years to accommodate several thousand Vietnamese who had either migrated or been re-located from the overcrowded coastal provinces. I did not know it then, but this influx of displaced Vietnamese was part of the running sore in the relationship between the Montagnard and the Vietnamese, both northerners and southerners. I was to learn more of this later — sometimes to my discomfort.

The prominent buildings of Ban-Me-Thuot were older structures. The most impressive was the huge, solid teak hunting lodge built by Emperor Bao Dai. Built on teak pillars to represent three Montagnard longhouses, it was linked by covered walkways. It was said that before the influx of Vietnamese shanties, the Emperor could shoot wild game at the jungle edge from its verandahs. In 1963 it was occupied by American advisers who called the huge building 'The Bungalow'. Years later, they accidentally burned down this magnificent structure.

South Vietnam
— Darlac and Phuoc Tuy Provinces

There was a Roman Catholic convent built along similar, but smaller lines on the north-east edge of town. One of the closeted Benedictine nuns was a great grand-daughter of the Emperor Franz Josef of Austria.

Apart from the large Catholic church in the old town square, the other outstanding building was the palace. It was a huge French-colonial building, set in large walled grounds. It was used by dignitaries visiting Ban-Me-Thuot.

Scattered around the province, on the more fertile tracts of land, were sprawling Vietnamese Land Development Centres (LDCs). These also were occupied by Vietnamese peasant farmers, again re-settled from the overcrowded coastal provinces, and even more resented by the Montagnard than the newer Vietnamese settlers in Ban-Me-Thuot itself.

Ban-Me-Thuot had two airstrips; the main civilian strip was fourteen kilometres east of the town. We landed on the second, a short, unsealed strip on the north-east edge of the town itself. We hired two cyclos to take us to Madame Ly-Tran-Ly's Hotel Darlac. This Vietnamese hotel was to be my home until I could find and rent a house.

Madame Ly was a comely lady, but she tightly controlled her family and business interests. She was from a wealthy and influential Vietnamese family. Her few bar girls were typical, young, provincial ladies, quite unlike their more sophisticated, money-hungry Saigon counterparts.

Madame Ly gave me a room in the separate annexe around the corner from the bar and restaurant. It was a simple room with a semi-open, Vietnamese-style bathroom in the corner and located at the end of a verandah on the second floor which overlooked a tree-shaded courtyard.

* * *

In Darlac Province the CIA supported two paramilitary/ political action programs. Salaries for members of all such activities in South Vietnam were paid by the CIA through the Vietnamese Ministry of Propaganda. Bryan Mills provided the logistic support, including weapons, direct to the controlling authorities in Darlac Province.

I should say that there were *supposed* to be two such paramilitary/political action programs. One was the Force Populaire, apparently consisting of two hundred Vietnamese and Montagnard under the control of the Darlac Province Chief. The other, the Armed Propaganda and Intelligence Teams of one hundred Montagnard was under the control of the Director of National Police for the Central Highlands Region. They were both financially and logistically supported by the CIA.

First Bryan took me to meet the controller of the first group, the province chief, Major Hoang-Thong. He was an aloof Vietnamese officer who appeared to have no interest whatever in me. He and Bryan spoke in French as Major Thong could not speak English. I understood very little of the conversation.

After the meeting, on our way to meet the National Police director, in charge of the second group, I said to Bryan:

'He didn't seem too bloody interested in me.'

'I don't think he likes the thought of you being around,' Bryan replied.

'Why?'

'Maybe it's because he thinks you'll find out too much. We're paying US$2500 a month in salaries alone to keep his Force Populaire going.'

'Don't you think they exist?' I asked.

He turned to me and gave me my first real job in South Vietnam.

'That's what I want you to find out.'

We arrived at the quaint, two-storeyed, teak National Police headquarters building where Captain Pham Tuong, the director, was waiting for us. He was an intelligent, alert, personable man whom I liked instantly. He spoke English well and Bryan clearly had great regard for him.

He also proved to be honest. Within the hour he took us out to see his one-hundred-man force. I did not know it then, but they were later to become the nucleus of my future guerilla force in the highlands.

Over breakfast the following morning Bryan Mills gave me a large package of Vietnamese banknotes.

'Here Barry, count this,' he said.

Amid the remnants of the hotel breakfast, I totalled 35 000 Vietnamese piastres — confetti money, worth only about us$350 — but at that time a considerable, and bulky sum in Vietnamese terms. A Vietnamese soldier was then paid vn1300 piastres (us$13) a month.

'That's your operational fund,' Bryan said. 'It'll be a revolving fund. Its replenishment will equal your expenditure. Keep a statement of expenses, supported by receipts, if you can get them, and that'll be replaced by the equivalent amount of money.'

For an army captain in those days to have a bag of money like that and the discretion to spend it, was a relatively big responsibility.

Mills, to say the least, was a nonchalent man.

'I'll be back in a couple of weeks,' he said. 'I'll buzz the town in my aircraft to let you know when I arrive.'

'How do I contact you in the meantime?' I asked.

'You can try the Vietnamese telephone system, if you're lucky,' he said blandly. 'If you can't get through that way, try the American advisers' telephone at The Bungalow. But try to stay away from those guys. You'll gain more credibility with the locals if they see you're not one of them.'

Bryan got up and to my alarm, gathered up his bag, quite ready to leave.

'Hey Bryan,' I said, 'You haven't told me what you want me to do up here in Ban-Me-Thuot!'

'Oh, just get to know the locals,' he said in his detached way. 'Find yourself a good interpreter and see if you can find a house to live in.'

He left — and I didn't see him for another six weeks.

I was rapidly learning about the CIA.

* * *

I was on my own in this quaint, colourful, yet somehow inscrutable highland town. I hardly knew a soul, had no grasp of the language, and was supposed to avoid the company of fellow Europeans — the Americans — as Bryan had advised. Worse still, I was not really clear what job the CIA wanted me to do, or what I was expected to achieve. I was something of a lost soul. We have a phrase for it in Australia — 'Left like a shag on a rock'.

I badly needed an interpreter but finding a suitable one was difficult. The few contacts I had were those I met around the hotel who spoke English of sorts, a couple of business people, and Captain Tuong, the courteous, but very busy police director. There was a limit to the time he could give me, despite our growing friendship.

There were probably as many as eighty Americans in Ban-Me-Thuot, mainly military advisers housed in The Bungalow, now surrounded by high, wire fences. For the 23rd Vietnamese Army Division was headquartered here. The Americans advised the Vietnamese commanders on military matters, and many operated outside Darlac Province. They had nothing to do with my work, which — as I imperfectly understood it — was principally connected with propaganda and intelligence. The Americans frequently extended invitations to join them in their club, at social gatherings and film nights, but I usually refused. To mix with them would make me one of them, in the eyes of both the Vietnamese and Montagnard, and Bryan Mills had warned me against that.

I was a 'loner', but although perhaps lonely too, I was not apprehensive, nor even particularly prudent about my safety. I had a CIA-issue 9mm Browning pistol, but did not even bother to carry it. I generally left it in a locked drawer in my room at the Hotel Darlac.

It was clear my first major task was to learn Rhade, the local Montagnard dialect. Someone suggested the American missionaries might help. The mission cantonment was on the southern edge of the town and the American Christian Missionary Alliance had been in Ban-Me-Thuot for almost thirty years. So I made an effort — for I am an agnostic — to mend my ways and go to church.

The Reverend Bob Ziemer was head of the Mission and had himself been in Ban-Me-Thuot for sixteen years. After the church service, he and his wife Marie invited me to lunch. Reverend Ziemer was a big, fine-looking man, but reserved. The Ziemers were very Christian — and still very American. Even lunch was American. There was hardly any local food on the table. Most of the fare was European, imported from Saigon.

Marie Ziemer said: 'We don't particularly care for the local food, except perhaps some rice, eggs and chicken.'

Her husband added: 'Nor do we approve of some of the Montagnard customs, particularly the traditional sacrifices of birds and animals, and certainly not drinking their rice wine. I hope you don't participate either.'

'What wrong do you see in it?' I asked, because I have always felt that if you want to achieve any kind of real empathy with people, you have to be prepared to share their way of life.

'We consider things like sacrifices and drinking as not particularly Christian,' Reverend Ziemer said.

I broached the subject of an English-Rhade dictionary.

'Oh yes' said Mrs Ziemer, 'We are preparing a dictionary. So far we have translated all the gospels and many of the hymns into Rhade. We hope to finish the dictionary one day.'

A sad note is that Bob Ziemer was killed during the Tet offensive. He courageously left the cantonment bunker to reason with the Viet Cong, but they shot him. Later, Ruth Wilting, a mission nurse, left the bunker to get medical supplies but she was also killed by the Viet Cong. They then threw a grenade into the bunker killing another of the mission staff and seriously wounding Marie Ziemer.

* * *

I made no progress with Mills's request in verifying the existence of the province chief's elusive two-hundred-man Force Populaire. I had already made inquiries with the American military adviser. He neither knew nor cared, because he didn't consider the matter of particular military importance. Nor did he seem to care about the province chief's civil administrative duties which were burdensome, to say the least. Still without an interpreter, I went to see the English-speaking deputy province chief, Captain Kha Vang Huy.

Captain Huy was a short, thick-set Vietnamese with an affable personality. I liked him, and we were to work together well during the next two years. But he hedged on this matter of the Force Populaire.

'I don't have anything to do with their operations,' he said.

'Where can I see some of them — or even someone in charge of them?'

'Quite a few have already left the force,' he said, and I could see that he was uncomfortable.

'Then, there must be at least some of them here,' I persisted.

'They would almost certainly be on operations, Captain Petersen. I don't know how you could contact them.'

He clearly did not like being pushed. From the outset, I had adopted the policy that I should not jeopardize my relationship with the Vietnamese by being too persistent. They had already had more than enough of this from some of the American advisers. So I dropped the subject.

I felt — and my latter dealings with him confirmed this — that Huy was an honest man, and that his evasiveness was due to his wish to protect his province chief, rather than himself.

He had told me nothing, yet I felt that I was well on the way to obtaining the information I was looking for.

About this time, I became aware that my room at the Hotel Darlac was being searched. I had been suspicious for some time and had set small traps.

My pistol, documents and the money Bryan had given to me were in a locked drawer at the bottom of my wardrobe. It seemed the safest place available in the mountain town, which did not even boast a bank. I had set my papers out in such a way that the slightest interference with them would be detectable. I saw that the documents were gone through almost daily, yet neither the money nor my pistol were taken. I could have carried the pistol, but Bryan's parcel of Monopoly money was far too large to tote about. So I left both where they were. Theft was obviously not the reason for the searches. My intruders weren't concerned with money or guns. I was the one they were interested in.

About this time also, a transport vehicle arrived, as promised by Bryan Mills. It was an old, battered, hoodless, three-quarter-ton ex-army truck. It was painted blue and looked terrible. But I was delighted. With it came a young, fit-looking Vietnamese named Vu, who announced that he had been provided by the province chief. I was equally pleased with this. Perhaps, I thought, the province chief, who seemed always aloof, was warming to me.

Then I discovered that Vu was related to the province chief and so almost certainly an informant. I said nothing and accepted him. Perhaps this was a mistake — Vu's standard of driving was to prove a greater threat to me than the Viet Cong!

*   *   *

Late one evening, I returned to my hotel room. For some reason I could not sleep and lay on the bed. The room was partly lit by the moonlight filtering through the barred windows. Suddenly, I had the feeling that I was being watched. I got out of bed. The moonlight allowed me enough light to search the room. The only hiding places were in the bathroom annexe and under the beds, which I checked. There was nothing. I again lay down, wide awake, on the bed.

There was a sound. Someone was attempting to push my keys out of the locked door from the outside. I sat bolt upright. My first thought was to get my gun. But I felt chilled as I realised I had foolishly locked it in the bottom drawer of the wardrobe, on the other side of the room. The key to the drawer was on the key-ring, already vibrating in the door. I had to make a judgement. Do I withdraw the bunch of keys to unlock my pistol? But their key only needed the removal of mine to enable the intruders to unlock the door and burst in. There would have been no time to unlock the wardrobe drawer. I grabbed the only weapon I could find — one of my heavy army boots. I half-sat, half-crouched on the edge of the bed, clutching it in my sweaty hand. The keys rattled more loudly as the attempts to dislodge them from the door became more intense. There was a series of thumps as shoulders were heaved against the door. Then all was quiet.

A moment later, two stocky Vietnamese were framed against the barred window facing the verandah. The moonlight was bright enough for me to clearly see them, even to define their features. I knew there was sufficient light in the room for them to see me as well. They just stood there as we stared at each other, for what seemed to be minutes. No-one spoke. It was quite clear that they were trying to intimidate me. Suddenly, they were gone.

Retrieving my keys, I unlocked my pistol, then the door, to look outside. It was as though nobody had ever been there.

I felt fear for the first time in Vietnam. I had been too cavalier by far. Never again did I allow that pistol to lie beyond my immediate reach.

I reported the incident to the National Police director the following morning. But it was only eighteen months later that he confirmed the incident had indeed been an attempt at scare tactics. But he never told me why.

In the Box Seat

The small, Air America Dornier aircraft swooped low over Ban-Me-Thuot. By its third circuit, Vu and I were already racing for the nearby town airstrip. Bryan Mills had said that he would return 'in a couple of weeks'! That had been six weeks ago.

I watched the aircraft taxi down the dusty airstrip towards us. It was an executive aircraft and could seat five comfortably. Bryan, using the magic arts of the CIA, had the plane to himself.

He was in no hurry to get down to business.

Much later, over drinks in a small Vietnamese bar, he sensed my anxiety. 'It's all right, I've got another bag of money for you.'

I was more than pleased to hear it. I was flat broke and had been so for two weeks. My creditors around town had been watching me like hawks.

'I've got some mail for you as well.'

'Did you bring my army pay?'

Being Bryan, it had probably been the last thing in the world to enter his head.

'No, but you have money in the package.'

I felt myself lucky I at least had my personal mail. I had been in limbo until he arrived.

Later — much later — he finally asked me:

'Have you found any of those elusive Force Populaire yet?'

'I don't think they exist, Bryan,' I said.

'That figures. This is the sort of thing that's been happening throughout the country. We've been paying for people who don't exist,' he said.

Bryan then told me that all American financial aid for psychological operations programs throughout Vietnam had ceased. As well, all financial support for Vietnamese Army units not actually on combat operations had also been stopped. That included the salaries of the élite Vietnamese Special Forces units comprising the presidential guard in Saigon — President Diem's personal bodyguard.

'What about our hundred men here in Ban-Me-Thuot under the police director's control?' I asked. 'They *do* exist.'

'It applies to everyone in our programs; but I've brought you enough money to feed, clothe and generally look after them,' he said. 'It could be some time before their salaries recommence.'

'How long do you think that might take?' I asked.

It didn't seem to worry Bryan.

'Oh, it could take weeks or even months,' he said airily. 'You'll just have to look after them.'

We talked about the rapidly deteriorating political situation in South Vietnam — the self-immolation of the Buddhist monks, the total banning of Buddhist processions, the effect of cuts in American financial assistance at all levels of government. Those who had been 'milking the purse' as well as those dependent upon it were feeling the effects. The whole country was rumbling with discontent.

'If anything does happen Barry, you'll be OK up here in quiet old Ban-Me-Thuot.'

The moment Bryan left for Saigon, I was out retrieving my credit rating around town.

* * *

One morning, in the courtyard below my hotel room, I was stopped by a fine-looking young Rhade.

South Vietnam
— Ethnic Minority Groups

'I believe you're looking for an interpreter sir,' he said in good English.

Y-Jut Buon To was nineteen, and had already served as an interpreter with the American Special Forces. From that moment, he became not only my interpreter, but a younger brother. Our fortunes have been linked to the present day.

The need to totally support the hundred-man Montagnard force under National Police control, enabled Jut and I to establish a rapport with those people who were to become the nucleus of our later force. I had an interpreter, money, and I suddenly found myself in the box seat. I was able to buy supplies of food, clothing and necessities for those men and their families. I found myself useful at last.

* * *

My Australian commander, Colonel Serong, flew in to Ban-Me-Thuot on Thursday, 31 October 1963. Late that afternoon, we could sense excitement in the air. There were claims that a revolution was taking place in Saigon. Colonel Serong, using the Vietnamese telephone system, tried in vain to call Saigon for details. We went around to The Bungalow, where the rumours were confirmed. There was trouble in Saigon, and the Ton-Son-Nhut airport had been closed. Other details were sketchy.

Purely by chance Captain Tuong, our regional director of National Police, was in Saigon. He sought refuge in Bryan and Betty Mills's villa. Radio Saigon fell into the hands of the revolutionary military junta led by General Duong Van Minh ('Big Minh') during the afternoon, and there were broadcasts of fighting in the streets of Saigon. The presidential palace was under seige.

As the night wore on it became evident that the government of President Ngo Dinh Diem was toppling. There was joy among many Vietnamese, particularly Madame Ly's bar girls who began to dance. Madame Nhu had banned dancing throughout the country. To be caught dancing by the police was to risk arrest. The bar girls abandoned all fears as the night wore on.

Y-Jut stayed with Colonel Serong and myself in my hotel room throughout the night, interpreting the Vietnamese radio broadcasts for us. Commanders of regions, military formations and regiments, as well as province chiefs, one by one, were publicly swearing allegiance to the new military junta.

In Darlac Province, both our province chief and Colonel Trong, commander of the Vietnamese Army's 23rd Division, held out until about midnight, when Colonel Trong was forced at gunpoint by his own subordinate chief of staff and the other staff officers to surrender his division, and to swear allegiance to the new military junta. Undaunted, our province chief, Major Thong, remained obdurate. Even as late as mid-morning the next day, he directed his Vietnamese Information Service loudspeaker-mounted vans to tour Ban-Me-Thuot, broadcasting an appeal to the citizens to remain loyal to President Diem.

What happened then is history, and well-recorded. President Diem and his hated brother Nhu escaped from the palace through a secret tunnel. Late the following morning, Radio Saigon broadcast the location and arrest of President Diem and his brother at a Catholic church in predominantly Chinese Cholon. They had sought refuge there. Radio Saigon later reported the assassination of the president and his brother which took place in in an armoured personnel carrier. Both had been shot and Nhu's body had been badly mutilated.

Major Thong was finally arrested around midday. An era in the history of South Vietnam had ended.

Morris West's book *The Ambassador* gives an accurate account of the lead-up to the *coup d'état*. After reading that book, I can certainly identify CIA agents I knew. I believe that during his research for the project, Morris West spent a number of weeks as a house guest of Colonel Serong in Saigon.

Captain Tuong stayed at the Mills's villa until the fighting ceased the following morning. He then tried to return to Ban-Me-Thuot by car. *En route*, while passing through the mountain town of Bao-Loc in Lam Dong Province, he was recognised by a revolutionary road block and arrested. I was not to see him again for another twelve to fifteen months.

Although most Vietnamese appeared overjoyed at the overthrow of the government of Ngo Dinh Diem and at the end of the influence of his family, they appeared genuinely sorrowful at the death of the president himself.

Ngo Dinh Luyen, Archbishop Thuc and Madame Nhu were out of the country when the *coup* occurred. Had this not been so, they would probably have faced execution like Ngo Dinh Can. Certainly the Vietnamese hated Madame Nhu. They wanted to behead Can, but had to be content with an execution by firing squad — they couldn't find a guillotine!

*　　*　　*

There was confusion for a week or so until new officials were appointed. The new regional director of National Police was an ex-Sûreté man, Ong Nguyen Binh. The Vietnamese word 'Ong' means 'Minister'. Ong Binh was obviously a highly experienced police officer.

The Vietnamese Sûreté were a type of security police, heavily involved in intelligence collection and internal security. They were a powerful section of the police force, and were generally feared by the average Vietnamese. Ong Binh could not speak English nor could his own chief of Sûreté, Ong Phan Tan Truoc. Ong Truoc was a cunning little man, distrustful of everyone. His weakness was that he was a heavy drinker and gifts of whisky could gain his temporary co-operation. Ong Binh, his director, was above graft. *His* weakness was hunting and we soon became good friends through that. I was a good shot, which he respected.

Madame Tuong, wife of the ex-police director, together with family, were evicted from their official residence. They had to find other quarters elsewhere in Ban-Me-Thuot. It was difficult for Madame Tuong as she was in an advanced state of pregnancy. I helped the family in every way I could, and later arranged an Air America DC3 Dakota aircraft to fly the family and furniture to Saigon after Captain Tuong was released.

The new province chief was another army officer, Major Le Van Thanh. He was to serve twice as province chief of Darlac Province while I was there, and was still in office when I left South Vietnam late in 1965. While Darlac province chief, he was promoted to the rank of lieutenant-colonel and I will refer to him as Colonel Thanh.

As a boy he lived in Dalat in Tuyen Duc Province. He spoke English well and he told me that when quite young he had come into contact with Australians — prisoners-of-war of the Japanese. They had been brought from Malaya and Singapore to work in Japanese-occupied Indo-China, building roads, bridges and airfields. Colonel Thanh used to smuggle food to the prisoners constructing the Dalat airfield.

Colonel Thanh and I became good friends, a friendship which endures to the present time. He now lives in Canberra with his second wife, Alice, and a daughter from his first marriage. His first wife and eight of his ten children were massacred by the Communists during the Tet Offensive in early 1968. The surviving daughter escaped to Australia with some of the Vietnamese refugees, the 'boat people'. His surviving son is still in the Socialist Republic of Vietnam, having been detained in a 're-education' camp for seven years because his father was a colonel in the South Vietnamese Army.

*   *   *

It took some weeks following the overthrow of the Diem Government before the salaries of the Armed Propaganda and Intelligence Teams were again paid. I approached Ong Binh, and convinced him that the Montagnard members of the teams should be housed in a nearby village. My argument was that they could better look after themselves in a location where they could keep chickens, ducks and pigs, and grow vegetables. In the overcrowded compound behind the police headquarters, they could not do this. My other, but secret reason for wanting to move them from police headquarters, was to separate them from the ever-watchful and suspicious Ong Truoc, the director's Sûreté chief. Ong Truoc was not allowing them to effectively carry out their role of constantly patrolling the province, disseminating propaganda, and collecting intelligence.

The police director and the new province chief, Colonel Thanh, did not seem to like each other. Each refused to discuss with the other the housing of the teams in a suitable Montagnard village. I became the go-between in efforts to re-settle them.

The place I selected was Buon Enao, a half-empty Montagnard village, only a few kilometres east of Ban-Me-Thuot. It had previously been used by the CIA-sponsored American Special Forces, as a training base. The province chief, Colonel Thanh, agreed to my use of it for the teams on condition that I sign for it. So I did. Here was more evidence of my improved status. I was signing for the buildings, livestock, and the care of seventy-five Rhade! Captain Huy and I, along with a few province officials, conducted the stocktake. Buon Enao is probably still on my signature.

Having acquired the village, I arranged with the police director to move the teams and their families there, and began building additional accommodation for a further two hundred people. One afternoon, much of Buon Enao burnt down when some cooking oil ignited and set fire to the village. We had to rebuild it.

By the time the salaries for the teams had recommenced, the teams were seeing a lot of me. My CIA operations fund had to feed, clothe and house them until their salaries recommenced. Truoc, the Sûreté chief, was more than a little annoyed at the way he was losing direct control and he stipulated I was not to go near the teams, unless he was with me.

I was being frustrated again. With great difficulty, I managed to phone Bryan Mills in Saigon.

'What's your problem, Barry,' he said.

'That bloody man Truoc is thwarting every attempt to get the teams operating. He's treating them as his own private army.'

'Don't worry about it, Barry. We'll sort it out.'

The problem with Bryan was that he always seemed to treat everything as a bit of a yawn.

I said: 'How are we going to do it, short of shooting him?'

'I'll be up there in a couple of days,' he said, as though other things mattered far more.

Using the Vietnamese telephone system was another exercise in frustration. Having gone through it, I hadn't advanced my position one iota.

A few days later, the familiar buzzing of Ban-Me-Thuot occurred again, this time the plane was a Pilatus Porter — fewer seats than the Dornier, but Bryan still had them all to himself.

Over the normal few drinks — Bryan always liked to calm the atmosphere before discussing business — he said:

'Why don't you just take over control of the teams?'

He spoke as though it was the most natural thing in the world to do.

'How the hell do I do that?'

'Just tell the police director that you've received directions from Saigon to take over operational control of them.'

'He wouldn't believe that,' I said.

'OK then,' Bryan said, 'we'll go around and see him and tell him we've received instructions that you're to do just that.'

'Is he going to believe it?'

'Leave that to me,' he said.

The police director wasn't at all convinced.

'I haven't received any instructions from my superior headquarters,' he said stiffly.

Bryan said casually:

'There must be some breakdown in communications from Saigon. Something's bound to come through very soon.'

Later Bryan said to me: 'I might just have to rig a letter, Barry.'

He flew out and was back within days. He had his letter, written on official American Embassy letterhead, and signed by a very senior official.

In essence, it thanked the police director for the smooth hand-over of operational control of his hundred-man force to me. It was glowing in its praise of the director for his past co-operation and good relations between his staff and me.

I read it with astonishment.

'How did you organize this?'

'Never mind,' he said with a smile. 'I think it'll do the trick.'

The director read the letter and shook his head with disbelief. He'd received no instructions from his headquarters in Saigon. Then he turned quickly to Truoc, his Sûreté chief, and spoke rapidly in Vietnamese. The next day, Bryan and I attended an official hand-over ceremony at Buon Enao.

I admired Bryan. His affable, easy-going style concealed a sharp brain. He was shrewd and understood the ways and tempo of Asia. I learned much of the importance of that from him in those early days. He also gave me an insight into the CIA, and an inkling of the subtleties and the power of their better operators.

As a result of his cleverness, I now had total control of a hundred-man force in the central highlands of South Vietnam.

4

Bruised Dignity

I had two permanent staff, Jut, my interpreter, and Vu, my driver. I still did not have a house, but Jut soon solved the problem. He found me a rambling, typically Vietnamese masonry dwelling in a large walled garden, located in the newer, less-attractive and overcrowded district, in Ton That Thuyet Street. It had five basic rooms in the main building, with a three-room structure for servants, plus a kitchen, at the back. The building was substantial, but the layout was appalling. To go from one room to another, it was sometimes necessary to walk through the whole house.

Bryan saw it and said:

'It seems all right. If there's anything wrong, use your operational funds and fix it up.'

I had no legal training, but Bryan told me to write out a contract because there was no solicitor in Ban-Me-Thuot. So I included a clause which enabled me to alter the building as I wished.

The bathroom at the rear had Asian 'squat' toilets and an open bathing area consisting of a huge earthenware jar of water and a dipper. The cooking facilities were two small bucket-like charcoal braziers and no water was connected to the house. Water had to be bought (from God knows where), and carried daily to the house on a cyclo fitted out to carry a full forty-four gallon drum. I had piped water installed, changed the layout of the main house by creating or sealing doors for sensible access, put a pedestal in one of the Asian toilets, and added a bathroom next to it. The laundry and cooking facilities were left as they were. Asian food is better cooked the Asian way, and laundry pounded on a concrete slab comes out just as clean as it does from a washing machine.

It took us no time to find a cook and a housekeeper. Nam and Hai were sisters, both married, content to come to work daily and stay as long as required. They were cheerful and clean. Although Nam could not cook Western food, I didn't encourage her to do so. Too many Westerners living in Asian countries try to make their staff cook European dishes and the results are often disastrous. They would be better off enjoying good local food, prepared in the way Asians know best. Perhaps the tragedy of Vietnam is that Westerners too often imposed their ideas and methods on a society that had got on perfectly well doing it their way for centuries.

H'Pam was another addition to the staff. She was in her mid-twenties, petite, very feminine and attractive. She was married with two children. Like Jut, she spoke English, French, Vietnamese and several Montagnard dialects. She lived on the outskirts of Ban-Me-Thuot with her family. H'Pam was not only my secretary, but looked after the operations fund accounting, the typing of my regular reports, instruction in English for potential interpreters and sometimes interrogation of captured enemy. In this role, her femininity and gentleness elicited more information than even the most severe interrogation might.

The house in Ton That Tuyet ultimately grew to twice its size. Eventually we had a radio room — manned night and day — a classroom for radio operators, an armoury, and accommodation for an eight-man security guard. The owner, old Mr Tran Dinh Quy, visited twice during those two years and each time, his face lit up like a beacon. The CIA not only paid the rent, but virtually gave him a new house.

The compound, surrounded by a high masonry wall, became a menagerie. The deposed police director, Captain

Tuong, left me his peacocks and a monkey, and, over the next year, the Montagnard gave me deer, gibbons, a young honey bear and a tiger cub. I called him simply 'Tiger'. His roars were to become as effective against intruders as all the security guards put together.

There was another pet, a leopard cub called Fatima. She had free run of the house, and was quite playful, climbing all over us, including guests. Occasionally, she would cause great consternation in the neighbourhood by climbing our wall, walking along the top of another and descending into neighbouring yards or into the local bakery. This always resulted in the rapid evacuation of the terrified occupants. We lost the peripatetic Fatima when she was fed a dressed chicken which Nam had bought at the market. I had laid down strict rules that no dressed meat would ever be brought into the compound. The Communists frequently used poison as an assassination technique. I insisted that all meat be bought live and slaughtered on the premises. This is no problem to a Vietnamese woman. This time Nam, to lighten her chores, took the risk by buying dressed chicken for the leopard. Fatima died, but I have no doubt the poisoned chicken she ate was meant for me.

*   *   *

By this time, Jut had taken me to many Montagnard villages. I was learning the Rhade dialect, and Montagnard customs as well as their problems. Montagnard of the central highlands are of two distinct ethnic backgrounds — the Malayo-Polynesian and the Mon-Khmer. The tribes in Darlac Province were predominantly the Rhade and some Jarai, both of Malayo-Polynesian background, while the M'Nong Gar were Mon-Khmer. The Rhade and M'Nong in Darlac Province totalled more than a hundred thousand. Seventy-five percent of these were Rhade — or Ede as they call themselves.

I could already speak Malay and was surprised to find that many of the words of the Rhade dialect were similar to

Malay. So I had the beginnings of a facility to understand and be closer to them.

In their villages, they lived as family groups in separate longhouses set in neat rows. Their pigs, chicken, ducks and dogs were free-ranging and the number of livestock was dependent on the food scraps available.

Physically the Montagnard are a strongly-built people, with broader shoulders than the Vietnamese and darker skin. They are quick to learn, loyal, as a rule very cheerful, but not afraid to fight courageously. They are descended from an earlier migratory group from the region of Yunnan Province in southern China.

Successive migrations of the Malayo-Polynesian groups were the forerunners of the present Malays, Indonesians and Filipinos, and even the Polynesians of the Pacific. The groups who settled the Annamite mountain chain of Indo-China overflowed west into parts of Kampuchea and of Laos. The highland tribes considered themselves owners of the land they occupied. The arrival of the lowland Vietnamese to take over their land in the 1950s was the source of continuing antipathy and suspicion. The Vietnamese, in turn, often treated the Montagnard as an inferior group. They called them 'moi' — meaning 'savage' — and the Vietnamese administrators were inclined to ride roughshod over the Montagnard. Most Vietnamese who held minor bureaucratic positions were guilty of this.

The Montagnard are a matriachal society and the women, although ostensibly subservient, really owned the wealth of land and property. A married man would take his wife's family name and become part of her family. The women were always consulted in decision-making.

* * *

Rice wine drinking sessions with the Montagnard were common during my next two years and I had to learn how to handle myself.

Whenever I visited a village, whether socially or on

operations, the village headman would insist on opening one or more jars of fermented rice wine. On most occasions, this was accompanied by the slaughter of at least one chicken, and occasionally a pig. Major events included the ceremonial sacrifice of a buffalo. To avoid offending a village headman, I could not refuse their rice wine and food, although I tried to dissuade our hosts from slaughtering their valuable livestock.

Rice wine is made by boiling rice, adding yeast and other substances and allowing the mixture to ferment in large earthenware jars, covered with rice husks and banana leaves. Fermentation of the glutinous mess occurs after one or two months, but can continue for up to eighteen months. Water is added to the base about twenty minutes before drinking.

In this matriarchal Montagnard society, the senior lady in the longhouse is, by protocol, the first to drink. She uses a bamboo straw, drinks a little then hands it to the honoured guest. It has to be passed from right hand to right hand, with a hand always on the straw.

Then the male head of the longhouse tells the guest how many containers of rice wine he is to drink. A figure between five and nine is not unusual but generally impossible to achieve. A young lad generally keeps count of the corresponding number of containers he needs to use, to keep the jar brim-full. The number of containers nominated by the host is a sort of hospitable challenge to the guest.

The rice wine is a little like cider in taste, whether it be sweet, sour or bitter cider. It is very filling, and after drinking four or five glasses through a straw in one go, I usually felt as though it was running out of my ears. There are few ways to escape drinking the nominated number of containers and the uninitiated generally returns bloated with rice wine to the sleeping mat, the hand-woven blanket and the cushion provided for his comfort.

A trick I soon learned was to drink some from the straw, then commence siphoning it into a glass — as if to drink from that. I found that it was polite to send, via young boys, a glass of wine to each dignitary present, plus another glass to the ladies — normally seated together towards the rear of the main room. By the time I did that, siphoning into and drinking from my glass all the while, the boy opposite generally lost count of just how much I had actually consumed. A nod from him, and I was free to hand the drinking straw back to the matriach of the longhouse.

But I had to learn this the hard way. My first heavy rice wine-drinking session was a disaster. It was late afternoon when we arrived at a village a short distance from Ban-Me-Thuot. By the time the rice wine jars were ready, it was already dark. My hosts seemed to be honoured by my visit, and I wanted to do the right thing by them.

On being invited to the jar, I was told by my host that I must drink seven or eight glasses of rice wine before I could hand the jar over. Now that's a lot of liquid in anybody's language.

I struggled through as much as I could physically hold, then I pleaded to be allowed to hand the jar over. My request was granted and I uncomfortably made my way back to my mat, my insides totally awash. As other drinkers took over the rice wine jars, to my horror they began to send me glasses of wine from their jars. At that stage, food was being served, and I received a bowl of rice with portions of meat and raw offal, and some fresh blood.

As diplomatically as I could, I ate some of the food and drank a little more wine, until I felt I was about to explode. One of my Montagnard offsiders then nudged me to indicate I was about to be invited to partake of another jar. Suddenly, I began to have difficulty in holding down the vast amount of liquid and the food I had already consumed. All I wanted to do was get rid of it. The fight between my mind and my gullet to hold it down, was causing me to perspire heavily. I knew that I had to get out of the heavy, smoke-laden atmosphere — and quickly. I mumbled an excuse and, getting to my feet, made a rush for the door.

Longhouses are built on stilts and ascent or descent is by means of a pole with stepped notches cut into it. As I lunged across the verandah, my paramount thought was to get down to the ground below as quickly as possible. I did just that as I cartwheeled over the high verandah edge. And as I sailed into space, my mind finally lost that fight with my gullet.

Help reached me in the form of my two Montagnard offsiders, as they peered over the edge of the high verandah into the blackness of night.

'Are you all right, sir?' Jut called into the darkness.

'No,' I replied forlornly.

Jut took me down to the nearby stream and helped me to wash the sour-smelling liquid off my clothes and myself. Fortunately the night was warm and the damp clothing didn't worry me as I dutifully returned to the longhouse. On entering, I was welcomed by polite, but obvious mirth. They had caught another 'new chum'.

My offsiders then told me that it is quite acceptable to quietly descend from the longhouse, go to a nearby thicket or bamboo clump, and regurgitate the sour liquid. After rinsing the mouth, you could then return to the drinking session ready to launch into it again. This procedure could be repeated until the stomach could take no more.

Acceptance is won in many ways, and diplomacy comes in many forms — even if one's dignity is occasionally bruised in the process.

There were other times when during a drinking session I would receive news of an approaching Viet Cong patrol, perhaps aware of my presence in the village. Such unwelcome news signalled a hurried departure from the village, rather than to try to shoot it out with the enemy from within the village. To do so would undoubtedly cost the lives of villagers, either during the inevitable crossfire, or as a result of later Viet Cong reprisals.

Such a warning was generally whispered to me, and it meant hastily slipping our boots on, laces still undone, picking up our equipment and weapons, and leaping out of the longhouse, heading rapidly for the jungle. I should point out that although I didn't like removing my boots on such occasions, it was rude to leave them on inside a longhouse.

Diarrhoea, I found, was a common complaint. It meant that I just had to keep the chocolate tasting, chalk-like, remedial powder with me at all times. It's quite suprising just how a healthy body will adapt to anything, and the stomach hardens.

* * *

On 29 January 1964, General Nguyen Khanh, Commander of the Vietnamese 2nd Army Corps in the north of South Vietnam, staged a successful *coup d'état*, overthrowing the ruling military junta led by General Duong Van Minh — 'Big Minh'.

One of General Khanh's first political moves was to order the release of most of the political prisoners imprisoned during the Ngo Dinh Diem regime. Among those prisoners was a Rhade elder called Y-Bham Enuol. Y-Bham Enuol, who was born in Buon Ale-A adjacent to Ban-Me-Thuot in 1913, was the president of the Bajaraka movement, which had been formed in early 1958 with the aim of maintaining the ethnic identity of the Montagnard despite the roughshod influx of Vietnamese into the highlands after 1954. The Bajaraka Movement sought from the South Vietnamese Diem Government at least the degree of autonomy they had previously enjoyed under French rule.

As early as 1957 Francis Sherry of the American CIA was a frequent visitor to the highlands from Saigon on hunting trips. He generally met Y-Bham and other leaders of the Bajaraka Movement during those visits and the South Vietnamese security police (the Sûreté) knew of this. Thus the CIA deliberately established contact with potentially dissident Montagnard.

In September 1958, Y-Bham and other leaders of Bajaraka were arrested by the Surêté. Y-Dhon Adrong and Y-Bih Aleo, supported by many others, petitioned President Diem for the release of the prisoners and organized a demonstration in Ban-Me-Thuot. About 2000 dissident Montagnard marched into the town. Armoured units of the Vietnamese Army's 23rd Division soon dispersed them.

Y-Bih Aleo was a former civil servant, had served in the French Garde Indochinoise and had been a member of the

Viet-Minh in their fight for independence from the French. To avoid arrest by the South Vietnamese Surêté he defected to the Viet Cong. The Communists quickly capitalized on his defection, promoted him to the rank of general and appointed him Chairman of the Committee for Autonomy of the People of the Western Plateau — a Communist-front organization purporting to support the Montagnard aspirations of autonomy in an effort to gain their support in the overthrow of the South Vietnamese Government.

Y-Bham had served over five years' political imprisonment, most of it under Diem's government. Colonel Thanh, the Darlac Province Chief, felt that greater political support from the Montagnard could be gained if Y-Bham could be returned to his people and given a senior Government appointment in Darlac Province. Although he saw this as necessary, Colonel Thanh also confided in me that he was concerned that Y-Bham might still harbour secret ambitions for Montagnard autonomy. However General Nguyen Khanh, the new prime minister, accepted this proposal and a ceremony was arranged.

In the Ban-Me-Thuot sports arena, in front of an assembled crowd of Montagnard wearing their traditional hand-woven loincloths and jackets, and a gathering of Vietnamese officials, Prime Minister Khanh arrived with Y-Bham Enuol. Khanh announced he was releasing Y-Bham Enuol, and returning this leader to his people, the Montagnard.

A few weeks later, Jut introduced me to Y-Bham Enuol. He seemed to like me and we became friends. Soon after, Y-Bham held a very large sacrifice to celebrate his freedom. It was held at his village, Buon Ea Bong, three kilometres north-west of Ban-Me-Thuot. I appeared to be the only non-Montagnard there. Although it was an honour, I had to be very careful not to sympathize with any autonomous aspirations Y-Bham might still have.

Y-Bham Enuol was to later play a major role in the politics of Indo-China as well as one affecting me, personally.

5

Training, Tactics and a Tiger

In 1964, with the hundred-man Montagnard force now firmly under my control, I realized I was in a politically precarious position. I was a foreigner, totally in command of a minority group — the Montagnard — in South Vietnam and I was vulnerable on many sides. There was always a possibility that the Vietnamese would move in and insert their own command structure. I wanted to operate the force so that it could be used to maximum effect and I did not want to risk the possibility of ineffective command. There was the other problem of the running sore of Montagnard resentment towards the Vietnamese. I had plans to develop a Montagnard command structure answerable to the Vietnamese in the last instance, but ethnically autonomous.

I needed a protector. Who better than the senior man in the province, the province chief? I went to him and said:

'Sir, would you be the Commander-in-Chief of the Armed Propaganda and Intelligence Teams? I will look after the recruiting, training and operational control for you.'

I knew perfectly well that the province chief was already titular commander of all military and para-military forces in the province — excepting the national army units. But there was something very grand in the title 'Commander-in-Chief' which I knew would appeal to him.

He agreed immediately, but I am not sure he understood

what I was really all about. I had deliberately linked the title, with the clarification of my position. He was commander-in-chief and I was, by definition, his chief executive. It meant I had virtually a free hand and was answerable only to him.

The command structure of the various forces in Darlac Province — throughout the whole of South Vietnam for that matter — was nothing less than a can of worms. There was not one single Vietnamese force, but many. There was the main force — the Army of the Republic of Vietnam (ARVN), with their own military commanders, and under central government control. Then, the province chief had his own Regional Force units which were concerned with the security of the province, and secondly, the Popular Forces which looked after the security of some villages and key installations.

The effect of all these commands was that the province chief was heavily overloaded. His responsibilities also included the civil administration of Darlac Province. He was frantically busy.

I told Bryan about the deal I had struck with the province chief.

'Great,' he said, 'let's recruit another hundred.'

'Hang on Bryan,' I said, 'I want to properly train the ones I've got first.'

'Yeah, but still recruit another hundred,' he said.

I liked the idea of increasing the size of the force, but I wasn't going to take the first hundred men I could lay my hands on. I wanted the right men. I wanted time to select, and I wanted every man to be trained properly.

I asked Colonel Serong if I could borrow an Australian warrant officer from the training team for a few weeks. He gave me Danny Neville. I knew him and he proved to be an excellent man for the job, as I knew he would.

The men I already had desperately needed basic training in weapon handling and minor tactics to handle any skirmish with the Viet Cong. At this stage, their basic role was to operate as armed teams throughout the province, disseminating propaganda and collecting intelligence.

No sooner had Danny Neville left than Colonel Serong made a visit.

'Barry,' he said, 'I think you could do with a full-time Australian assistant up here. Could you use one?'

'Yes sir,' I said, and I really meant it.

Within weeks, Warrant Officer Bevan Stokes arrived. He had been serving with an American Special Forces 'A' Team in a province further north. I knew Bevan very well. He had served as a corporal with me in Australia some years before. Bevan was a fit, enthusiastic, likeable and very capable young man. I couldn't have been given a better person to help me.

Bryan Mills turned up again about this time. He seemed to like the way we were going about things.

'Recruit another one hundred and fifty men Barry.'

'Jesus, Bryan, we haven't even finished recruiting the second hundred yet.'

'You've got the authority to go to three hundred and fifty as soon as you can handle it,' he said.

I knew the reason for the swift expansion. Viet Cong activity was increasing throughout the country. The highlands were the key to the security of South Vietnam because the North Vietnamese were using the Ho Chi Minh trails which ran from the north, through the highlands of Indo-China to the south, to infiltrate the country. Men and equipment were being poured into South Vietnam in increasing numbers. The Montagnard, scattered throughout the highlands were in the best position to help block the growing North Vietnamese invasion. Teams of trained Montagnard, working amongst the scattered population, were best suited to gain the people's support, and to collect the most useful information about the Viet Cong and North Vietnamese movements.

I realized a force of three hundred and fifty would need its own command, and training and logistics support elements. Bevan's principal task was to organize a training cadre who, in turn, would instruct the new recruits.

The members of the original hundred-man force were predominantly Rhade, with some M'Nong and a few Jarai. With the increase in numbers, I could see the M'Nong operating in their own tribal area in the south of the province. The M'nong represented a quarter of the total force, and I decided to keep it that way, because their tribal area was roughly a quarter of Darlac Province. The M'Nong lived in the geographically-isolated Lac Thien District. 'Lac' is the Vietnamese word for lake and Lac Thien District surrounded Dak Lac, a large lake in the basin-like area surrounded by mountains. In fact, Darlac Province was named after that lake and has now been correctly renamed by the present Vietnamese Government.

Following training of the expanded teams, I planned that Bevan should establish an operational base in Lac Thien, and thus control the M'Nong teams from there. I would control the operations of the larger group of Rhade and Jarai teams, and oversee the operations of all the teams in Darlac Province.

I had already decided to organize the force into eight-man teams. Each team would have a light machine gun and two automatic sub-machine guns; the rest of their arms were rifles, mainly 30-calibre carbines, sniper rifles or shotguns. These were weapons which were obsolete in the American Army, acquired by the CIA, and issued to those para-military forces supported by them throughout the world. I only had to ask, and I would receive.

Each team would have at least one member trained as a radio operator and one as a medical orderly.

My plan was to organize the teams, according to the geographic location of the villages of the members. For example, I would choose a group of four or eight neighbouring villages, and each eight-man team would ideally comprise an equal number of members from each of those villages. The teams would be directed not to stay overnight in a village, but instead, set night ambushes on tracks approaching one or another of the villages, in their area of responsibility. To avoid becoming a Viet Cong target, they would be told not to remain in the same location on two consecutive nights.

I realized that my directions would not be implicitly obeyed; however, the composition of each team would induce it to move from one village to the next. At each village, at least one member of the team would be a local youth, and could gain intelligence from his fellow villagers.

The plan sounded good, but first we had to fully train and organize the teams, and the new reinforcements Bryan Mills had authorized.

I had by this time clarified the roles of my force and had cleared them with the province chief. The objectives were still the dissemination of anti-Communist propaganda and the collection of intelligence; but now also the disruption of Viet Cong activities; ambushes; small-scale raids; and the kidnapping or assassination of Viet Cong agents and officials. In due course, the force would conduct long-range raids into Viet Cong controlled areas in order to destroy their safe bases and to rescue their captive labour.

One other role I had in mind was to use the force as the nucleus of a resistance movement, should the central highlands ever fall into Communist hands. I revealed this only to Colonel Serong, my Australian commander, and in a secret paper dated 1 June 1964, to the Covert Action Branch of the CIA. Although Colonel Serong regarded it as a remote possibility at that time, a few Americans in the Covert Action Branch told me that I had a defeatist attitude in thinking that any of South Vietnam might ever fall to Communist North Vietnam. I still have a copy of that paper.

* * *

Bevan was settling in well. I told him he would be going to Lac Thien with the M'Nong teams to control their operations and that he had to get to know the senior leader of the M'Nong teams and their customs. As with other Montagnard tribes, the rice-wine-drinking ceremony was an important event.

The new province chief, Major Bui Huy Gia, was to pay an official visit to the teams in Buon Enao, and a sacrifice with a

rice-wine-drinking ceremony was to take place that afternoon. It would be Bevan's first taste of the Montagnard rice
wine.

That morning, Bevan, Jut and I, together with Y-Tin, our
other interpreter, went to Buon Enao to check on preparations. We saw ten or twelve large rice wine jars in a long line,
each tied to its own pole. A Rhade elder thrust his hand
down into the jar nearest us and withdrew a small portion of
the claggy, fermented rice. It was moving. It had been blown
by flies, and the resulting maggots made the globules of rice
appear alive. Such a minor detail wouldn't mean the waste of
a good jar of rice wine. The old man, as official taster,
approved the jar.

Bevan was horrified.

'Sir,' he said, 'I'll do anything else you ask of me, but I'm
not going to drink that bloody stuff.'

I assured Bevan the tiny holes drilled into the bottom of
each plugged reed straw were too small to allow maggots, or
any other sediment through. 'Just clench your teeth as you
drink,' I said, 'and you'll filter them if they do slip through.'

Bevan was adamant. Under no circumstances was he going
to drink any rice wine that day or any other.

Major Gia arrived and, following his formal inspection of
the teams on parade, the reception commenced. The sacrifice
was preceded by a number of beers. As there was no refri-
geration, the 'Bia La Rue' — the local brew — was cooled
slightly by chunks of brown, Ban-Me-Thuot ice, and drunk
from thick glasses. Vietnamese ice, like their sugar, always
appeared to be brown, probably due to the dust in the dry
season.

When the ceremony commenced, Bevan was nowhere to be
found. I was annoyed as he had a role to play. I later found
he was still drinking Bia La Rue, in the company of the
leader of the M'Nong and a few of his men. Even when
Major Gia was leaving with his escort late in the afternoon,
Bevan was still in hiding.

Darkness fell and, at about 8 o'clock, I was invited up from
my mat to drink at yet another jar of rice wine. The Montag-

nard bronze gongs and buffalo-hide drums had been thundering their beat into the dark, surrounding jungle. After a while they stopped. Quietness prevailed, broken only by some raucous laughter from the end of the line of 'dragon' jars. I leaned forward to identify the source of the laughter, only to see Bevan, drinking from the very jar we had seen tested that morning. Sitting beside him, drinking from the next jar, was the semi-toothless M'Nong chief. They had arms across each other's shoulders and they were obviously becoming acquainted. I forgave Bevan instantly.

Bevan was to totally accept the way of life of the M'Nong and they, in turn, totally accepted him. The life style at Lac Thien left Bevan no choice but to eat and drink what the M'Nong ate and drank, including bush rats. When, many months later, Bevan left to return to Australia, he said that he was able to identify five different types of worms in his faeces. The price of diplomacy and acceptance is sometimes quite high.

*   *   *

Although our clashes with the Viet Cong were still very limited at that time, they were certainly about. On one occasion I was visiting a Rhade village east of Ban-Me-Thuot. The villagers told us of a tiger which was taking some of their livestock. They said that each time it attacked, it became more confident and they were afraid that it might one day take a child. They asked me to shoot it. I wasn't too keen on the idea, but realizing the danger of a potential man-eating tiger, I agreed to try.

Inexperienced as I am at tiger hunting, I recalled how it was done in the adventure books I had read as a boy. First you have to select an area the tiger frequents. Then you tether a sacrificial goat to a stake in a clearing in that area, allow the tiger to take the goat, then repeat the performance at least two more times.

Prior to these preparations, you must construct a platform in a tree overlooking the sacrificial clearing. You then position yourself on the platform in the tree after tethering the sacrificial goat for the third and last time, and as the tiger takes his victim, you get him. Bang! No more tiger.

It seemed a fairly simple and safe method of dispatching a dangerous animal. We decided to adopt the plan and commence preparations. I asked the villagers to take us to a suitable spot frequented by the beast. It was a glade in a predominantly bamboo forest. As we entered the glade, I could smell the tiger. I had experienced that distinctive odour of stale urine previously in Malaya. We knew that the tiger's lair was quite close. We beat a hasty retreat from the bamboo clearing and chose a suitable area nearby as the 'killing ground'.

While the platform was being built, I arranged for the purchase of a small goat from the villagers. It was tethered to a stake and left overnight. Sure enough, the next morning it was gone. I didn't like the sacrifice of the goat, but I was delighted with the confirmation this seemed to give to my memories of the 'ripping yarns' that had engrossed me in childhood. I ordered another goat to be tethered there on the next suitable night.

In the *Boys' Own* stories it was always made clear that the tethering of the goat had to occur either during or before rainfall. This was to ensure that the rains washed all human smells from the area around the goat. Several days later, there was suitable rain, and the next morning, the second goat had vanished.

The plan was working. The tiger had established a safe food source. The tree platform was soon completed. Several days later there was more rain and a third goat was duly tethered. That evening, Jut and I, both armed with Springfield 30·06-calibre sniper's rifles, climbed onto the platform and waited. It was a very hot evening, and still clammy despite the rain. The humidity had hardly abated at all when darkness came. I could see the goat tethered below and quite close to the tree. It was bleating plaintively. I was not insensitive to its predicament. What a dreadful fate lay in store for it. But the tiger was endangering a village, and might perhaps have taken a child. The goat was the necessary sacrificial offering, to avert such a tragedy. I hoped I could get the tiger before it got the goat.

It was not at all comfortable on the platform. There must have been a termites' nest nearby for they began their mating flight. Termites have a remarkably swift and spectacular mating ritual. At the right time, both sexes take to the air for a brief but vibrant half-hour or so as winged creatures. As they land, they seem to shed their wings, mate and find a suitable home if not taken by nocturnal predators. Jut and I were almost at the centre of this exposition of Nature's wonder. We lay on the platform in a cloud of mating termites which stuck to our perspiration-drenched skin. Through the darkness, lit only by a quarter moon, I felt I saw something move in the bushes behind the goat. With infinite care, I raised the rifle to my shoulder, taking careful aim. I was determined to get that tiger.

I had the clump of bushes firmly in my sights and my finger had closed on the trigger when the silence was interrupted by jabbering. I looked down and saw villagers beneath the tree, beckoning to us.

I signalled to them urgently to go away, but they did not seem to get the message.

I turned to Jut.

'For Christ's sake,' I hissed, 'tell them to piss off.'

Jut shinned down the ladder and I resumed my aim at the tiger's previous position. The villagers and Jut were in animated conversation. I was furious, for the tiger would have had to be stone-deaf and drunk on rice wine not to hear the jabbering.

'Sir,' Jut called, half-whisper, half-shout.

'Quiet,' I hissed.

'Sir,' Jut said, his voice several octaves higher. 'The Viet Cong!'

I took several seconds to assess the situation. It was clear that I was a sitting duck lying on that platform. Even Tarzan of the Apes could not have got out of that tree with greater speed.

Later, I heard from the villagers that local Viet Cong had

been aware of my plans for the tiger and had been moving in through the jungle to ambush me. We must have got out just in time.

I never did catch sight of the tiger.

6

Plots and Counterplots

I had been in South Vietnam for more than nine months. The training and infant operations of the teams had gone exceptionally well. We had almost reached a three-hundred-and-fifty-man force, although some were still undergoing their initial training. Not too bad for an army captain. In the Australian Army, an infantry company is commanded by a major — one rank higher — and my force numerically equalled three companies. We had come a long way since the day I first landed with Bryan in Ban-Me-Thuot. I now knew what I was doing and where we were going. I couldn't have said the same thing during those first few months.

Bryan Mills was impressed. On one of his visits, again over drinks, he suggested I create an élite group by giving the force their own distinctive badges, uniforms and title.

'Like the Gurkhas under British command, Barry,' he said. 'Give them a real identity, a bit of oomph.'

I was apprehensive about creating what could appear to be a private army, but I saw the value in being distinctive. It would certainly boost morale if our teams could see themselves as part of a special force. At some time in the future, I decided to design a distinctive beret badge for them.

Months later, when our hit-and-run and propaganda operations began to have a real effect, the Viet Cong began to refer to our teams as the 'Tiger Men'. The name probably came from the type of camouflage uniform the CIA warehouse issued as our operational uniform. Captured Viet Cong documents clearly indicated our operations were hurting them, and warned all their units to be careful of the Tiger Men. So I chose the head of a tiger as our symbol, and ordered one thousand 'silver' tiger-head beret badges to be made in Saigon. They were in fact simple alloy badges depicting a tiger's head and they carried no wording.

A later province chief, Lieutenant-Colonel Nguyen Dinh Vinh, gave our teams the title 'Truong Son Force'. 'Truong' is Vietnamese for 'very long' and 'son' means 'mountain'. The Vietnamese call the Annamite Mountains, 'Truong Son'. The Truong Son Force was to gain considerable respect and fame.

*   *   *

My Truong Son Force was not the only Montagnard force in the central highlands of South Vietnam. At that time there were the Civil Irregular Defence Group (CIDG) units, scattered in outlying areas of the provinces and ostensibly commanded by a Vietnamese Special Forces 'A' Team, the Luc Luong Dac Biet (LLDB). There was an identical American team of twelve, an 'A' Team of the United States Special Forces (USSF) commanded by a captain — my rank — to advise them. The Americans called the Montagnard forces 'strike force companies'. They used them principally as reaction forces when Viet Cong were located, or when a village came under Viet Cong attack. They tended to operate in groups of a hundred or more, which made them formidable — if they managed to surprise the enemy. But too often these groups were too big and cumbersome.

Sometimes the Viet Cong drew these reaction strike force companies into prepared ambushes by deliberately attacking a nearby Montagnard village.

In response, a large strike force company of a hundred men or more on motor vehicles would take the shortest possible route to relieve the besieged village. The Viet Cong would anticipate their reaction. The road was often mined so that the lead and perhaps rear vehicles of the convoy were blown up and thus the vehicles and personnel in between were trapped. Heavy machine-gun, rifle and even mortar fire could often inflict heavy casualties on those trapped. The Viet Cong could then quickly disappear after a highly effective hit-and-run tactic — just because the incoming force was too large and too predictable.

My aim was to keep the Truong Son Force a group of small, mobile, hard-hitting and elusive elements which could play the Viet Cong at their own game. The deal I had struck with the province chief, for him to act as commander-in chief, had proved enormously valuable. Bevan and I had a free hand to operate, without the constriction of having Vietnamese counterparts who might well argue over our own operational techniques. Later results proved the effectiveness of this strategy.

Fighting in South Vietnam from the earliest days was beset by mistakes, confusion, and sometimes quite outlandish follies stemming from differing perceptions, priorities and methods.

For example, an incident occurred when a Montagnard village in the east of Darlac Province came under heavy attack by the Viet Cong. They were running low on ammunition, and called the province headquarters by radio asking for more ammunition.

The American advisers at the province headquarters requested an American helicopter from Pleiku. None were stationed in Ban-Me-Thuot. They intended to parachute additional ammunition by helicopter to the besieged village.

After the helicopter arrived at the Ban-Me-Thuot town airstrip, a radio message was received by the US 23rd Advisory Group, reporting that a sergeant member of the USSF 'A' Team at Buon Mi Ga had badly cut his hand while 'whittling' (woodcarving) with his bowie knife. The wound required suturing. The team medical sergeant, despite the extensive para-medical training which equipped him to do the job perfectly well himself, wanted to send the injured man to the American Army medical officer with the advisory group in Ban-Me-Thuot.

American casualties in South Vietnam received top priority in helicopter tasking and the Pleiku helicopter was diverted to collect him. Only after delivering him to Ban-Me-Thuot was the helicopter then loaded with the precious ammunition for the besieged Montagnard village. On arrival over the village, the American advisers saw it in flames. There was no sign of life below. A village had died.

It was one of the stupidities of that war — and there were many of them — that the inhabitants of a village could be cruelly wiped out because an American had cut his hand, carving a bit of wood.

*   *   *

July, August and September 1964 were months of rumour in Darlac Province, and especially in Ban-Me-Thuot. I received a large number of varying reports, and was able to gather considerable intelligence during conversations with important people. One was the province chief, Major Bui Huy Gia, a lover of intrigue who also loved discussing it.

The CIA's Covert Action Branch had given me a two-piece transceiver. Both parts — the transmitter and the receiver — were small enough each to fit inside a cigarette packet. The receiver could be connected to any size tape recorder located within three to five kilometres of the transmitter. When visiting the province chief or director of National Police, I would strap the small transmitter to my waist. I could then feed the combination antenna-cum-microphone lead up and through my T-shirt, pinning the microphone just behind a button of the shirt which I wore over all. The microphone was so sensitive that I had to sit very still when recording conversations. Even the slightest movement of my shirt cloth would be loudly amplified to the tape recorder, some distance away. As a wire could easily be seen through a light cotton shirt, most of my T-shirts ended up with a small hole in the front.

One day, I had an important meeting with both the province chief and the National Police director at my house in Ton That Thuyet. I had taped the small transmitter beneath the top of a cane table. The receiver, attached to the long-playing, reel-to-reel tape recorder, was in the locked office, elsewhere in the house.

During our discussions over Vietnamese tea and drinks, I suddenly saw something out of the corner of my eye. The small transmitter had come loose, and was dangling by part of the adhesive tape beneath the table top. I was acutely aware of it. Neither Major Gia nor the police director and their officers had seen it. If they had, I'm sure that I would instantly have been expelled from the province, or possibly even arrested.

I was ostensibly an Australian Army captain, although both these senior Vietnamese knew I worked for the CIA. They probably suspected me of some espionage activity, but I did not want to be caught red-handed practising it on them.

Almost distracted in my anxiety, I had to sit through the remainder of the lengthy conversation. Fortunately that one piece of adhesive tape still prevented the small transmitter from clattering to the tiled floor.

I could use parts of taped conversations for reports to the CIA's Covert Action Branch. In late 1965, my complete records were confiscated by the CIA. They did not realize I kept a copy of every report I had written in South Vietnam during my attachment to them. I also passed a copy to my own Australian Army commander.

* * *

During a conversation in his office one day, the province chief, Major Gia, told me that as a young officer during the 1940s he had received training at Wampoa, a Chinese military academy in a part of China still under the control of Chiang Kia-shek. Major Gia was a member of the VNQDD (Viet-Nam Quoc Dan Dang), the Vietnamese nationalist party modelled on Chiang Kai-shek's Kuomintang Party of China.

Major Gia told me of existing resistance movements in the border region between Laos and North Vietnam. The Kha, Meo, Thai and Muong tribes were evidently involved, as were the Zin-Poong (a warlord army of opium traders). He seemed to have details of their strengths, weapons and radio equipment, and he deliberately furnished that detail to me in a report meant for the CIA. Major Gia also told me he had some contact with elements of the Muong resistance movement in that northern region of Indo-China and Laos. I gave the report to the Covert Action Branch.

More importantly, Major Gia gave me my first insight into French involvement in the war in South Vietnam.

On 27 January 1964, the French President Charles De Gaulle recognized China's Communist Government and called for the 'neutralization' of the former Indo-Chinese states — Laos, Cambodia and the two Vietnams. This policy apparently meant that all foreign powers should cease any intervention in the affairs of these countries, and thus, of course, the Americans would be forced to withdraw from South Vietnam. I believe that the French were jealous of the American takeover of their colonial role in South Vietnam, following the French defeat at Dien Bien Phu. The French naïvely believed that a neutralist South Vietnam would enable both their own government and French expatriates to retain their commercial interests in that country.

It was strongly rumoured that the French Government actively and financially supported the neutralist movement. I know that plotting and intrigue did occur.

Major Gia named Monsieur Marcel Coronel, a local coffee planter, as the French Government's organizer of the neutralist movement in the central highlands. He also named the Director of National Police for the central highlands, Ong Nguyen Binh, as another member of the movement, as well as a number of prominent Vietnamese and Montagnard.

Major Gia told me that in September 1964, the French had actually sent one of their helicopters across the border from Cambodia to a French plantation in Quang Duc Province, just to the south of Darlac. In those days the inadequate radar cover of South Vietnam enabled foreign aircraft to move in and out of the country virtually undetected. Major Gia said the helicopter had picked up Y-Char Hdok, a prominent M'Nong, who was taken to Phnom Penh then flown to Paris, to attend a conference on the organization of the Neutralist movement.

A few years later Jut confirmed that the same French helicopter had actually picked up Y-Bun Suor (later known as Bun-Sur) — also a M'Nong, and a graduate of Lycée Yersin (a French high school) in Dalat in Tuyen Duc Province of South Vietnam. He was a secret intelligence agent of the French Government's Service de Documentation Extérieure et de Contre-Espionnage (SDECE) and the Cambodian Sihanouk Government's Deuxième Bureau.

I also learned that other French SDECE agents operated in Darlac Province — principally French owners or managers of tea, coffee or rubber plantations. They also included the French 'résident' (the French Embassy's representative in the central highlands), Monsieur Noel Mercurio. Even Father Bianchetti, the senior French Jesuit priest in Darlac Province, was a secret agent of the SDECE and so, presumably, were many of his subordinate priests. I can only assume their principal operation in the central highlands in those days was the active promotion of the French Government's neutralist proposal for Indo-China — a proposal supported by Prince Norodom Sihanouk and his Cambodian Government.

7

Unrest Among the Montagnard

Unrest among the Montagnard was on the increase during the months of August and September, 1964. There were growing rumours of an impending Viet Cong attack on the town of Ban-Me-Thuot. The unrest seemed to stem from the treatment given the 'moi' or 'savages' as some called the Montagnard, by some Vietnamese petty bureaucrats. The centre of the trouble appeared to be the special forces base at Buon Sarpa, in nearby Quang Duc Province.

In July 1964, the Montagnard commanders at Buon Sarpa had sent a detailed letter of complaint to the Darlac province chief, Major Gia. Probably because Buon Sarpa was in Quang Duc Province, Major Gia did not interfere. A copy had also been given to the American captain in command of the USSF 'A' Team in Buon Sarpa. I sent a copy to the Covert Action Branch in Saigon.

The complaint was basically against Captain Thuan, the commander of the Luc Luong Dac Biet — the Vietnamese Special Force 'A' Team. It accused him of bad administration of the Montagnard CIDG, misappropriation of salaries, collaboration with the Viet Cong, and the encouragement of dissention between the Americans and the Montagnard.

* * *

On 6 September 1964, Jut reported that a secret meeting of Montagnard elders was taking place in the American Christian Missionary Alliance Hall in Buon Ale. Y-Bham Enuol, the assistant province chief in charge of Montagnard affairs, and titular leader of the Dega (the collective term for Montagnard or 'sons of the mountain' tribes), had called the meeting. Jut said that Y-Bham would tell the Montagnard leaders that he had established contact with General Y-Bih Aleo, the Rhade elder mentioned earlier who, following the 1958 Montagnard Revolt, had defected to the Viet Cong.

Y-Bham was to tell the others of General Y-Bih's claim that the Viet Cong would attack Ban-Me-Thuot on an unspecified night and that they planned to destroy all key installations and public utilities. Y-Bih was supposed to have told Y-Bham that American personnel would not be harmed, unless they played an active part in the defence of Ban-Me-Thuot. (I thought that a very strange statement for a Viet Cong general to make, and that something was amiss with the information. The Viet Cong would never give such assurances about Americans. They would kill or capture them on the slightest pretext.)

However, I reported Jut's conversation to the Covert Action Branch. I also knew that two Rhade school teachers, Y-Dhon Adrong from Lac Thien District and Y-Nuin from Buon Kram, were named as the liaison officers between Y-Bham and General Y-Bih. Some weeks earlier, the province chief had told me that he had received an intelligence report that these school teachers had disappeared. Y-Dhon, at least, was to play an important role in the near future.

As the days passed, rumours were rife, but nothing happened. Then, on the morning of Saturday 19 September, Bevan Stokes and Y-Tin returned from Buon Enao to tell me that our Truong Son base had been developed into a fortress, and there was tension in the air. That day we were expecting two Air America DC3 Dakota aircraft, loaded with more weapons and ammunition for our Truong Son Force. We had a busy day ahead of us.

By early afternoon, we learned there was to be a Montagnard uprising against the Vietnamese administration that night. The second Dakota aircraft was on the airstrip being unloaded. I realized I needed to get a message to Saigon, yet avoid a hasty over-reaction from either the Americans, or the Vietnamese. I held the aircraft until I could get Bevan and Y-Tin aboard it. I had decided to send Bevan direct to Colonel Serong in Saigon, and allow him to pass the information on to the CIA. It was far too late for either the CIA or Colonel Serong to fly into Ban-Me-Thuot that day. I was pleased. The last thing Darlac Province needed that night, was a bunch of CIA operatives and a senior Australian Army officer flying in *en masse*, further generating Vietnamese suspicions. Anyhow, what could they do about an impending Montagnard revolt, apart from further adding to the confusion?

We had a Filipino communications instructor who worked for the CIA on loan to us, to help train our Truong Son Force radio operators. We told him to pack, and return to Saigon with Bevan and Tin, aboard the Air America Dakota. Using a spare identity card he had, we made up a forged Filipino identity card for Tin — a Montagnard — to protect him from possible arrest in Saigon.

Later I received a visit from Ong Binh, the Director of National Police for the Central Highlands Region. He was with his Sûreté chief plus a protective escort. When Ong Binh and I had met before, our exchanges had been invariably cheerful. We had been friends and shooting companions. When he arrived at the house at Ton That Thuyet that afternoon, it was clear his attitude towards me had changed.

We first settled down to the customary Vietnamese tea. Then he said:

'Captain Petersen, have you heard anything about a Montagnard demonstration in Ban-Me-Thuot tomorrow?'

'No sir,' I lied.

'We have reports that there is going to be a demonstration.'

'I know nothing about a demonstration,' I said. This was true. He had got it wrong. It was to be a revolt.

'I'm surprised you know nothing about it,' the director said. 'I trust that none of your men intend taking part.'

'I know of no demonstration, sir,' I said.

Then he said ominously:

'If there is a demonstration Captain Petersen, we will expect you to bring your own men into Ban-Me-Thuot to help quell it.'

I could see myself becoming a scapegoat.

Soon after, the province chief, Major Gia, and a few of his officers arrived. He asked me the same questions and received the same professions of ignorance.

Major Gia said quite deliberately:

'Captain Petersen, if any demonstration does occur tomorrow, you are to stop your men from taking part.'

'Sir,' I said, 'they're not just my men, they're your men as well. You're their commander-in-chief.'

'No, Captain Petersen.' He was looking at me very coldly. 'If anything happens, if any demonstration occurs, you will be held entirely responsible.'

The province chief's attitude seemed to me quite unreasonable.

'Sir,' I said, 'I don't control all the Montagnard in this province.'

He looked at me very hard indeed.

'Captain Petersen, you heard me. I'm holding you entirely responsible for anything that happens.'

I *was* to be the scapegoat! My head really was on the block.

I suppose I could have taken all this as a back-handed compliment. It seemed the province chief and the police director both believed that I — a foreigner, and a mere army captain at that — had sufficient influence to prevent not only my own Truong Son Force from demonstrating, but all the Montagnard. Yet the problem was not a demonstration, but a widespread Montagnard revolt against the Vietnamese Government. I was as powerless to prevent this as the province chief and the police director themselves.

My predicament was very clear: if a revolt occurred, and

the Truong Son Force took part, I could well be arrested by the Vietnamese. If I was absent from Ban-Me-Thuot when the revolt occurred, then I would be seen by the Vietnamese to be implicated. I had to avoid both being implicated and being arrested.

Jut and I drove to our Truong Son Force base at Buon Enao. It was dusk and we found it well defended by additional armed Montagnard. On our arrival, we obviously interrupted a conference. Y-Bham Enuol was emphasizing to the elders that the Montagnard were not going to revolt.

Jut whispered: He's only saying that because there are secret agents of the Vietnamese Sûreté here.'

After the meeting, I called Y-Bham aside and asked him not to be implicated in any way.

'If you are seen to be involved in the revolt,' I said, 'it could lead to mass arrests by the Vietnamese of Montagnard elders and intellectuals.'

He was an old man, very quiet and considered.

'I know,' he replied.

'You should stay in your official residence in Ban-Me-Thuot and we'll provide a guard to protect you and your family. I'll give you a hand gun. Do you know how to use one?'

He nodded.

I gave him a Colt .45-calibre semi-automatic pistol and directed that a Rhade guard return with him to Ban-Me-Thuot.

Without consultation with me, the Rhade guards were later replaced by M'Nong members of the Truong Son Force. The M'Nong were not as keen on revolt as the Rhade and Jarai.

We returned to the house in Duong Ton That Thuyet; Jut and I found that our own Rhade security guards had also been replaced by M'Nong. That didn't particularly worry us. We prepared a demolition charge, and positioned it without its detonator against a wall of the house. Should the situation become serious, my plan was to set it off and make it look as if Jut and I had been abducted against our will. It seemed the only way to make it legitimately appear that we had nothing to do with the revolt.

Jut and I settled down to face the night. Our main concern was the part the Viet Cong and North Vietnamese might play, should they take advantage of this delicate and dangerous situation.

8

The Montagnard Revolt

It was Sunday 20 September 1964. I awoke at first light to an eerie stillness. Jut and I were alone in the house, save for the M'Nong guards in the compound. I had slept fitfully, expecting to be woken by the sounds of gunfire and explosions, or to hear the 'enemy' — perhaps the Vietnamese, perhaps the Viet Cong, perhaps the rebel Montagnard — around the house or at the entrance in an attempt to arrest, capture or kill both of us. Nothing had happened.

I checked the demolition charge we had positioned the night before. It was as I had left it. I looked outside. Normally, even on a Sunday, there would have been activity in the street at this hour. The house was in one of the more populous areas of the town and there was a market only a block away. People and vehicles — cyclos or motor scooters or the occasional truck — should have filled the streets. But they were almost deserted. It was as if Ban-Me-Thuot had been partly evacuated. Yet I could see figures and faces at doors and windows of the adjacent houses. People were clearly not venturing outdoors, unless it was really necessary.

Jut was already up and about, and that was comforting. He seemed the only ally I had. My relationship with the Vietnamese authorities was tense, and I was uncertain how I stood with the Montagnard, particularly with those who led them in their new rebellious mood. Jut was my constant support. He had been with me most moments of each day since the time I had employed him, almost a year before. He was my interpreter, adviser, companion and friend. I trusted him. I think he trusted me.

'Is there anything on the radio?' I asked him.

'I've tried it, aie (sir),' he said. 'It's dead.'

The government radio station — Radio Ban-Me-Thuot — was on the outskirts of the town. Normally it would be broadcasting Vietnamese music, pretty even to a foreign ear, and news or propaganda in Vietnamese or a Montagnard dialect. Its silence was ominous.

I had no telephone in the house in Ton That Thuyet then. They were rare and cantankerous instruments possessed by only a few. The occasional calls I made were through the province headquarters, or from the Bungalow where the Americans had installed more powerful, but still imperfect, radio-relay telephones. I still had not established my own radio communications system from the house.

I was cut off without any idea of what was going on, and in a delicate situation, both with the Vietnamese and the Montagnard. I was out of contact with my own teams stationed at Buon Enao, a few kilometres outside the town. I did not know whether they had also joined the revolt and, if they had, what their attitude would now be towards me. To go straight out to Buon Enao would, in Vietnamese eyes, implicate me.

Jut and I went by jeep to the official residence of Y-Bham, the Montagnard titular leader in Ban-Me-Thuot. My first priority was to establish his safety. His M'Nong guards were still on duty. There had been no trouble overnight, and no need for Y-Bham to use the pistol I had given him.

We then went to the province headquarters. I needed to find out if I was still in the Vietnamese hot seat. We seemed in the clear. The information they had on the revolt was still very sketchy. It was confirmed that Radio Ban-Me-Thuot was in rebel hands and that a force of about five hundred Rhade, M'Nong and a few anti-government Cham, had captured the strategic 'Bridge 14' on the southern route to

Saigon. The Montagnard rebel group had established their operational headquarters at the nearby village of Buon Mbre.

The revolt had begun. But it was too early to assess its scope and seriousness.

By mid-morning, an Air America aircraft was buzzing Ban-Me-Thuot. My message, sent to Saigon with Bevan Stokes, had reached Colonel Serong and the CIA. We drove quickly to the town airstrip. Colonel Serong was aboard the aircraft with Stu Methven of the CIA's Covert Action Branch. Methven's arrival was the first real indication I'd had that Bryan Mills had been phased out and Methven had replaced him as my agent handler. Mills had been tranferred from Saigon although I was never to be told where. The CIA seemed to work that way. I've not seen Bryan Mills to this day.

I knew Stu Methven. He was a familiar personality around the Covert Action Branch offices in Saigon. He was a big man with an olive complexion and a large Mexican-style moustache. In fact he looked a bit like a Mexican bandit. Methven was a flamboyant man, with a pronounced air of confidence — although he was certainly not loud-mouthed.

I drove Colonel Serong and Stu Methven back to the house and briefed them on what I knew and of my confrontation with the province chief and director of police the previous afternoon. We then went to the province headquarters. During the next few hours, messages about the extent of the Montagnard revolt began trickling in.

It seemed that about three thousand Montagnard were associated with the revolt — more than two thousand of them actively. At that time, there were five special force bases of armed mountain tribesmen in the area around Buon-Me-Thuot, each ostensibly under the command of a twelve-man Vietnamese Special Forces 'A' Team — and in turn 'advised' by identical twelve-man 'A' Teams teams from the American Special Forces. Three of the bases were in Darlac Province, and the other two in the adjoining Quang Duc Province. Our Truong Son Force, the only one totally supported by the CIA and run along different lines to the others, brought the number of bases involved, directly or indirectly, to six.

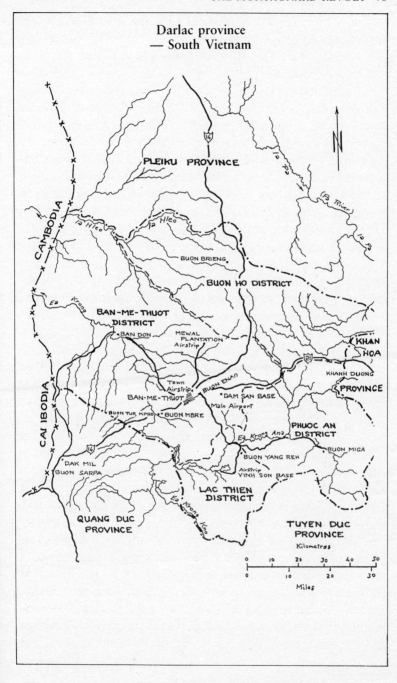

Darlac province
— South Vietnam

The reports coming in showed that the uprising had been both large-scale and bloody.

At Buon Sarpa base in adjacent Quang Duc Province, rebels had disarmed and held as hostages members of the American Special Forces 'A' Team, and an American International Voluntary Service volunteer, Tracy Atwood. Nine of the corresponding twelve-man Vietnamese Special Forces 'A' Team had been shot or had their throats cut.

In another area of Quang Duc Province near the Cambodian border, another five hundred Rhade and M'Nong had overrun a Vietnamese Civil Guard outpost and massacred the occupants, and had then occupied the small town of Dak Mil, taking the Vietnamese district chief as hostage.

A further five hundred Rhade and a few M'Nong at Buon Mi Ga base in Darlac Province had disarmed their American Special Forces 'A' Team then executed, by shooting, all twelve Vietnamese counterparts. The Montagnard from this camp had moved in and occupied the main Ban-Me-Thuot airport, about fourteen kilometres from the town.

During the night, a total of four, fully-armed Montagnard groups had begun to close in on Ban-Me-Thuot. The Vietnamese and Americans had almost completely lost control of their Montagnard charges, although in two cases, the American commanders had exercised some degree of influence. At Ban Don base near the Cambodian border to the west of Ban-Me-Thuot, the rebels held hostage both their Vietnamese and American Special Forces 'A' Teams. Captain Terry, the leader of the American team, persuaded the rebels to take him with them as they advanced on Ban-Me-Thuot. As they approached the town, Terry persuaded them not to participate in the revolt. This force then turned back, but still held hostage Terry and the other Americans and Vietnamese.

At Buon Brieng, another special forces base to the north of Ban-Me-Thuot, the commander of the American Special Forces 'A' Team, Captain Vernon Gillespie, dissuaded Y-Jhon Nie, the commander of the Montagnard five-hundred man strike force, from participating in the rebellion. The

Buon Brieng force remained inactive, but its Montagnard leader was later to be vilified by his own men. He resigned as commander and soon after appeared to have lost his sanity. Jut and I discovered him some weeks later, prostrate in the middle of a road in Ban-Me-Thuot. He had thrown himself face-down in the road, to die under the wheels of passing traffic. We took him back to the house in Ton That Thuyet for a few days, then he disappeared, probably to complete the task we had interrupted. Loss of face can be as lethal as a bullet.

The piece of information that concerned me most of all was that my Truong Son Force of three hundred and fifty men had not carried out their role in the revolt. I learned later that their orders were to capture the smaller airstrip on the edge of the town, to occupy the radio and telephone relay station, and to surround the northern perimeter of Ban-Me-Thuot. But a pre-arranged signal involving the firing of three 81mm mortar rounds into the town did not occur — so nothing happened.

Although my force was implicated, they had emerged fairly 'clean' — primarily because of a failure in communication.

Then came news I had not expected: Y-Bham Enuol had been abducted. A jeep and an enclosed van filled with armed, dissident members of the Buon Sarpa force had crashed through the Vietnamese defences and road block on the south-west edge of town. They had gone to Y-Bham's official residence, bypassed the M'Nong guards and abducted him without opposition. The agitators with the Buon Sarpa force now controlled the unofficial leader of the Montagnard. He had been taken out of Ban-Me-Thuot.

The Montagnard revolt had now reached a state of crisis. Vietnamese and American control had been seriously challenged and the titular Montagnard leader was in the hands of the rebels. The central highlands, which were the key to the security of South Vietnam, were in ferment and ripe for takeover by the Viet Cong.

* * *

By late afternoon a Vietnamese airborne regiment had flown in to reinforce the defences already established around Ban-Me-Thuot.

General Co, the Vietnamese corps commander, also flew in that day and set up his headquarters in the large presidential residence — the 'palace' — which was set in roomy grounds, and surrounded by a high wall. It was used as a temporary official residence by the president, the prime minister or other important officials on their visits to our mountain town. Late on that Sunday, Stu Methven told me that General Co wanted to see me. I wondered why — I was only a captain. Methven could not give me a reason.

When I entered the large reception room at the palace, there were some very senior people present:

General Hoang Xuan Lam, Commander of the Vietnamese 23rd Army Division; Colonel John F. Freund, the American deputy senior adviser at General Co's headquarters in Pleiku; Colonel Donald Kersting, senior American adviser at General Hoang Xuan Lam's division headquarters in Ban-Me-Thuot; Colonel Serong; and Stu Methven.

At the meeting, General Co turned to me.

'You know these people,' he said. 'Do you think you could get some of the rebel leaders together and bring them in to see me? I'll give you safe conduct passes to get through our defences.'

'I'll try sir,' I said, knowing full well that this could be quite a problem. I would be attempting to persuade rebel leaders to enter a lion's den. Some of their men in the last twenty-four hours had been slaughtering Vietnamese soldiers.

Colonel Freund interjected:

'General,' he said, 'I don't think that's necessary. I have already established contact with the Buon Sarpa rebel leaders. I have a meeting arranged with them tomorrow morning.'

General Co was a proud and very senior Vietnamese officer. He seemed to resent being told what he should do by a more junior American officer.

'I want Captain Petersen to bring some of the rebel leaders in to talk to me tonight,' he replied coldly.

It was nine o'clock on Sunday night. As Jut and I were making our way out to our jeep, Colonel Serong said:

'I think I'll go with you, Barry.'

Colonel Kersting, the American senior adviser in Darlac Province, standing nearby, overheard Colonel Serong.

'There's not much I can do here,' he said. 'Do you mind if I come too?'

With both colonels in the back of the jeep, Jut and I, armed with General Co's safe conduct passes, drove through the strong Vietnamese defences which now ringed Ban-Me-Thuot.

Normally, as a mere captain, I could have found it intimidating to have two full colonels looking over my shoulder, while I did a job. But I had so much on my mind, and such a demanding task ahead, I could not have given a damn.

Rain was falling, and the tracks were slippery. We drove slowly and carefully in the darkness, through the rubber plantations and jungle towards Buon Enao, until we located the first of the Montagnard rebel ambushes. We stopped the jeep. Jut and I walked in front of the headlights so that the tense Montagnard could identify us. I'm sure that had we been Vietnamese we would now be dead. Because I was Caucasian and Jut was Rhade, they permitted us to speak. Although not all the ambushes were manned by Truong Son Force members, all the rebels had heard of me, and either knew or knew of Jut. Once we had identified the two colonels in the jeep, they allowed us through. This procedure was repeated several times, until we reached the fortifications of Buon Enao.

The rebels were gathered in a dirt-floored hut used as a lecture room. Although I knew some of them well, they did not greet me in their normally cheerful way. Their attitude was guarded. It was clear they thought we were going to interfere with their revolt. They were jumpy, and the tension increased as Jut and I told them that General Co wanted to talk with them.

Their initial response was one of total refusal. Under no circumstances would they even consider it, they said. They clearly had lost a degree of faith in Westerners.

My theme was that a meeting with General Co was their opportunity to put their grievances to a very senior Vietnamese official. I pointed out to them that I felt that General Co's intentions were honest and that he was genuinely concerned with sorting out the Montagnard problems. It took some effort to convince them that the Vietnamese were not going to arrest them, whatever the outcome of the meeting.

The discussions went in stages. I would put the case and we would all wait in another room for them to talk about it at length. This procedure was repeated a number of times. Our patience was wearing thin when Colonel Serong drew me aside and whispered:

'Barry, you've got to make them agree to come back with us.'

'Sir, it is a decision they are going to have to make themselves,' I said. 'I can't *make* them do anything. All I can do is try to persuade them.'

He leaned towards me, very angry.

'Don't you speak to me like that,' he hissed. 'I can have you out of this country within twenty-four hours!'

I waited a moment. I didn't know what to say. Perhaps I *had* been insubordinate.

'Sir,' I replied simply.

I was just as tense and as impatient as he — if not more so. And perhaps he recognized it then. The subject was dropped.

Finally, a small group of the rebel leaders agreed to return with us to Ban-Me-Thuot. We arrived at the palace around midnight. We left our weapons on the verandah and entered the large reception room. General Co had organized Vietnamese tea and whisky, which was served as we sat in a large circle. The same group of Americans and Vietnamese were present.

General Co conducted an excellent discussion, which lasted three hours. He gave the rebel leaders every opportunity to present their demands. Despite the belligerent manner of some of them, the general did not allow anything to upset him.

Among other things the Montagnard wanted:

* A Montagnard elected representative in the National Assembly.
* Montagnard to be commissioned as officers and to command Montagnard troops.
* District chiefs and perhaps province chiefs to be Montagnard appointees in the central highlands.
* Their own Montagnard flag.
* Montagnard children in schools to learn their own tribal dialect before Vietnamese.
* The right to own the land they actually cultivated.
* Higher academic and tertiary education opportunities for Montagnard school children.
* American aid, destined for the Montagnard, to be given direct to the Montagnard, and not administered by the Vietnamese.

General Co said that some of the requests were quite reasonable, and that he would implement those within his power almost immediately.

'Others,' he said, 'will require consideration at national level.'

Then he asked, 'Now, do you still want to fight me?'

The rebel leaders agreed to return to their bases to wait and see.

. General Co appeared delighted with the meeting. He asked me to ensure that the leaders visited each rebel group to tell them of the outcome of the descussions. This would happen at daybreak.

Colonel Freund interjected and told General Co that the rebel leaders present should instead be flown across to Dalat to meet Prime Minister General Khanh, who was on a visit. He said he could arrange an aircraft.

General Co's reply was curt:

'Colonel Freund, I am the prime minister's representative in this region,' he said. 'My word is all that is necessary. I want these men to brief each dissident force on tonight's discussion.'

I felt that Colonel Freund, an American, was bloody rude in trying to interfere in what was basically a problem between the Vietnamese and the Montagnard.

The meeting between the rebel leaders and General Co had continued until three o'clock on Monday morning. At sunrise, the rebel leaders briefed our Truong Son Force and elements of other dissident groups and villagers in Buon Enao. They told them of General Co's concessions and promises. Some questions were asked and answered, then they unanimously agreed to temporarily cease hostilities against the Vietnamese and to quietly return to their bases and villages.

Accompanied by Colonel Serong, Stu Methven and the rebel leaders, Jut and I commenced our visits to each of the other dissident groups. We began with the Buon Sarpa force headquarters at Buon Mbre. We found that Colonel Freund had arrived ahead of us. He had with him Major Edwin E. Brooks of the American Special Forces, Captain Gillespie, and Howard Sochurek, the journalist. I was surprised to see both Captain Gillespie, who was way out of his territory, and Sochurek — a civilian. Howard Sochurek had approached me without success for a story some days before the revolt.

Colonel Freund then stunned us by emphatically stating he was not going to permit the rebel leaders to speak with the Buon Sarpa force. Here was an American senior officer, an adviser only, defying the senior Vietnamese commander in the region and trying to take over control of the dissident Buon Sarpa force. Additionally, he had a journalist present to witness it.

I thought perhaps he was trying to gain personal prestige, in being seen to be defusing a dramatically tense confrontation between the Montagnard and the Vietnamese.

Both Stu Methven and Colonel Serong tried to reason with

Colonel Freund. He remained adamant that the dissident Buon Sarpa men should not hear of the result of the discussions with General Co. Colonel Freund was trying to get the Buon Sarpa force to return to its base, still ignorant of the Vietnamese general's attitude. He had his own meeting with the Buon Sarpa rebel leaders that morning. He was giving greater priority to that than to the general's wishes.

The Americans managed to get the angry and confused Buon Sarpa troops aboard their vehicles and, 'Pied Piper' fashion, Colonel Freund led them back towards their base, still ignorant of General Co's concessions and promises.

However, other dissident groups listened to the outcome of the discussions with General Co and quietly withdrew from their aggressive positions.

Bevan Stokes and Y-Tin had returned from Saigon as Colonel Serong and Stu Methven left Ban-Me-Thuot. Within hours both were arrested at gunpoint by South Vietnamese soldiers and temporarily imprisoned. Jut and I were away from Ban-Me-Thuot and returned to find that Colonel Kersting, the American senior adviser, was negotiatiing their release.

Both Bevan and Tin were shaken by their experience. Bevan had insisted on not being separated from Tin and had probably saved his interpreter from a beating, or even worse. Many Vietnamese, in addition to those in the special forces bases, had been massacred, and shooting incidents were still occurring. The Vietnamese ill-feeling against the Montagnard ran high.

* * *

Vietnamese senior officers and Montagnard later told me of what happened at the Buon Sarpa base. When the dissident force returned, Colonel Freund offered himself, a senior American officer, as sole hostage in return for the release of the other American and Vietnamese hostages.

Y-Dhon Adrong, the Montagnard and suspected Communist sympathizer believed to have led the revolt, retained apparent control of the Buon Sarpa force for the next few days despite attempts to arrange a meeting between the former and General Co. On one occasion, the erratic Y-Dhon sent a message to General Co to the effect that he was too busy cooking his rice to meet him — an insult to both Vietnamese and Montagnard. General Co was rapidly losing his patience. He threatened to attack the Buon Sarpa base with aircraft. Perhaps the only factor restraining him was the presence in the base of Colonel Freund.

Y-Dhon Adrong together with the real organizers of the revolt, eventually saw the writing on the wall, and decided to decamp with their supporters who included some dissident Chams. They left Buon Sarpa with weapons, ammunition, radio equipment, rations, and as many other supplies as they could carry. They also took the abducted Y-Bham Enuol with them.

The deserters moved into Cambodia, and proclaimed a new autonomy movement, the 'Front Unifié de Liberation des Races Opprimées' (FULRO) — (the Front for the Liberation of the Oppressed Races). Y-Bham Enuol was named General Y-Bham Enuol, President of the High Plateau of Champa. Y-Dhon Adrong was appointed Y-Bham's political adviser. Thus the movement, purporting to be truly nationalist, was politically controlled by the suspected Communist agent — Y-Dhon Adrong.

With Y-Dhon and his rabid supporters gone, Colonel Freund persuaded the young and faint-hearted leader of the rest, to officially surrender to the Vietnamese at Buon Sarpa. The capitulation was made to Prime Minister General Nguyen Khanh.

Howard Sochurek's article in the American *National Geographic* Volume 127 No 1, January 1965, indicates why I felt that Colonel Freund was trying to gain some personal glory from the situation. Sochurek's article portrays Colonel Freund as the man who had defused the confrontation between the Montagnard and the Vietnamese. However, I believe differently. Because he refused to allow the rebel leaders to pass on General Co's assurances, I blame Colonel Freund for prolonging, not shortening, that confrontation.

The Buon Sarpa force, although it returned to its base with Colonel Freund, remained in a dissident mood for a further week.

The official surrender caused a loss of face to the Montagnard. It also lost Colonel Freund any respect the Montagnard might have had for him. The base was abandoned, and the remnants moved by the Vietnamese into a Vietnamese-controlled Regional Forces' base on the outskirts of Ban-Me-Thuot.

*　*　*

Y-Dhon Adrong's story is an interesting one. He was born in Buon Emap near Ban-Me-Thuot around 1933 and was educated at the French Lycée Yersin in Dalat. He was the first Montagnard to gain the French First Baccalaureat and became the Director of Primary Education in Lac Thien District in 1950. In July 1964, shortly before the September revolt, Y-Dhon took charge of the Bajaraka Movement (the original ideology of which was based on the maintenance of the Montagnard ethnic identity) at Buon Sarpa. He, together with other Montagnard Bajaraka representatives, met with senior officers Les Kosem and Um Savuth of the Royal Khmer Army in the forests of Cambodia's Mondul Kiri Province. Colonel Les Kosem was a Cambodian Cham, a Muslim and an officer in Prince Sihanouk's Army. Les Kosem succeeded in persuading Y-Dhon Adrong to merge the Bajaraka Movement with the Front for the Liberation of Champa and the Struggle Front of the Khmer of Lower Cambodia. (The flag they designed had three horizontal stripes of blue, red and green with three stars representing the Cham, Khmer Krom and the Montagnard.) It was reported by a dissident, Ksor Kok, that Les Kosem's French adviser proposed the merger. This explains the presence of Chams with Y-Dhon Adrong at Buon Mbre and the dissident Buon Sarpa Force.

Y-Dhon Adrong was subsequently executed on the orders of General Y-Bham Enuol. He was accused of trying to destroy the FULRO movement. Ksor Kok reported that Y-

Dhon was buried to his waist then executed. His body was then thrown into the river.

And Colonel John F. Freund, I later learned from American sources, was decorated by his government for courage displayed during and following the Montagnard revolt of September 1964.

9 The Story of FULRO

The morning after Bevan and Y-Tin were released from the Vietnamese cells, they accompanied Jut and me to Buon Enao. We expected to find a much quieter Truong Son base.

Buon Enao at that time was still a large, traditional Montagnard village consisting of high-set longhouses in rows plus a number of timber and bamboo huts at ground level. The three hundred and fifty members of the Truong Son Force lived here together with their families and other villagers. It was surrounded by a pallisade of bamboo stakes, fiercely pointed, a common form of fortification for villages in South Vietnam at that time.

Only two mornings before, we had seen the Montagnard acceptance of General Co's concessions and promises. We expected our force to be back to normal training. Instead, on entering the gates of Buon Enao we saw almost the entire force assembled on the ground at the end of one of the longhouses. On the verandah at the end a newly-arrived Rhade, Y-To Nie, was haranguing them. Y-To was one of the rebel leaders who was in Buon Enao on the night they met with General Co. Now he was behaving like someone in control of our Truong Son Force. As we drew within earshot, it was clear he was bent on aggravating the anti-Vietnamese feelings of the Montagnard. He had whipped his audience into a high pitch.

He was beating his chest, waving his fists in the air, and his voice was strident. Only the Montagnard had the right to elect their leaders, he screamed. Nobody else.

'... not the Vietnamese ...!'

There was a resounding roar of approval.

'... not the French ...!'

A further, but slightly lesser, cheer.

'... not the Americans ...!'

A further cheer, but less emphatic. Knowing we were within earshot, Y-To shouted:

'... not even the Australians!'

There was an audible murmur of approval, but it was not a cheer. We four looked at one another. Bevan and I knew we could trust Jut and Tin, but we cast our eyes around the gathering to identify others who might show a hint of loyalty to us. It was difficult to tell who was for and who was against us — or how many were being swayed by peer group pressure.

Y-To was delivering his final sally.

'... Any foreigner who stands in the way of Montagnard autonomy will be crushed!' he screamed.

There was no roar, only a murmur of approval. But it was clear we were not in control of the force.

Intelligence reports later showed that Y-To Nie was a suspected Communist agent and, for almost two years, had been imprisoned in Hue by the South Vietnamese Government for his earlier activities.

Y-To then nominated himself as the Montagnard leader of the Truong Son Force. He was duly elected.

The man he replaced was Y-Djap Kpor, a placid old man whom I inherited from the National Police as commander of the original one-hundred-man force. I did not see him in the crowd. I learned later that at that very moment he was attempting to hang himself in a nearby hut. He was cut down before choking to death and smuggled out of Buon Enao by loyal members of our force.

Bevan and I — unlike the Americans — were at no stage disarmed by the Montagnard.

Following the revolt, Y-To Nie's continued control of the Truong Son Force was a thorn in our side. We couldn't very well get rid of him until we had won over more supporters to our side.

However, Y-To became his own worst enemy, and played into our hands. He busied himself by travelling around the special forces bases and villages in the province, promoting the FULRO movement. During the few times he participated in combat operations, he refused to fight the Viet Cong. He arranged truces with them. He then became boastful and over-confident, traits not respected by the Montagnard. Indeed, they have a saying similar to ours — 'Empty vessels make the most sound'. He lost the respect of the Truong Son Force.

This gave us our opportunity. On his return together with a few close aides from one of his propaganda tours, we confronted him with a larger group of armed members of the Truong Son Force and disarmed him at gunpoint. I told him that he and his supporters were to instantly leave the Truong Son Force and never return. I warned him I would shoot him if I saw him again. He didn't resist and departed quietly.

Y-To Nie crossed into Cambodia and joined the FULRO Movement. A report later came back to us that he had become the commander of Y-Bham's presidential guard. In later years we learned that Y-To Nie was the liaison between the Viet Cong General Y-Bih Aleo and the dissident FULRO movement. Although he apparently was a Communist secret agent and had no trouble contacting Communist units, either North Vietnamese or Viet Cong, Y-To Nie was later killed by the Communists.

*   *   *

Both the National Police director and the province chief, Major Gia, had threatened me on the eve of the revolt. They had intimated dire consequences for me should our Truong Son Force participate or even if a demonstration occurred. I heard nothing from either senior official throughout the period of the revolt. I neither heard of nor saw Major Gia

again. General Co removed Gia and appointed Major
Nguyen Dinh Vinh as the new Darlac province chief, promoting him to lieutenant-colonel. Vinh was the commander of
the Vietnamese airborne regiment which relieved Ban-Me-
Thuot during the revolt.

I was to become both friend and confidante of Colonel
Vinh.

*   *   *

Jut learned later from his personal liaison with General Y-
Bham Enuol and other leaders of the FULRO movement
of the involvement of the foreign secret intelligence services
of both the French and Cambodian Governments in the
Montagnard Revolt. I offer this furthur information to give
a better understanding of the behind-the-scenes policial manipulations by both these governments. It seems that French
interests would be served in stirring up troubles among the
Montagnard and thus discrediting both Americans and Vietnamese.

I spoke earlier of the French helicopter from Cambodia
which flew into South Vietnam to collect Bun Sur, the French
and Cambodian secret agent. Bun Sur, together with General
Y-Bham Enuol, titular leader of the FULRO movement, was
later taken to France, where they publicly met with the senior
French General Jean-Victor Simon. We know that further
meetings occurred later in France and in Phnom Penh.

I believe Bun Sur was a secret agent of both the Cambodian Sihanouk government's Deuxième Bureau and the
French Government's Service de Documentation Extérieure et
de Contre-Espionnage (SDECE). (The Sihanouk Government
had modelled their Deuxième Bureau on the French SDECE,
which has since been replaced by the DGSE — Direction
Générale de la Sécurité Extérieure — the agency responsible
for the sinking of the *Rainbow Warrior*, the anti-nuclear
protest ship, in Auckland Harbour in 1985.)

Bun Sur was born of the M'Nong tribe in South Vietnam
and was educated at the French Lycée Yersin in Dalat. He
could well have been recruited then as a prospective secret

agent of the French Government. He was later promoted to the rank of lieutenant-colonel and held that rank in the Cambodian Army. He was appointed province chief of Mondul Kiri Province in eastern Cambodia — the province adjoining Darlac Province in South Vietnam — by the Cambodian Sihanouk Government.

We know now that the Montagnard revolt of September 1964 was directly organized by the anti-Vietnamese Chams who were with the Buon Sarpa Force. And two of the principal leaders were Chams living in Cambodia — Chau Dara (born in Phan Rang on the South Vietnamese coast) and Les Kosem (born in Chau-Doc south of Saigon). They have also both since been identified as secret agents of Prince Sihanouk's Deuxième Bureau. Information I have indicates they were also secret agents of the French Government's SDECE and that they too worked for the French General Simon. They also worked with the French SDECE secret intelligence agents in Darlac Province at the time — among them I have mentioned Monsieur Noel Mercurio (the French 'résident') and Father Bianchetti (the senior French Jesuit priest). I occasionally met French Jesuit priests during my movement throughout Darlac Province. They always appeared arrogant, and I felt uneasy in their presence. It was safer not to trust them although they were men of the cloth.

It seemed that the French could move anywhere throughout South Vietnam without interference from the Viet Cong. It was strongly believed by American and Vietnamese intelligence agencies that the French obtained and gave intelligence information and even weapons to the Viet Cong. An American intelligence officer once told me that the American Army sergeant in charge of a US PX canteen was buying captured, confiscated or stolen weapons from American servicemen, and then selling them to the French planters in Darlac Province. They, in turn, were apparently giving them to the Viet Cong. He asked me if I had been approached by the sergeant offering to buy weapons, as I held quite a large reserve for the Truong Son Force and we also captured a number from the enemy.

French collusion with the Viet Cong was apparent in the delivery of large ex-army vehicles to me in Ban-Me-Thuot, for use by our Truong Son Force. The twelve or so trucks given to me by the CIA were driven from Saigon by a Frenchman. He was supposed to have had a vehicle repair business in Saigon. On his arrival in Ban-Me-Thuot with a truck (always during darkness) I would pay him the delivery fee, plus a reimbursement for the taxes he had paid to the Viet Cong checkpoints *en route*. I would do this out of my CIA operational fund. That was the only way a truck could be delivered intact to me in the highlands!

Yet another story concerns an American intelligence sergeant who initially got close to the French expatriates in Darlac Province. We became quite good friends. He was actually a French-Canadian by birth, however he looked and spoke like a Frenchman. To avoid distress to his family, I shall call him Bill Duval. He told me he worked for the US Defence Intelligence Agency, which operated in Ban-Me-Thuot under the cover name of the Field Sociological Society.

On two occasions when I had met him over a beer in Ban-Me-Thuot, Bill had told me the French were trying to kill him. I scoffed at him, saying that he, of all the non-French in Darlac Province, had entrée to their rubber, coffee and tea plantations. He assured me it was very much restricted at that time. I still didn't take his assertions seriously.

One morning, on my return to Ban-Me-Thuot from operations, I was told that Bill Duval had been murdered in his apartment. He lived on the first floor of a building in the same street as our house, and not in the military advisory compound as did all other Americans. Bill had been shot with his own handgun, through the mosquito net and the back of his head — a difficult angle for him to adopt if he had killed himself. His handgun was clasped loosely in the wrong hand. The Vietnamese police who first arrived on the scene agreed that it was undoubtedly murder and treated it as such.

American Army investigators arrived by air in Ban-Me-

Thuot a few hours later, removed Bill's body and personal effects and declared that he had committed suicide. Bill Duval no longer existed.

I cannot be sure that Duval's murder was the work of agents of the French Government SDECE, although they may have had good reason to eliminate him. None of the French expatriates seemed to miss their earlier friend.

* * *

Realising that Y-Bham Enuol, chairman of FULRO, was a figurehead for the Montagnard, it was clear that he would be of greater value to us if we could retrieve him from indirect Communist control in Cambodia. I decided to attempt to bring him back into South Vietnam. I chose Y-Pam Enuol, his younger brother, and a favourite of the old man, for the task. Y-Pam was young, fit and intelligent and was prepared to try to persuade his older brother to return to Darlac Province.

My plan was to send Y-Pam, with an armed escort from the Truong Son Force, into Cambodia to the FULRO base. They were to pretend to be deserters. Y-Pam would try to convince his older brother of the value of his place back among his people and hopefully have him willingly escape from his mentors.

I had the total support of the province chief and of the Covert Action Branch through Stu Methven.

The Communists must have learned of my plan. On 1 February 1965, Y-Pam Enuol, Y-Uih Enuol (an older brother), and Y-Miao (an uncle of Y-Bham) died in their village of Buon Ea Bong. They were the only close male relatives of Y-Bham. Captain Jones, the US Army medical officer with the American advisory group in Ban-Me-Thuot, investigated the cause of their sudden deaths. All three, although living separately, had been poisoned. My plan to recover Y-Bham had to be abandoned, because I no longer had an effective go-between.

Some few weeks after the deaths in Buon Ea Bong, I

received a similar intelligence report from both the province chief and Montagnard sources: Y-Bham's wife and seven children had been abducted from Buon Ea Bong.

The report indicated that approximately two weeks after the poisonings, an old Peugeot car was driven by unidentified men, said to be Cambodian Communists, into Buon Ea Bong. Y-Bham's wife and seven children were squeezed into the car. The province chief later told me that the car had been found abandoned near the airstrip at the French-owned Mewal rubber plantation approximately twenty-one kilometres north of Ban-Me-Thuot. He said the group was then flown from that airstrip into Cambodia by an unidentified aircraft. He told me the Vietnamese Sûreté strongly suspected the complicity of the French in the kidnapping.

Jut has since told me that Y-Bham's wife and family were taken to Ban Don to the west of Darlac Province and from there by elephants to Krechea in Mondul Kiri Province in Cambodia. They then joined Y-Bham at the FULRO base.

So Y-Bham was re-united with his family. But subsequent events were to prove that there was to be little security for any of them in Cambodia.

On 31 December 1968, two battalions of Prince Sihanouk's Royal Khmer Army surrounded the FULRO headquarters base north of Camp de Rolland in the forests of Cambodia's Mondul Kiri Province. The FULRO force were ordered not to resist, and General Y-Bham and members of his family were taken to Phnom Penh where they were placed under house arrest. Y-Bham had apparently been suspected of seeking a compromise with the South Vietnamese government to return the Montagnard FULRO forces to South Vietnam. The arrest was to prevent what the Cambodians saw as a sell-out. Y-Bham remained under house arrest until April 1975, when the Communist Khmer Rouge overthrew the Lon Nol Government and entered Phnom Penh.

At that time, as those who have seen the film *The Killing Fields* will be aware, hundreds of refugees of all nationalities had sought sanctuary in the French Embassy. Among the refugees were General Y-Bham Enuol, President of the High

Plateau of Champa and chairman of the FULRO movement. With him was Colonel Y-Bun Suor, the French and Cambodian secret agent and General Y-Bham's close adviser, and approximately one hundred and fifty loyal Montagnard members of FULRO.

On Saturday 19 April, Khmer Rouge officials commenced pressuring the French Vice-Consul, Monsieur Jean Dyrac, to hand over approximately eight hundred refugees. In his book *Cambodia — Year Zero*, Father François Ponchaud, who was in the Embassy at the time the FULRO highlanders were forced by the Khmer Rouge to leave, wrote: 'I can still see one hundred and fifty FULRO mountaineers, men and women who had fought the Saigon regime, the Viet Cong in Vietnam and the Khmers Rouges in Cambodia to defend their territory. They had counted on France, and she let them down. They marched away sorrowfully but with their heads high. Mr Y-Bam [Y-Bham], founder of the movement, and Colonel Bun Suor, their chief, led the way.'

The Khmer Rouge first took them to Lambert Stadium for preliminary processing. A survivor, a lieutenant-colonel in the former Khmer National Army, told Jut a few years later that they were then taken to a soccer field on the northern outskirts of Phnom Penh. Men, women and even very young children were then made to run from goal post to goal post as the Khmer Rouge shot them down as moving targets. Some scattered — the colonel was one — and he managed to escape.

10 Truong Son Force Operations

October 1964 brought rumours of a further revolt in the highlands. Desertions from the special forces bases were alarming. The Vietnamese closed down the Poste de Bu Prang base in nearby Quang Duc Province and Ban Don base in Darlac Province, near the Cambodian border. They moved the remnants of those bases to the north of Pleiku Province. This meant even more defections to the FULRO movement in Cambodia.

Our Truong Son Force, on the other hand, was growing stronger and stronger. Its operations were becoming increasingly effective. Our base, however, was still in Buon Enao — within Vietnamese artillery range of Ban-Me-Thuot. I knew we had to move, because a further souring of Montagnard/ Vietnamese relationships was always a possibility. I did not want the Vietnamese to shell the base if this occurred.

Bevan and I reconnoitred a base for his M'Nong teams in Lac Thien District. It was adjacent to the road, about forty kilometres south of Ban-Me-Thuot and a few kilometres north of district headquarters at Poste du Lac. Across the road was the M'Nong village of Buon Dia. Bevan and his men lived there until he had constructed the operational base which we called Vinh Son after the province chief, Colonel Vinh.

I asked Stu Methven for permission to construct an airstrip

next to the base, because there was no airstrip in the isolated Lac Thien District. This can be a costly business and the Covert Action Branch initially refused. Nevertheless, I told Bevan to commence building, using work-elephants and village labour. The Lac Thien District was geographically cut off from the remainder of the province by mountain ranges. I foresaw the mountain passes becoming targets of Viet Cong ambushes.

Using our CIA operational fund, Bevan hired his elephants and labour and commenced construction of Vinh Son airstrip. We learned then how temperamental work-elephants can be. They were big, unpredictable and sometimes exasperatingly stubborn.

In Vietnam, elephants were part of the wildlife. They were either captured young, or, if born in captivity, were released to roam in nearby jungle after weaning to build up their strength. After about eighteen months they were then re-captured. The Montagnard did not train their own elephants. They were sent north into Laos because Laotians are re-nowned in Indo-China as elephant trainers. They were then sent back to their Montagnard owners.

We used the elephants to knock over smaller trees and remove debris from the airstrip site. Shackled to each end of a heavy log, a pair of them would then grade the airstrip surface. If they felt like working, the elephants were highly effective. If they didn't, they would 'strike', refuse to move, or go roaming for fodder. It was a nightmare for their handlers to get them working again.

Bevan and his Montagnard labourers finally cleared the area — and in doing so became much wiser about the cussed ways of elephants.

When Stu Methven, my handler in the Covert Action Branch, saw how well our unauthorized work on the airstrip was progressing, he recommended to the CIA station chief in Saigon that official approval be granted. We received the assistance of an American civil engineer, 'Dutchy' Ackerson, and a small team of American 'Sea Bees' — specialists in the construction of military airstrips. They surfaced the strip with pierced steel plating and Air America aircraft commenced landing there to support Vinh Son base and the Truong Son Force.

On his first official visit to the Truong Son Force base at Buon Enao, I asked the province chief, Colonel Vinh, to present the newly-manufactured Truong Son beret badge I had designed for the force. The simple, silver alloy tiger's head was to be worn on their green beret when not on combat operations. It was obvious that the men were delighted with their new insignia.

Soon afterwards I chose another site for a major training base for the Truong Son Force. It was growing rapidly and we needed a suitable location close to permanent water, where we could later build an airstrip if necessary. It too had to be beyond the range of Vietnamese artillery in Ban-Me-Thuot should another Montagnard revolt occur.

Buon Enao was to remain a secure village for the dependants of the Truong Son Force. Its twenty-bed hospital and school offered excellent facilities. It was not an operational base, so was unlikely to be attacked — and we deliberately planned it this way. The hospital staff and schoolteachers were paid from my CIA operational fund. Both establishments were fully supported with equipment from the generous CIA warehouse in Saigon.

The site for the main Truong Son Force training and command base was twelve kilometres east of Ban-Me-Thuot. Almost half the perimeter was surrounded by a deep, wide stream. I decided that the above-ground buildings should be built like Montagnard longhouses, but of more substantial materials. The defences were to be strongly constructed and maintenance-free. I wanted to tie down as few men as possible in the defence and maintenance of the base.

All recruits to the Truong Son Force were to be trained here including the M'Nong from Lac Thien District. In this way we could ensure the highest standard. After their initial training, they would be used in a major operation to 'blood' them before returning them to their own village areas.

This main base was to later be named the Dam San base.

* * *

Late in 1964, following the Montagnard revolt, General Nguyen Khanh, the Vietnamese Prime Minister, had asked both the American and Australian Embassies for my removal from the central highlands. I was told of this by Stu Methven. He said General Khanh had suspected I might have been instrumental in the Montagnard revolt of September 1964. Methven said that both embassies had resisted the prime minister's efforts and General Khanh eventually stopped pressing.

Stu Methven was an extrovert. He lived with his wife, Joy, and their young family, in a large villa in one of the outer, more insecure areas of Saigon. It was originally the official residence of the Korean Ambassador and the walled gardens contained peacock and deer.

Stu occasionally invited me to a Sunday brunch at his villa. He would insist that my next monthly or six-weekly visit to Saigon should coincide with one of these brunches. He would have his car and driver waiting to meet me at the terminal at Ton Son Nhut airport and I would be whisked out to the villa.

The brunches would generally get underway with 'Salty Dog' (a concoction of half-gin and half-grapefruit juice, with a dash of salt). The 'Salty Dog' would be ladled from a large, hand-crafted, solid-silver Thai punchbowl.

The brunch visitors would increase in numbers as the day wore on, mainly CIA operatives and journalists. Journalists are sometimes a good source of intelligence information, and are useful for deliberate leaking of information.

My visits to Saigon, which took place every four to six weeks, were to submit my periodic reports; to replace my operational fund receipts with a suitcase of Vietnamese piastres; and to submit my indents for additional weapons, ammunition, uniforms and other equipment.

During one visit I met Colonel Lou Conein, a retired US Army lieutenant-colonel working for the CIA. As a major, he had served in Indo-China during the French/Viet Minh war. The Vietnamese majors he had befriended during those days were now generals. Some of the officers who engineered the *coup d'état* which overthrew the government of Ngo Dinh Diem, had first consulted the American Ambassador, Henry Cabot Lodge, through Lou, to gain assurance of American support following a successful *coup*. Lou was with these generals of the junta prior to, during, and immediately following the events, and kept Ambassador Lodge informed.

Lou was also a very good friend of Prime Minister General Nguyen Khanh. According to a story Lou told, General Khanh had wanted his official limousine discreetly armour-plated. He asked Lou if the CIA workshop near Ton Son Nhut airport could do the work. Lou assured him that it could, and took the limousine out there. A week or two later, Lou returned the limousine to the prime minister's palace. Then he invited General Khanh to see the finished product.

The work was so well done General Khanh couldn't notice any difference. He asked Lou for an assurance that the armour plating was really effective. Lou told the driver to get into the limousine. He then fired all six cartridges from his revolver into the side of the highly polished limousine door. An ashen-faced driver sat petrified on the other side of the bullet-ridden door. General Khanh was apparently stunned, but suitably impressed by Lou's demonstration. It took a further week to fly a replacement door out from America.

There were several attempts to remove General Khanh by some of his fellow Vietnamese generals. One, the commander of the Vietnamese Army's 4th Corps, telephoned Lou — his friend — to tell him confidentially that he was planning a *coup d'état*. He wanted Lou to find out if the American Government would support him should he succeed.

Political stability was considered essential in South Vietnam at that time. Lou told his friend that if he attempted to overthrow the prime minister, then he, Lou, would personally punch the general on the nose.

Lou felt he should inform Ambassador Taylor of the incident in case a *coup* was attempted. Ambassador Taylor and General Khanh, the Vietnamese prime minister, were not on speaking terms — Conein was the go-between. Lou told us that when he reported the incident to Ambassador Taylor, he reprimanded him for speaking to the Vietnamese general in such an insubordinate manner. Lou said that Ambassador Taylor told him to leave South Vietnam immediately which he did — only to be recalled within a couple of days. He was the only person able to maintain any contact between America's ambassador to South Vietnam and that country's prime minister.

* * *

Following the Montagnard revolt, the Viet Cong stepped-up their activities in Darlac Province. They moved units from the coastal provinces up to Darlac. The Vietnamese in the Land Development Centres in Darlac had originally been resettled from these overcrowded provinces, and some had relatives in the Viet Cong units. The units relied on the LDCs for food, intelligence and recruits. The Viet Cong even moved in to some settlements and fortified them. They then operated from them, and attacked surrounding Montagnard villages.

Units of the Vietnamese Army's 23rd Division were heavily committed elsewhere in the highlands, and the problem of clearing these fortified LDCs fell to Province Chief Colonel Vinh. He had his Regional Force units, and promptly deployed some of them to attack Thang Thanh, one of the LDCs. The Viet Cong, however, had mined the roads, tracks and trails around the fortified LDC and using ambushes and mortar fire, easily prevented the vehicle-mounted Regional Force troops getting near it.

Colonel Vinh called me. He was a dynamic man, about thirty years of age, young for his rank. He was very resolute but fair-minded, a quality that gained him the respect of the Montagnard in Darlac Province. The close bond which developed between us was the result of a mutual understanding of the plight of the people in the province, both Vietnamese and Montagnard. Our friendship was such that there was no formality, he called me 'Pete'.

On this particular day, he told me of his worries about Viet Cong units encroaching on the Vietnamese LDCs. He described his Regional Force units as being far too road-bound to get anywhere near the fortified villages without alerting the Viet Cong. They were running into mines, booby-traps and ambushes. The Viet Cong were firing mortars at the approaching convoys as well.

'I don't think they're capable of operating in any other way, Pete,' he said. 'At least, not without a great deal of re-training. I could use artillery or air strikes on the Land Development Centres, but that would cause too many casualties among innocent villagers. I'd like to try a different way.'

He asked me if the Truong Son Force, lightly equipped and basically operating on foot, could attack the fortified settlements and clear out the Viet Cong. After we had captured the LDC he wanted every house searched. Those harbouring Communist weapons, ammunition, flags, propaganda, or any other incriminating items, were to be burned to the ground as an example to other villagers. The owners of the burned houses, as well as every male of military age were to be brought back to Ban-Me-Thuot for interrogation by the Vietnamese.

Colonel Vinh and I both felt that this was the more positive way of ridding the villages of Viet Cong and their supporters. It would avoid the indiscriminate killing that often occurred during artillery-fire, aerial bombing or napalming — methods too often used by both Vietnamese and American forces as the war progressed.

To burn the house of a Communist sympathizer may seem brutal, but it is an effective method of eliminating the enemy. The Viet Cong, on the other hand, did not hesitate to burn whole villages and indiscriminately to kill the occupants. Murders and maiming of village officials, teachers, agricultural officials and families of South Vietnamese soliders and also those of our Truong Son Force were commonplace. Viet Cong methods of murder or maiming were often horrific.

The Truong Son Force already had a number of teams patrolling among the Montagnard villages around Thang Thanh. We had radio contact with each patrol and had much information on the Viet Cong unit occupying it. Our teams had already clashed with some of them. We sent additional teams into the area to strengthen existing patrols. I took an extra eighty-five men as an assault force.

I decided the attack should take place in the early afternoon — siesta time. There was usually little activity during this period. The Viet Cong normally attacked the surrounding Montagnard villages in the late afternoon or at night.

After positioning the teams in blocking forces around the settlement, our assault force moved in an extended line towards the open flank of the village. Those villagers we encountered working at the charcoal kilns in the hills or in the fields we took prisoner, to prevent them from warning the settlement of the attack.

Our plan was to take the fortified village by surprise, opening fire only when the Viet Cong reacted. Eighty-five men, spread out in groups of two or three, merge with the terrain and do not give the impression of a massed force.

We were into the outskirts of the village before the surprised occupants were aware of our presence. At first the villagers saw only two or three armed men in camouflage uniform approaching their small plot of land. Only then did they commence to shout out warnings to adjacent houses.

It was some minutes before the enemy realized that many small groups of armed Montagnard were entering their defences. They must have expected to receive some sort of warning — which we had anticipated. The first Viet Cong shot rang out and the village suddenly came to life. People ran for the trenches and to underground bunkers which they had apparently been ordered to prepare.

Although there was only sporadic firing as we moved through the village checking trenches and bunkers, more intense noise could be heard from the far side of the settlement. Some Viet Cong trying to escape our assault force had run into our teams lying in ambush around the outer flanks.

I was in the middle of the extended line. A shot came from

a clump of banana trees. I immediately fired a short burst back into the clump. Silence fell as I cautiously approached the trees. Lying crumpled among the trunks I saw the Viet Cong I had badly wounded. He was obviously dying and no longer a danger. I picked up his weapon and continued on my way. From behind I heard a shot. The commander of my training cadre, Y-Bu, an ex-Viet Cong himself, had killed the wounded man. He grinned at me, muttering cheekily that I should have done the job properly.

In fact, had I killed the wounded man myself, Y-Bu would have had less respect for me. Although the Montagnard would kill a wounded or captured Vietnamese Viet Cong without any compunction, they expected Bevan and me to be above such an act.

On all such major combat operations, Y-Bu would appoint himself my personal bodyguard and, like my shadow, was always close to me.

Y-Bu, Jut and I were deep into the settlement. There was sporadic firing and explosions, shouts and the howling of the villagers. Occasionally there were signs of Viet Cong running for cover or seeking escape through the settlement perimeter.

I was directing the clearance of a bunker. A woman, dressed in the traditional, black, pyjama-like peasant dress, climbed out. She was carrying a small baby. When she saw me, her eyes widened with fear and she suddenly dropped her baby. This shocked me. I felt I looked less fearsome than some of my Montagnard — my 'savages' as some of the Vietnamese called them.

'Why the hell did she do that?' I yelled, outraged. 'Ask her Jut.'

Jut, equally shocked, was shouting the question at her.

I cannot remember anyone ever looking so terrified of me.

'She says Americans eat babies, aie,' Jut said in disbelief.

'Tell her I'm not an American.'

'Aie, most Vietnamese think you and Mr Bevan are Americans,' he replied.

I felt quite helpless. Someone had picked up the baby and

it was crying. They handed it back to its distraught mother who cradled it, cowering against the wall of a hut.

I have never forgotten that moment. The power of propaganda on simple villagers could make them believe the most appalling lies.

The province chief had asked me to bring back to Ban-Me-Thuot not only the Viet Cong prisoners but all males between approximately fifteen and fifty years of age. Then, where possible, we identified the owners and occupants of the few houses which contained evidence of Communist support and set fire to them.

Our fight to capture the fortified village was over and suspects had been rounded up, when I entered a hut occupied by an old couple. They were terrified. There was no evidence they were connected with the Communists, but they were shaking with fright. In an effort to calm them I asked the old man if his wife could make a pot of Vietnamese tea for us all — which she did, and the poor old people began to calm down.

There were dead and wounded outside, and the houses we had set alight were still burning. I did not want to press the old man with any questions that could be interpreted as an interrogation. So, through Jut, I asked him about his farming, his children and his home province, with my questions couched, I hoped, in a humane and concerned way.

He sipped his tea and answered as best he could and I could see his terror abating. I thanked them both, and we left.

It was an odd little tea party — exchanging pleasantries in the wake of war. Yet I hoped that those people could pass on to the other villagers the message I was trying to get across: that we were performing our duties as soldiers, and that they could see we were not ogres.

We left Thang Thanh with our prisoners and the captured weapons and equipment just as the sun was setting. We had not lost a single member of the Truong Son Force.

Colonel Vinh was delighted with the result. He had avoided bombing or shelling the settlement and had not caused unnecessary casualties among the genuine villagers. Those who had suffered were Vietnamese who resisted, or those who lost their houses because of their collaboration with the Viet Cong. And I know my presence on those larger combat operations prevented indiscriminate killing by the Truong Son Force. They had little love for the Vietnamese, and even less for those who were Viet Cong.

The clearing of Thang Thanh was to be the first of a series of such sorties. The province chief immediately nominated two more Viet Cong-occupied and fortified LDCs — Le Giao and Khue Dien — and said that he would like them cleared in the same manner.

I didn't participate in one of the later operations because just before it was due to commence, I was suddenly called to Saigon by the Covert Action Branch. With all the preparations already made, I allowed it to proceed in my absence. On my return from Saigon I was told the operation was another success. The force had captured one hundred and thirty assorted weapons. I was delighted and asked how many prisoners were captured.

'Sir,' I was told, 'none were captured. They all fought until they were killed.'

After that, I made certain that I didn't miss another major fight.

※　　※　　※

I have often been asked what it is like to kill a man. When you are being fired at, it is instinctive to fire back. During the heat of battle, it is a matter of 'you kill him or he kills you'. At that moment, it is matter of survival of the strongest. It is after the act that there is time to ponder; to feel remorseful, particularly if the enemy was carrying photographs of his family, or personal mail. It is at night, when you are trying to sleep, that you most consider the life you have taken.

It would take a callous, perverted person who could kill another, unless his life were threatened. I have never killed anyone unless this were so, nor do I think I could.

※　　※　　※

At first, Bevan and I had difficulty in teaching the eight-man teams of the Truong Son Force that they were far more effective and safer operating as small teams rather than larger-sized units. By early 1965, our men were thoroughly convinced. They could be elusive, attack with impact and quickly withdraw to be elusive again. They were merely using the same tactics used earlier by the Viet Cong, and they had the added advantage of operating in the region of their own villages.

To try to counter the devastating effect these hit-and-run sorties had on the enemy, the Viet Cong increased the strengths of their units when operating in areas where there were Truong Son Force teams. The larger-sized Viet Cong units were unable to properly conceal themselves and became more susceptible to our attacks. This meant very few casualties among the Truong Son teams.

The Rhade could be extraordinarily courageous. On one occasion, two eight-man teams attacked a Viet Cong ambush awaiting a large Vietnamese Government convoy.

The South Vietnamese were moving the very isolated Phuoc An District headquarters, situated in the swampy south-east area of Darlac Province, to a more secure area. It entailed hauling vehicles through deep swamp, using work elephants. The convoy was large, slow, and very vulnerable to ambush, despite its heavily armed escort of Regional Force troops. The Viet Cong knew of the move, and prepared a trap.

Our two Truong Son teams discovered one end of the long ambush while patrolling. The Viet Cong were expecting the convoy from the other direction and evidently hadn't seen our teams. Not realizing they had discovered one end of a hundred-man linear ambush, the teams attacked. As they later said: 'We kept running and firing, and still did not reach the other side of the Viet Cong position'.

Only five Viet Cong bodies were later found, but judging by the amount of blood, others were wounded. The Viet Cong abandoned their attempted ambush and the government convoy was saved. Nobody from the Truong Son teams was even wounded. The teams were elated at their success and obviously relieved at coming through unscathed. A later examination of the ambush site showed that there were about one hundred Viet Cong in the ambush.

On another occasion, one eight-man Truong Son team was harrying the perimeter defences of a Viet Cong battalion position of over four hundred men. The Viet Cong battalion had established a fortified bunker system (a defensive position of underground bunkers) just south of Thien Hanh, a Vietnamese LDC. Although their orders were to harass only, the Truong Son team became too enthusiastic and assaulted a machine-gun position. They captured a Russian 62mm beltfed machine gun. They didn't know how many Viet Cong they killed or wounded, but seven of that eight-man team were wounded. It was a brave but foolish act for the small band of guerillas.

Most of our Truong Son combat operations were hit-and-run and this consistently netted small numbers of Viet Cong casualties and prisoners, while we sustained minimum casualties ourselves.

Many members of the Truong Son Force were decorated for bravery by the South Vietnamese Government. The Vietnamese High Command's opinion of the Truong Son Force was best expressed in the citation of a gallantry award they made to me. Among other things, it said: 'The Truong Son Force has attained one of the best combat records in Vietnam by inflicting heavy casualties and equipment losses on the Viet Cong while sustaining a minimum of friendly losses'.

*   *   *

By late 1964, Viet Cong activity had been stepped up not only in Darlac Province, but throughout South Vietnam. The 'pin-prick war' had begun to assume another guise, and the pins were hurting, to the extent that even the American public was beginning to notice.

As early as October 1964, the Viet Cong were shelling the American/Vietnamese air base at Bien Hoa, north of Saigon, with mortars. In December, a car bomb was detonated beneath the Brinks bachelor officers' quarters in Saigon, blowing out many of the rooms on the lower floors of one wing. The administrative staff of the Australian Army Training Team occupied part of the building and had their premises damaged, although only one Australian officer, Captain Stuart Cochrane, received minor injuries.

By February 1965, the Viet Cong were attacking American air bases in Pleiku, and soon after, a Viet Cong bomb was detonated by a suicide sapper on the ground floor of the American bachelor enlisted men's quarters in the province of Qui Nhon, killing twenty-one and injuring twenty-two.

On 29 March 1965, a car bomb exploded in the street outside the American Embassy. It was estimated that one hundred and thirty-five kilograms of plastic explosive was used. Two Americans were killed and fifty-two injured. But the Vietnamese toll was far worse: twenty killed and one hundred and thirty injured.

The Americans began to move in combat troops to protect American installations. US Marines were the first major units used to protect the Danang air base in the north of the country.

Many of these events seemed far removed from our little war involving the Montagnard in the highlands. The Truong Son Force operations were becoming widespread and more successful day by day. There was more to do but there was a bigger and better force to deal with it.

A set-back — and a sadness — at this time was the departure of Bevan Stokes. He had spent well over twelve months in South Vietnam and needed some minor medical treatment on his return to Australia. Bevan left his mark with the Montagnard and they often fondly spoke of him as 'Mr Bevan'. His replacement was Warrant Officer Harry Pope, who served ably commanding the M'Nong part of our Truong Son Force. So did Warrant Officers Larry McGarry and John 'Jock' Roy who took over from him in turn.

Just before Bevan left, the increased Viet Cong activity reached Ban-Me-Thuot. A bar opposite the Hotel Darlac was the target of a grenade attack. The bar was frequented by

American and Vietnamese servicemen. I had been there a number of times myself.

One evening, when the bar was packed with American and Vietnamese servicemen, Ngoc, a Vietnamese orphan boy came in. Ngoc made his living by polishing the shoes and boots of the bar patrons, and I knew him as a nice kid, always with a grin on his cheerful face. That evening he entered the bar from a side entrance, with a hand grenade in each hand. The safety pins had already been removed and he had to hold the safety levers down with his fingers to prevent the striker pins detonating the charges. He made his way onto the centre of the small dance floor, squatted on the floor and released the safety levers.

The blast killed Ngoc and many others including an attractive and personable bar girl, Co Than, a good friend of mine. She was a mother and widow who also had to work as a bar girl to support her child. The action and death of the young Ngoc stunned me. How could such a likeable and popular lad be coerced into carrying out such terrible act and kill himself as well? Surely he was too young to have a sufficiently strong political ideology to voluntarily carry out such a deed.

But the war in Vietnam was intensifying and things were happening that I for one, and perhaps most of the world outside, had not believed could ever occur.

11 A Change of Scene

In March 1965, after nineteen months in South Vietnam, I was told to take a break. I found myself in Melbourne. It was a world far removed from the Montagnard and the highlands of Darlac Province.

It was autumn, the best time of the year there. I have always thought of Melbourne as being socially cold, the people more reserved and less approachable than those in the more northern cities. But it is a beautiful city. I love the parks and the trees which seem to be everywhere. The leaves were touched by the change in the season, creating a character and warmth far removed from the green jungles of South-East Asia.

I was not officially on leave. Colonel Serong had told me that the Australian Secret Intelligence Service (ASIS), then headquartered in Melbourne, wanted to see me. So did the Department of External Affairs and the Australian Army Directorate of Military Intelligence in Canberra.

'We'll call it a break, Barry,' he had said, before I left. 'You can fill them in and the change will give you a chance to unwind. You probably need it.'

Colonel Serong was serving his last days as Commander of the Australian Army Training Team Vietnam. He was leaving to take up another appointment in Saigon, ostensibly with the United States Operations Mission. It was obvious to me that

he was not cutting his ties with the CIA. His successor was to
be Colonel Oliver David Jackson, a former Director of
Infantry at Army Headquarters in Australia.

I did need that break. I hadn't realized it at the time — I
had been too busy — but I had been under a lot of strain. I
stopped off in Singapore and then in Brisbane to see my
parents on the way, and it was only then, when I reached
home, that I recognized how tense I had become.

The Australian Secret Intelligence Service was then found
under a cover name in part of Victoria Barracks in St Kilda
Road, opposite the Shrine of Remembrance and the beautiful
Royal Botanic Gardens. I was debriefed by officers of the
service, then interviewed by General Sir Walter Cawthorne,
then the director. He took me to lunch at the Melbourne
Club afterwards.

It was an occasion far removed from the life I had been
leading. The Melbourne Club was the home of the
Melbourne 'establishment', and located at the top end of
Collins Street. At that time Collins Street retained its Parisian
touches. Many of the beautiful old Victorian buildings had
not yet given way to the steel and concrete towers there
today.

I was awed by my surroundings. I had spent nineteen
months with the Montagnard, eating with chopsticks or, as
often as not, my fingers. I was acutely aware I would have to
watch my table manners! The Melbourne Club was solid,
Victorian and very starchy. More importantly, it was filled
with elderly, distinguished gentlemen lunching on soup and
roast beef and conversing about matters that, no doubt, were
of profound importance. I was certainly the youngest person
there for I was not yet thirty, and, as an army captain,
probably the lowliest.

Sir Robert Menzies, the Australian prime minister, was
lunching with others at the table next to General Cawthorne
and myself. Sir Walter and Sir Robert exchanged greetings
and then the general turned to me.

'Have you met Prime Minister Menzies, Barry?' he asked.

'No sir,' I said.

General Cawthorne then took me to the prime minister's table, introduced me and told Sir Robert something of my work with the Montagnard in South Vietnam.

Sir Robert paused over his soup while he listened, then shook my hand.

'Well done, young man,' he rumbled. 'Keep up the good work.'

I had received my accolade for that day.

During lunch I told General Cawthorne about the career change I had been considering. I was enjoying the intelligence work and was thinking about giving up my army career to join ASIS. I thought it a good opportunity to get a word in with the top man.

General Cawthorne heard me out.

'If you applied, Barry, I'd certainly back you,' he said. 'But are you sure that sort of job would suit you?'

'I've been thinking very seriously about it, sir,' I said.

'In ASIS you won't get as much work in the field as you do in the army. You'll spend most of your time behind a desk,' the general said.

'Oh ...,' I said. 'I hadn't realized that.'

That was the end of my aspirations to join ASIS. I hate desks.

Before lunch was over General Cawthorne asked me another, more oblique, question:

'Barry, what do you think would be the effect of sending Australian combat units to South Vietnam?'

I knew American combat units were already moving into South Vietnam. But I had heard no suggestion of Australian Army involvement, other than the training team already there. I was not really prepared for the question because I had not thought about the possibility.

'I see no problems, sir,' I said, too glibly. Had I had a chance to think about it, I might have advised against the combat units in favour of a stronger advisory effort.

In Canberra I was debriefed by the Directorate of Military Intelligence, then told that the Chief of the Australian General Staff, General Sir John Wilton, wished to see me. He was know througout the army as 'Smiley' — because he rarely did. However, during our conversation over coffee, I found him amiable enough, in fact a very likeable man. Near the end of our conversation, he put to me the identical question asked by General Cawthorne about Australian Army combat units in South Vietnam.

I still had not thought the thing through, and I gave him the identical answer — that I could see no problems. But now I was putting two and two together.

The next session was with the Department of External Affairs, now Foreign Affairs. It was conducted by the desk officer for South-East Asia, Arthur Malcolm Morris. This meeting was anything but congenial. Morris sat behind a large table, with two other departmental officers on either side of him. From the outset he launched into an inquisition. There were no introductory handshakes. My chair was set almost two metres out from the main table, so that my every movement or mannerism was exposed.

'You were involved in fomenting the Montagnard revolt of last September,' Morris rapped.

'That's not true, sir.'

'We have evidence that you did.'

'Sir, that evidence is incorrect!'

'The South Vietnamese Government have a clear indication that you supported the uprising and assisted the Montagnard in their actions,' Morris said, his voice cold and emphatic.

I was off-balance and angry. I hadn't expected this. I was being judged guilty and required to prove my innocence.

'The Vietnamese Government have been incorrectly advised. I had nothing whatever to do with the revolt nor did I encourage it,' I said.

'You're going to have to convince us of that, Captain Petersen,' Morris said.

I responded as firmly as I could:

'Sir, in trying to keep my Truong Son Force together, the last thing in my interest was a Montagnard revolt. There was no way in the world I would seek that nor want it,' I said.

'But you sympathize with the Montagnard and their aspirations for autonomy, don't you Captain Petersen?' Morris said, and I could sense the search for a crack — for 'the wedge'.

'Sir, I admire those people and I understand their aspirations,' I said. 'But Montagnard autonomy is very much a secondary matter. Montagnard rebellion is against the interests of my program, and our fight against the Communists.'

The questioning continued for an hour or more. It was like the School of Torture all over again. Gradually I could see I was beginning to convince them. Finally the questioning ended and Morris and his officers were smiling. I was 'clean'.

The interrogation — and that was the appropriate word for it — clearly stemmed from the suspicions held about me by the Prime Minister of South Vietnam, General Nguyen Khanh. Methven had warned me that Khanh wanted me out of South Vietnam. In a sense, the Department of External Affairs was justifying the stance they had taken in defying Khanh's wishes. That really was something, for Australian Government departments had a reputation for pussyfooting when dealing with foreign governments. The Americans had a better reputation in this regard. This time the Department of External Affairs had established my *bona fides*, and were prepared to back me, despite the exalted rank of the complainant.

After all, a prime minister had demanded the removal of a mere Australian captain. The Australian Government had declared him wrong, and had said 'no'.

Arthur Malcolm Morris, OBE, later became Australian Ambassador to South Vietnam. He held that appointment during my second tour of duty there years later — which turned out to be of great significance for me.

I was so drained by the interrogation that I hardly felt up to my next meeting with Sir James Plimsoll, Permanent Secretary of the Department of External Affairs. But fortunately he, like Walter Cawthorne and John Wilton, was the soul of geniality. Then, just as I was leaving, he also asked me about the introduction of Australian combat units into South Vietnam.

I was certain then that the Australian Government was intending to take action along these lines.

When I got back to Saigon I reported this to my new Australian commander, Colonel Jackson.

'I know nothing about it, Barry,' he said, and he seemed most surprised.

'I think they're going to put combat troops into South Vietnam, sir,' I said. 'If they do that, you'll probably be promoted to brigadier to command both the combat troops and the training team.'

And that's exactly what happened.

* * *

I was seeing a lot of Stu Methven following my return to the highlands. We had been working together now for about six months. He had been a frequent visitor to Ban-Me-Thuot during this time, and there were the occasions in Saigon where I'd shared his brunches and swapped stories in the restaurants and bars in Saigon. I felt we were getting on well. Perhaps I didn't have the same empathy with him that I had with Bryan Mills. But Bryan's style had been quieter, even vague — although he had proved extremely acute, and true to his promises. Methven was a different personality — far more the extrovert, perhaps less reliable in coming up with promises given.

But there was still a lot to learn about him.

He flew into Ban-Me-Thuot one day and talked about an additional task he had for me.

'I want you to get a couple of counter-terror teams together, Barry,' he said.

'What are counter-terror teams?' I said. I wasn't clear what he meant.

'Sort of hit-men,' he said. 'They play the same game as the Communists — carry out reprisals, identify and knock off

Viet Cong agents; put the squeeze on their sympathizers.
They're working well in other provinces.'

I didn't know it at the time, but what he was proposing
later became an element in the Phoenix Program. This
program, instigated and funded by the Covert Action Branch
of the CIA, was to gain some infamy in South Vietnam in the
future.

When I first heard the proposal from Methven, I didn't
know the full story. But I didn't like the idea at all.

'You want me to form teams of professional assassins,' I
said.

'Call them that if you like,' Methven said. 'But we need
them. Start looking around for the right guys and build up a
couple of teams.'

Basically, the proposal was that we should do to the Viet
Cong what they were doing to us.

It was reportedly quite common for the Viet Cong to carry
out reprisals on South Vietnamese Government officials and
their families, intelligence officers or agents and propa-
gandists. It was not unusual for a village chief to be
beheaded or disembowelled and for his wife to have her
breasts cut off. At times, complete families of government
officers or agents were executed to the last infant. It was as if
they were following the precedent set when the Bolsheviks
executed the Russian Czar, his complete family and closest
attendants during the Russian Revolution. In such instances,
not a trace of the immediate family was left to later avenge
their martyred parents.

The proposed counter-terror teams were to carry out the
same techniques on the Viet Cong, their agents or supporters.
I strongly objected to the idea of having whole teams of
professional assassins operating in that manner. Surely if the
province chief were to identify a Communist who had to be
killed, we could arrange it using selected members of the
Truong Son Force.

I discussed this with Colonel Vinh, the province chief. He
totally agreed with me and together, we rejected the CIA

pressures to raise special counter-terror teams. We were worried that such professional assassins could ultimately become Frankenstein-like monsters. Stu Methven did not agree with us.

He kept badgering me about the counter-terror teams, but I was adamant.

'I won't have any part of it,' I kept telling him.

'They work quite well in other provinces, Barrry,' he insisted. 'We've got to get 'em going here.'

I kept refusing him — perhaps to my cost, as events were to prove later.

Then, during one of his visits to Darlac Province, Stu told me he wanted to send a young, newly-arrived CIA officer up to Ban-Me-Thuot. He called him Bill Smith and said he had CIA experience with the Montagnard tribes in Laos. Stu said he wanted Smith to look at my programs in Darlac Province for a few weeks and generally to assist me. With the benefit of hindsight, I now believe Stu was considering Bill as my ultimate replacement. I had, at that time, spent nearly twenty-one months with the Montagnard in the highlands.

I agreed to take Bill Smith on, providing he did not interfere in any way with my operations in Darlac Province. Stu accepted.

Smith finally arrived in early May 1965, after missing two Air America aircraft. He seemed a pleasant, if somewhat brash and over-confident young man. He was quick to find and point out to me any fault he found in my programs and seemed full of ideas, particularly about raising counter-terror teams.

The CIA's Covert Action Branch sponsored a number of different programs in South Vietnam and each was somebody else's bright idea. The CAB headquarters in Saigon wanted these programs conducted in each area, regardless of their suitability. The CAB appeared too inflexible to be able to create programs to suit special circumstances. Our Truong Son Force in Darlac was unique in South Vietnam and did not conform with any of the other 'brain-child' programs of CAB officers.

A typical tree-lined boulevard in the older part of Saigon in 1963.

Looking down on the courtyard of the Hotel Darlac, photographed soon after my arrival in Ban-Me-Thuot.

Above: *On the way to the highlands. Typical lowland Vietnamese countryside showing mature rice fields almost ready for harvest.*
Left: *Y-Jut Buon To, my young Rhade interpreter and offsider.*

A street in Ban-Me-Thuot at the time of my arrival in 1963.

The Bungalow, the Emperor Bao Dai's teak hunting lodge in Ban-Me-Thuot, used by the American military advisory team.

Right: *Bryan Mills taking a nap in one of the CIA's Air America aircraft.*

Below: *An Air America Dornier plane on the Ban-Me-Thuot airstrip.*

One of my Vietnamese assistants with our pet leopard cub, Fatima, and the honey bear cub, Bozo. Fatima later died when she ate poisoned chicken meat meant for me.

My pet tiger cub in his carrying cage.

The entrance to a Rhade village of longhouses.

Truong Son Force members during training.

Ba Nam (front) *and Ba Hai* (rear), *our cook and housekeeper at the house in Ton That Thuyet.*

Above: *Myself wearing Rhade ceremonial jacket and loincloth, with Y-Kren Nie, one of my offsiders, and Warrant Officer John (Jock) Roy, and members of drama team members of the Truong Son Force. These teams toured outlying Montagnard villages and disseminated anti-Communist propaganda in plays and songs.*

Above left: *Our airstrip at Vinh Son base in Lac Thien District. An Air America Caribou aircraft has just departed after delivering bundles of pierced steel plating for the airstrip surface.*

Montagnard work elephants.

Young Rhade girls wearing their traditional hand-woven jackets.

Truong Son Force members on patrol. One carries the radio used for communications back to Buon Enao, Dam San Base and the house in Ton That Thuyet.

Truong Son Force on parade at Dam San Base.

General Nguyen Huu Co with Lieutenant-Colonel Nguyen Dinh Vinh behind him, decorating members of the Truong Son Force for bravery in combat action.

Above: *Y-Tin, myself (looking rather angelic) and Bevan Stokes, searching for a suitable firing range near Buon Enao.*

Dorsey Anderson, of the CIA's Covert Action Branch, visiting a Montagnard village with Truong Son Force members behind him.

Members of the Truong Son Force aboard one of our typical armour-plated trucks. We had a fleet of about twenty-five vehicles.

Above: *Myself, Colonel Lou Conein, Stu Methven, and Captain Vernon Gillespie, Commander of the US Special Forces 'A' Team at Buon Brieng. Taken at Buon Brieng in front of our Air America plane.*

Right: *Rhade elder wearing traditional dress inside a longhouse. A rice wine jar stands in front of him.*

Myself (right) *meeting the* FULRO *rebels on their secret return from Cambodia to Darlac Province in July 1965.*

Below: *A typical eight-man team of the Truong Son Force on normal operations.*

Viet Cong and suspects taken prisoner during an attack on a Communist-fortified Vietnamese Land Development Centre in Darlac Province. The banner on the wall behind is Communist propaganda.

Below: *A group of typical young members of the Truong Son Force. Note the tiger head badges on their caps.*

A member of the Truong Son Force with two captured Viet Cong flags. He is holding the actual Viet Cong flag — top half red and the bottom half blue, with a gold star.

Parachuting supplies to Truong Son Force patrols near a Rhade village. One of the parachutes dropped from the Air America plane can be seen falling in the clearing to the left of the village.

Rhade ceremonial sacrifice of a buffalo for a rice wine ceremony.

My farewell to Dam San Base — the rice wine ceremony. The brass bracelets and necklace were presented to me during the ceremony.

General Y-Bham Enuol, titular leader of the FULRO movement. He was taken prisoner by the Cambodian Khmer Rouge in April 1975 and is reported to have been executed.

Right: *Y-Jut Buon To, my interpreter and friend, now lives in the USA with his wife and family.*

Left: *Borneo 1965. Members of the British M16-sponsored guerilla force in training at Kubaan in the Bario Highlands of Sarawak.*

Above: *Borneo 1965.*
Some of the guerilla
fighters sponsored by
the British dancing
while balancing
plates. Not an easy
feat, as I can testify!

Typical members of
the British M16-
sponsored force which
operated into
Indonesian
Kalimantan from
Sarawak in 1965.

Charlie Company,
Vietnam 1971.
Lieutenant David
McPherson, artillery
forward observer, on
operations in Phuoc
Tuy Province.

*Phuoc Tuy. Moving artillery into position in a
proposed fire support base where support could
be given to infantry combat operations.*

*Vietnam, 1971. Resupply of Charlie Company
and a section of the 2 RAR Mortar Platoon
during operations in Phuoc Tuy Province.*

From time to time, Stu would authorize me to increase the strength of the Truong Son Force, usually by two or three hundred at a time. We were rapidly approaching the strength of one thousand. Stu also pressed me to recruit one hundred members of the Muong tribe, expatriates from North Vietnam. He said he wanted them to be part of the Truong Son Force and operate in the same manner. There was only one Muong refugee village in Darlac Province and I felt that one hundred Muong were proportionately too many for that one village. There were just over nine hundred Rhade, Jarai and M'Nong members of the Truong Son Force to cover more than one hundred and forty Montagnard villages in the province. I also knew that the Muong were basically very different people to the South Vietnamese Montagnard tribes. I suspected Methven's real motive in raising a Muong force was to use them to infiltrate into North Vietnam. Such infiltration programs were really the prerogative and responsibility of the Studies and Observation Group, and not the Covert Action Branch of the CIA. Methven was evidently convinced of the feasibility of an elaborate infiltration plan originally given to me by a previous province chief Major Bui Huy Gia — himself a Muong.

What I didn't realize was that Methven had instructed Bill Smith himself to go ahead and do the recruiting. Evidently to enable him to do just that, I was called to Saigon for a few days on another matter.

When I returned to Ban-Me-Thuot, Y-Jut told me that Colonel Vinh, the province chief, wanted to see me and wanted me to bring Bill Smith along. I asked Smith if he knew what the province chief might want. He said he didn't know. He didn't tell me anything else.

We arrived at Colonel Vinh's office, where the province chief, after making us comfortable with Vietnamese tea, proceeded to tell me of Smith's interference in our Darlac Province programs.

During my absence in Saigon, Smith had recruited one hundred Muong by offering them the Truong Son salaries, which were higher. Unfortunately, many of them were already on the province chief's Regional Force or Popular Force payrolls. Colonel Vinh was justifiably annoyed as he hadn't been consulted. I apologised for Smith's impetuous action.

Colonel Vinh then went on to say that Smith had been trying to persuade province headquarters staff that counter-terror teams were highly desirable. The province chief then reminded us that he and I had agreed that Darlac Province did not require counter-terror teams, and that we had an excellent working relationship with our Truong Son program as it was.

Colonel Vinh turned to Smith and said:

'Mr Smith, remember you have to learn to walk before you can run.'

The rebuke did not seem to faze Smith. As we left the office he said in a voice loud enough for the province chief to hear:

'He's like any other Vietnamese. He can be bought.'

I was acutely embarrassed that Colonel Vinh had heard and I was furious with Smith. I worked closely with the province chief and trusted him as a friend. I had no doubt about either his integrity, or his honesty.

I turned on Smith.

'Shut up!' I hissed with real anger.

On arrival at the house in Ton That Thuyet, I telephoned Wynn Oliver, the deputy head of the Covert Action Branch in the absence of the chief, Tom Donahue. I told Wynn what had happened and asked for an Air America aircraft to collect Smith from Ban-Me-Thuot the following morning. Wynn told me he wanted a written explanation as soon as possible — which I duly provided.

Bill Smith's premature return to Saigon, together with my written account of events, angered both Methven and Tom Donahue. They felt I should rewrite the report as the first one would harm Smith's CIA career. Rather than aggravate an already strained relationship with Methven and Donahue, I did so. I still have copies of both reports.

12 Dam San

I was now something of a veteran in South Vietnam. I had been in the highlands for almost two years, while the normal tour of duty for both Australian and American personnel in the region was twelve months. I was certainly the longest-serving Caucasian in Darlac Province. Both the Montagnard and the Vietnamese there seemed to think of me as a fixture and that was not a bad thing. They knew me, and knew me well, albeit 'warts and all'. More importantly, I had a deepening affection with them. I was not a transient, but felt myself a sort of partner with that place and those people. I was beginning to understand and to sympathize deeply with them.

I had come to Ban-Me-Thuot as a green young officer in August 1963. By 1965 I considered myself an experienced commander, a seasoned soldier, and a man far wiser in the ways of the world as they applied in that part of South-East Asia. I was still only a captain while most of my contemporaries back in Australia had been promoted to major. I wouldn't be promoted while still in Vietnam, but I couldn't have cared less. I had a rare and wonderful job with what was, in army terms, undreamed-of autonomy. I was the effective commander of almost one thousand men and had the charter to recruit, train, organize and lead them virtually unfettered. I was responsible for bags of money, had considerable influence within my own area and, I felt, had also the trust of 'my' people — the Montagnard. It is not a boast but a fact to say that my job was unique within the sphere of Western involvement in the war in South Vietnam.

No other Australian, American or any other Caucasian had quite the same free hand. Maybe I was only a minor monarch, but I was as close as anyone got to being the absolute ruler of his own little cabbage patch. I never, for a second, envied or coveted my contemporaries back in Australia now a rank above me — commanding under-strength companies or battling with a storm of paper-work behind those wretched desks. I had a gem of a job and I loved every moment of it.

I was basically a military man, but I was also privy to the undercurrents that were so constantly present in the conduct of that seemingly inscrutable war. There were intrigues, manoeuverings, political manipulations, double-crossing, and downright bungling. In many senses the seasoned veteran among those who fought with the Americans was measured not so much by courage or soldierly virtues, but how case-hardened he was to these — rampant throughout the history of the war. In fact, a veteran, by definition, was a connoisseur of the 'cock-ups' and that meant his own as well as everybody else's.

I was asked to give minor assistance in the training of Vietnamese special operations teams for airborne infiltration into North Vietnam. The Studies and Observation Group which carried out the training wanted me to provide a secure area of tall jungle, into which the teams could parachute by night for practice, from unmarked CIA-sponsored aircraft. The planes were grey-painted Hercules C130 cargo aircraft fitted with extra fuel tanks on the wings. They had no markings, and were generally flown by Nationalist Chinese civilian pilots employed by the CIA. I often spoke with them when they delivered cargo or jeeps to me in Ban-Me-Thuot.

The Americans were keen that I learn as little as possible of the infiltration operation. But by talking to the various instructors, I picked up quite a lot of information.

The program was occasionally referred to as Project Delta or Operation Delta. It was sponsored by the 1st Observation

Group, but the whole thing appeared to be overseen by the Studies and Observation Group. The Vietnamese chosen for the infiltration were young, fit and hand-picked, and born in North Vietnam. They were trained as an élite part of the Vietnamese special forces, the Luc Luong Dac Biet. They appeared to be trained in Long Thanh, twenty kilometres east of Saigon.

I think it was on the third practice drop that one of the night parachutists broke his neck falling through the tall trees. The American Special Forces captain in charge on the ground had the body, still in its clothing and equipment, taken to the Ban-Me-Thuot hospital. There it was placed in the morgue. The clothing and equipment worn by the trainees was 'deniable'. That is, there were no markings, and the styling was anonymous so there could be no link to the American or the South Vietnamese Governments — this very lack of identification made it stand out.

I heard of the fatality when I returned from the airdrop area to Ban-Me-Thuot. I also learned what the American captain had done with the body. I asked where the captain was and was told that he had gone to the International Bar in Ban-Me-Thuot. I eventually found him, still in his own unusual uniform, wearing his low-slung handgun and sitting on the small stage with the Vietnamese band, thumping away on their drums. He couldn't have been more obvious to all in that bar — Vietnamese and Americans alike.

I called him aside and suggested to him some of the implications once the casualty's body was examined the following morning.

'Won't the body raise embarrassing questions, clothed as it is, and with a broken neck?' I asked.

'Jeez!' the young American captain exclaimed, 'I hadn't thought of that. Is there any way we can get the goddamed thing back?'

'I'll try' I said, and suggested that he change his specialist clothing and equipment to attract less attention.

I then had to arrange the only 'body-snatch' from a morgue I've ever carried out in my life.

I knew the only way I could officially get the body released would be to get the authority of Dr Ton That Niem, medical superintendent of the Ban-Me-Thuot hospital. This seemed undesirable due to the high security classification of the operation. Y-Tin announced that he knew the morgue attendent, who was an aged Montagnard.

'Do you think there's any way we could bribe him?' I asked Y-Tin.

'He likes whisky, aie,' Y-Tin replied.

'Good,' I said, 'Take a couple of bottles down there and see if you can get him well and truly plastered.'

The plan worked like a charm. The old fellow made a hole in one bottle and Y-Tin gave him the other. He headed off into the darkness with a bottle under each arm, happy as a lark. Y-Tin and some others loaded the body into a van and it was brought back to our house in Ton That Thuyet. We kept it in a small storeroom overnight.

The contrite young American Special Forces captain allowed us to load the shrouded remains aboard an Air America aircraft the following morning.

It says something about the ordinariness of death in South Vietnam at that time that to my knowledge, neither the morgue nor the hospital authorities ever bothered to inquire of the body's whereabouts.

*   *   *

Because of the large variety of American intelligence agencies in existence in South Vietnam in 1965, the Americans felt that some coordination was required.

A situation could arise where one agent or informant provided the same piece of information to two or more different intelligence agencies, and was paid for it by each of them. Each agency would then pass the information to their higher headquarters or other selected intelligence agencies. In the latter case, an agency would jealously refuse to divulge the identity of the source of the information. It was found that exchange of similar information was often regarded as corroboration.

To rectify this, the American Government decided to place

a State Department curb on the differing American advisory and intelligence agencies in each Vietnamese province. They appointed a State Department officer of third secretary status to each province. His role was to coordinate activities, and to maintain some degree of rationality in intelligence collection and collation. The Americans then termed each province group of American operatives as the 'Country Team', with the State Department third secretary being called the 'Country Team Leader'. Because I worked for the American CIA, I became a member of the Country Team in Darlac.

I shall call the man appointed as our Darlac Province Country Team Leader Bob Riverwood.

Some months after taking over, Bob approached me one evening and confessed he had been having an affaire with the wife of a Frenchman who owned a small coffee plantation near Ban-Me-Thuot.

She was a beautiful and well-educated woman. The French expatriates in the central highlands had a sort of consul they called the 'résident'. He was the man called Noel Mercurio, and the planter held an unofficial title under him — representative for the 'Cultural Section of the French Embassy' in Saigon. The Cultural Section of the French Embassy was the cover for the French Government's SDECE. In other words, he was a secret agent.

He was able to take his wife on an extended honeymoon in France following their marriage. They were absent about six months — a very expensive holiday for a modest coffee-plantation owner from war-torn South Vietnam. It is quite possible that she herself had received some secret intelligence training from the SDECE, during the six-month 'honeymoon' in France.

When Bob Riverwood told me of his secret *affaire* with her, he asked me to quash any stories that might be passed around.

I pointed out to Riverwood that his principal worry should be not what people might think but what the State Department might say if they learned that a career officer had been so compromised. I also asked him to think about what the

French would do in the future, if he ever became an ambassador for the United States of America.

My assessment of his potentially disastrous indiscretion stunned him. He obviously hadn't even considered that aspect of it. He immediately reported the matter to his superiors in Saigon and was removed from South Vietnam.

* * *

Some of the village chiefs, learning of the success of the Truong Son Force, came to see me at Buon Enao or even into Ban-Me-Thuot. They would arrive like a group of emissaries, dressed in their hand-woven, traditional loincloths and bearing gifts. All were important people in their own right. Many delegations had to travel long distances on foot until they reached some form of public transport. They looked rather quaint even in Ban-Me-Thuot, moving in file through the streets of the town, each carrying a woven bamboo bowl of brown rice with an egg or two perched on top. (Eggs are very valuable to tribal people of South-East Asia, each is regarded as a potential chicken.)

It was embarrassing for me as a young Australian Army captain to have to receive delegations of such important chiefs. Their request was always the same:

'Aie (sir), would you please send the Truong Son Force to protect our villages?'

My reply was always, 'As soon as we can we will protect your area, but you must be prepared to give us your fit young men to train.'

The delegations usually returned with all their fit, young men in tow. It was then even more embarrassing to me, because some of the delegations came from areas we were not yet able to saturate with Truong Son patrols and securing their areas could be months away. It took six to eight weeks to give Truong Son Force recruits their basic training and we were already heavily committed. They would have to wait their turn. Yet it was discourteous not to accept their gifts. I also reluctantly had to accept their young men because, as often as not, the Viet Cong might otherwise take them as unwilling, unpaid conscripts. Members of our Truong Son Force were paid, willing volunteers.

* * *

During the construction of our main base east of Ban-Me-Thuot, I first heard the Montagnard referring to it as Dam San base. I asked them the reason. They replied that the base was named after me, and that Dam San was the Rhade name they had given to me.

They told me that one of the Rhade legends was a story about a Rhade warrior named Dam San. That legendary warrior was victorious in all his battles. None could conquer him except the Spirit of the Sun. One day he challenged the Spirit of the Sun to a duel. He chose a huge, high rock face on the mountainside above his village of Buon Yang Reh, in the south of Darlac Province and on the ancient Montagnard salt trails to the coast.

During the battle, Dam San ran up the rock face, throwing his spear at the sun. The Spirit of the Sun then struck him dead.

I was honoured by the title, but what did it mean? Dam San was a brave warrior, unconquerable, until he attempted the impossible. He considered himself worthy of doing battle with the sun, and then perished for being so foolish. Was Dam San then a fool? I don't think the Rhade saw me that way. Perhaps the Americans might. Would they have seen me rising up, then over-reaching myself only to burn up and disappear before a far greater power?

The Americans rarely got the Montagnard names right. Would 'Dam San' the noble warrior become 'Damn Sam' the fool who was struck down because he became too big for his boots?

I had been presented with numerous beautiful, handwoven Rhade blankets, and traditional garments during the previous year. Suddenly I was presented with the finest handwoven loincloth and shirt I had ever seen. They must have taken months to make for they were woven from locally grown, spun and dyed cotton and patterned and embroidered in the most intricate way. The jacket was basically black, with long sleeves. It had a large rectangle of red piping across the chest. Around the upper arms there was patterning and piping in red and white, overlaid with silver embroidery and with a row of small spherical brass buttons. The loincloth was a long, broad scarf-like affair about one-third of a metre wide and five metres long. This was wrapped between the thighs then around the waist a number of times, then the finely-decorated tasselled ends were turned and allowed to drape on either side, back and front. The sides of the legs and thighs were bare. These garments are now displayed and I hope preserved forever in the Australian War Memorial in Canberra.

I found that increasingly I was regarded more as a paramount chief among the Montagnard rather than as an Australian adviser. Jut and some of the other interpreters continually told me of my new-found status among the Montagnard. There was no ceremony, no fanfare, not even an announcement. It had simply occurred before I was made aware of it.

The whole situation was somewhat of an embarrassment to me as well as being potentially dangerous. Stu Methven was already calling me 'Lawrence of the Highlands' and I was being told that I was creating a personality cult among the Montagnard. The last thing I wanted the Americans to know was that I was regarded as a paramount chief.

I certainly did not reveal that the Montagnard called me by that name. To be frank, I would have felt foolish about anyone knowing, apart from the Montagnard themselves.

*   *   *

Earlier in April 1965, Stu Methven had told me CIA headquarters in the United States had approved the raising of the numbers of the Truong Son Force to one thousand two hundred men. This was fortunate because I had already had to expand, due to the pressures from the Montagnard village chiefs.

My CIA operational revolving fund was increased to five

million Vietnamese piastres — a huge increase from the thirty-five thousand given to me less than two years before. The revolving fund had to be justified with a monthly statement and supported by receipts where available. I presented these to the accounts section of the CIA during my periodic visits to Saigon. I was given cash for the monies spent and I would return to Ban-Me-Thuot with a suitcase full of Vietnamese piastres.

However, the money was not mine to spend entirely at will. Most of it was absorbed by the salaries for the Truong Son Force; the drama teams which we used to perform propaganda playlets and songs in outlying villages; the school-teachers and our hospital staff; and payments to intelligence agents and informants. My responsibilities to the Covert Action Branch also included reports on the operations of all these support elements.

In Saigon a few months before, Stu Methven asked me if I was entertaining people.

'What do you mean "entertaining"?' I asked.

'Having people to dinner or taking them to dinner when you're in Ban-Me-Thuot — that kind of thing,' he said. 'Giving them the odd bottle of whisky or cognac.'

'I can't afford that,' I said. 'My pay isn't much and I can't use the operational fund for that.'

Methven eyed me as if I were terribly naïve:

'Hell, Barry, that's what your operational fund is *for* — you can also include booze on your normal requisition forms for weapons and equipment.'

Then he added, half turning away:

'Jeez Barry, the way you're carrying on, you're embarrassing the rest of us.'

I did as I was told. When the next re-supply aircraft arrived in Ban-Me-Thuot with weapons, ammunition and equipment, I found crates of liquor, some of them marked 'Expressly for the Diplomatic Corps'.

On one of my earlier trips to Saigon, I was sitting in the cockpit beside the Air America pilot and I admired the fine twenty-four-hour Swiss watch he was wearing. He told me it was CIA-issue to Air America and Vietnamese Air Transport pilots.

In Saigon I was ordering my return aircraft to Ban-Me-Thuot when Jim Woods, the Air America operations officer, asked me if I could get three 9mm German Luger pistols for three of his pilots who wanted them.

'The CIA won't issue our pilots with anything but .35-calibre Smith and Wesson six-shooters,' Woods said.

'Hey Jim,' I said. 'What makes you think I can get them?'

Woods looked at me as though I was a little simple. He said:

'Barry, you can get anything you ask for. You have *carte blanche* on anything in the CIA warehouse. You are one of the very few people in the whole country who has. Didn't you know that?'

I shook my head incredulously.

'No, I had no idea!' I said.

Woods said: 'Anything that's sent up to you in Ban-Me-Thuot is written off immediately it's despatched from the warehouse. Didn't you know that?'

I was stunned. 'No,' I replied.

'Well believe you me, it's true,' Woods said.

I added three 9mm Lugers to my requisition form and behold, in the next re-supply aircraft, three beautifully reconditioned Second World War German Luger pistols arrived. I took them back to Saigon on my next trip and gave them to Woods. He was delighted.

'See. I told you that you could get anything you asked for,' he said. 'Incidentally, there's a package for you on the desk over there.'

I unwrapped the package. I found a small wooden box containing a beautiful twenty-four-hour wrist watch made by Glycine and Altus of Bienne, Switzerland — identical to the one worn by my Air America pilot friend.

I thought, if I do have *carte blanche*, I should be able to get some of these watches for our Truong Son Force radio operators.

I indented for twenty watches. They arrived with the next re-supply aircraft.

It seemed I could do no wrong — with the Montagnard, the Vietnamese, and the Americans.

* * *

In May 1965, I received a message to report to the Covert Action Branch in Saigon. I flew down and reported to Stu Methven. Methven asked me to prepare a brief on the Truong Son Force program. He said that His Excellency the American Ambassador, General Maxwell Taylor, was to be briefed that evening on programs sponsored by the Covert Action Branch in the central highlands of South Vietnam. The only other CAB-sponsored Montagnard program at that time was a training centre in Pleiku Province.

I asked if I was required to give the brief personally and was told that it was not necessary. So I prepared the papers for Stu Methven then handed in my statement of expenditure plus receipts from my operational fund. I then submitted my requests for equipment and ordered an Air America aircraft to take me back to Ban-Me-Thuot the following morning.

I got back to Ban-Me-Thuot late on Friday morning, to be told that the American senior adviser to the province chief had a message for me. I went straight to the province headquarters, and was told that the American Ambassador himself was coming to Ban-Me-Thuot the next day. The message said that the purpose of Ambassador Taylor's visit was to be briefed personally by Captain Barry Petersen.

'But he was briefed on the Truong Son Force program in Saigon last night!' I protested.

'Well, he's coming here, and he wants one from you personally' was the reply. 'Colonel Browne has arranged the briefing in the Bungalow with the necessary security protection for Ambassador Taylor.

I was stunned. I wondered what had transpired in Saigon. I had heard nothing from the Covert Action Branch and they could have got a message to me prior to my departure from Saigon that morning.

I heard later that during the briefing of Ambassador Taylor in Saigon on the Thursday night, he had been highly impressed by the effectiveness of our Truong Son Force program. He had asked who was running the program, and had been told that it was a field case officer from the Covert Action Branch. His close questioning of the CAB briefing officers had revealed that the Truong Son Program was in fact run by an Australian Army captain. He then decided to meet me and receive a detailed personal briefing from me in Ban-Me-Thuot. Everything, including American and Vietnamese military police protection, was organized. I was clearly the last person to be informed of the arrangements.

I was both puzzled and a little nervous when the ambassador's group arrived at the heavily-guarded Bungalow. I was introduced to Ambassador Taylor and the other officials on the wide verandah of the huge teak hunting lodge, then we moved into the briefing room, which was also guarded.

With Ambassador General Maxwell Taylor were General Nguyen Huu Co, General Lu Lan, Colonel Laurence E. Browne — the US senior adviser to General Lan, an unknown senior officer from the United States Operations Mission in Saigon, and Larry Flannigan, the USOM representative in Darlac Province, Province Chief Colonel Nguyen Dinh Vinh, Stu Methven, and a few aides.

The briefing lasted about thirty minutes and dealt generally with my operational concept. Ambassador Taylor and the Vietnamese generals appeared impressed.

Then Ambassador Taylor said: 'This is the type of operation we should be conducting throughout the whole of South Vietnam.'

I agreed my operational concept would be effective in *some* other parts of South Vietnam, particularly among the Montagnard, but on other counts I had to silently disagree with the ambassador. I did not think my program could be applied universally. It simply would not have worked in many places. It was tailored for certain areas only.

Ambassador Taylor thanked me for the information, saying he was impressed with the effectiveness of the Truong Son Force program. This was a big boost to my morale and vindicated my stand against Tom Donahue, head of the Covert Action Branch, and Stu Methven. They had argued for months that my program should conform with other CAB-supported programs throughout South Vietnam. While the other programs might have produced effective teams for work among the Vietnamese, I remained unconvinced that they were the overall panacea for South Vietnam's problems, particularly among the Montagnard in the highlands.

As the group was departing, one of the ambassador's aides leaned towards me and said:

'Did you hear what the ambassador said to your CIA friend?'

'No,' I replied.

'He asked why the CIA had to use an Australian to run this sort of program,' he said. 'He wanted to know why an American was not capable of doing it.'

Ambassador Taylor's visit was the pinnacle of my career in the highlands. It was also to prove the turning point.

13 Delicate Negotiations

Soon after this, General Co, Commander of the Vietnamese Army's 2nd Corps, was appointed Minister for Defence and Deputy Prime Minister to Air Vice-Marshal Nguyen Cao Ky.

Ky, together with General Nguyen Van Thieu, had taken over the government in February 1965, assuming the roles of prime minister and president respectively.

Our province chief, Colonel Vinh, was a favourite of General Co and the general asked Vinh to be his chief-of-staff in Saigon. Colonel Vinh told General Co that he would prefer to remain in Darlac Province, where he found the work more rewarding. But in June 1965, Colonel Vinh reluctantly had to leave Darlac Province. His departure was a personal loss to me because we had developed a very close friendship. It was as if we had grown up together. We thought alike and could laugh together over the same things.

Colonel Vinh had an understanding for his people, Vietnamese and Montagnard alike, regardless of their rank or status. He was very much admired by both Vietnamese and Montagnard in Darlac Province and was a sad loss.

Fortunately, his replacement was Lieutenant Colonel Le Van Thanh. This was Colonel Thanh's second tour of duty as province chief during my time in Vietnam. He had preceded Major Bui Huy Gia as province chief following the overthrow of the Diem Government. The Vietnamese Government couldn't have chosen a better officer. He knew Darlac Province well, and understood the people and politics of the region. We were already friends. He now lives in Canberra, Australia, and we are still on excellent terms.

* * *

By the end of June 1965, the strength of the Truong Son Force was at one thousand two hundred and our operations were progressing well. The Vietnamese authorities had developed a lot of confidence in the effectiveness of the force.

The new Commander of the Vietnamese Army's 2nd Corps, General Vinh Loc, was both anti-Montagnard and anti-European. He also hated the American Central Intelligence Agency. He was a bull-necked, arrogant, overbearing and overweight Vietnamese officer, not much liked nor respected by his own countrymen.

Colonel Thanh recently told me that General Vinh Loc was a prince of the Vietnamese royal family — a relative of the deposed Emperor Bao Dai. As a young man he was once an aide-de-camp to the emperor.

General Vinh Loc sometimes visited Ban-Me-Thuot from his headquarters in Pleiku. On these occasions, the province chief would hold an official dinner for the general. I was invited to one such dinner, where I witnessed General Vinh Loc's rudeness to General Lu Lan and even to Colonel Thanh, his dinner host.

I think the only reason I did not also bear the brunt of his bad temper was because of the tremendous success of the Truong Son Force operations. The general instead merely chose to ignore me totally.

Colonel Thanh also told me that General Vinh Loc didn't like him and wanted him replaced as Darlac province chief by a lieutenant-colonel from Thu Duc Military Academy. What General Vinh Loc did not realize was that both the president, General Thieu, and the prime minister, Air Vice-Marshal Ky, had asked Colonel Thanh to accept the appointment as Darlac province chief, and had no intention of replacing him.

* * *

In early July 1965, I was asked by Stu Methven to go to Saigon. No reason was given so I didn't hurry down. On Monday 19 July 1965, I was contacted by Y-We Eban, a messenger from General Y-Bham Enuol, president of the rebel FULRO movement in Cambodia. He told me that Y-Preh, another member of the movement, wished to see me.

My immediate reaction was one of anger. I knew that any liaison with the rebel movement could mean the kiss of death for our Truong Son Force. Y-We had previous proven contacts with the Communists.

Y-We then told me that three battalions (approximately one thousand armed men) of FULRO troops had entered Darlac Province from Cambodia and were approximately fourteen kilometres west of Ban-Me-Thuot. This information almost matched recent intelligence reports of a suspected Viet Cong battalion of approximately three hundred men sighted some seventeen kilometres west of Ban-Me-Thuot, and moving south. Perhaps the suspected Viet Cong battalion might be FULRO troops instead. Y-We's story could be true to some degree

Y-We then told me that General Y-Bham and the FULRO movement had realized that Viet Cong activities in Darlac Province were harming the Montagnard people. They were now prepared to fight the Viet Cong. If this were correct, a swing of the FULRO movement to the South Vietnamese Government's side from that of the Communists would be a resounding political victory.

I immediately contacted Tom Donahue in Saigon. I told him that secret liaison with the rebels could be politically dangerous, and suggested I should inform the Vietnamese authorities of the situation and let them handle it. I told him I would first check on the authenticity of Y-We's story before informing the Vietnamese authorities. Tom agreed with my plan.

Before leaving Ban-Me-Thuot, I went to see Tom Burke. He was a CIA officer working for the Liaison Branch of the agency — the branch directly and primarily responsible for intelligence collection and interrogation. That branch had

been set up in Ban-Me-Thuot in mid-1964. Tom Burke worked directly with the national and provincial police and other
intelligence agencies in Darlac Province.

I was surprised to find Dorsey Anderson with Burke.
Dorsey was an American officer working for the Covert Action Branch in Saigon. As he worked for the same branch as
myself, I expected him to pay me the courtesy of letting me
know when he entered my area of responsibility. He was a
friend of Y-Preh, the FULRO representative who wanted to see
me. Dorsey had with him Nay Luett, a member of the Jarai
tribe and a representative of the Department of Montagnard
Affairs in Saigon.

With the benefit of hindsight, it would not surprise me if
Dorsey Anderson knew that Y-Preh was back in South Vietnam at that time. I now believe that, through Y-Preh, Dorsey
was the CIA's contact man with the FULRO movement in
Cambodia, and probably had been since the previous year's
Montagnard revolt. I think that the Vietnamese became
aware of that connection, because he was later banned from
visiting the central highlands.

Dorsey wanted to accompany Y-We, myself, and my interpreter offsiders, to meet the FULRO representatives. I could
hardly refuse as it might appear that I was concealing something from the CIA.

We were guided to the Rhade village of Buon Tur Mpro,
thirteen kilometres south-west of Ban-Me-Thuot. There we
waited until the FULRO delegates arrived. They were dressed
in an assortment of military uniforms with their own badges
of rank and other small insignia. They were armed with an
assortment of weapons of American origin, obviously those
taken from the disbanded special forces bases.

They handed me six letters, five addressed to me and one to
the 'Country Team Leader' — the US State Department third
secretary in Darlac Province. They confirmed that the three
rebel battalions were back in South Vietnam to fight the Viet
Cong. He said General Y-Bham Enuol, the FULRO leader, had
told them to contact me and ask for my advice.

I immediately told them they would have to liaise directly

with the Vietnamese Government authorities. They protested
they would not be prepared to do that. They wanted to
remain an autonomous force, receiving direct support from
the Americans. I abruptly told them that was not possible,
and that by contacting me directly, they were jeopardizing my
own Truong Son Force, which was proving itself an effective
force against the Viet Cong.

Dorsey Anderson intervened, telling me I should be more
diplomatic with the delegates. I knew I had the upper hand
and therefore ignored Dorsey's advice. After all, he wasn't
invited to the meeting. He had invited himself. I was annoyed
at the obstinate attitude of the FULRO delegates and at the
danger their direct liaison with me posed to our Truong Son
Force. I didn't feel that I had to be nice to any of them.

When they persisted in refusing to negotiate with the Vietnamese authorities, I told them abruptly I wanted nothing
further to do with them. They had their orders from General
Y-Bham to accept and follow my advice. This left them with
no option. They agreed to meet General Lu Lan if I could
arrange a meeting with him and we separated on that note.

On my return to Ban-Me-Thuot, I reported directly to
General Lu Lan, Commander of the Vietnamese Army's 23rd
Division, and the most senior Vietnamese officer in Darlac
Province. He agreed to a meeting with the FULRO delegates at
2 pm on Tuesday 20 May 1965 — the following day.

I returned to tell the FULRO people of the arrangements for
the meeting. I told them they should confine their discussions
to their willingness to fight the Viet Cong under Vietnamese
Government control. I warned them not to make any of the
time-worn autonomy demands. They agreed to follow my
advice, and, at the pre-arranged time, I collected the delegates
in two Truong Son Force jeeps and took them to General
Lan's headquarters. On arrival, we found a number of Americans in attendance. They were Colonel Theodore Mataxis —
senior adviser to General Vinh Loc's headquarters in Pleiku;
Colonel Laurence E. Browne — senior adviser to General Lu
Lan, the 23rd Division commander; William Beachner — US

State Department representative in Darlac Province; and Dorsey Anderson.

I was annoyed at the massive presence of Americans at a meeting which I considered principally a Vietnamese/Montagnard affair. I said I did not wish to remain during the discussions but Colonel Hoang Manh Dang, General Lan's chief of staff, told me that General Lan wanted me to remain.

The meeting took place in Vietnamese and the Rhade dialect, and the Americans did not understand it. Then the FULRO delegates rudely refused to speak Vietnamese and demanded an interpreter. Y-Rit, one of my offsiders, acted as interpreter, much to his embarrassment. Autonomy demands dominated the discussions, and little mention was made of FULRO preparedness to fight the Viet Cong. I was both annoyed and embarrassed. The unsuccessful meeting concluded, photographs were taken, and we left Ban-Me-Thuot.

I remained angry and silent. Y-Senh was aware of my anger, as I intended. When he asked me for the reason, I abruptly told him I thought they wanted to fight the Viet Cong and instead they were chattering like old women.

They asked for a further meeting with General Lu Lan, but I refused to arrange it, telling them I didn't want to waste any more of General Lan's time. They continued pestering me for another meeting, while all the time I tried to embarrass them as much as I could.

Finally, I reluctantly agreed to try to arrange another meeting for them with General Lan, with certain provisos. I wrote down for them a list of points they were to discuss. They were to accept Vietnamese liaison officers with their FULRO battalions, to operate under Vietnamese military control against the Viet Cong, and in areas where accidental clashes with Vietnamese Army units were not possible. They also were not to ask for additional weapons, nor for ammunition and rations above their immediate requirement for survival, until the Vietnamese authorities could fully trust them.

I warned them they would have to endure inconvenience and distrust until the Vietnamese Government was assured of their loyalty. They agreed and promised to adhere to the points I had written down for them.

On my return to Ban-Me-Thuot, I again reported to General Lan, and gave him a copy of the points I had already given to the FULRO delegates. He was very happy and agreed to another meeting the following day.

On the night of 20 May, Tom Burke, the CIA Liaison Branch officer in Ban-Me-Thuot, received a telephone call from Colonel Browne, the US Army senior adviser in the province. He asked Tom to come to the Bungalow with Bill Beachner (the State Department official), Dorsey Anderson and myself. Colonel Browne was full of self-importance and liked to think that he ruled Darlac Province. He asked me for a briefing on the latest developments. He then said that as General Lan's senior adviser, he wanted a copy of the list of points to be discussed the following day — the points I had already given to both the FULRO delegates and General Lan. He also asked for a map, marked with a proposed area of operations where the FULRO battalions could operate. He directed his requests to Bill Beachner to whom I was locally answerable. I had to provide the information and did so in good faith, believing that Colonel Browne wanted it only for his own knowledge.

As a group, we then all agreed that the following day's discussions between the FULRO delegates and General Lan were a Vietnamese and Montagnard affair. We mutually agreed that no Westerners would attend.

The following morning, I again collected the FULRO delegates and delivered them to General Lan's office. Colonel Dang, the chief-of-staff, again asked me to remain during the discussions. I pointed out to him that the matter was not my business, and that I would prefer to remain downstairs. I then politely excused myself and left the room.

Dorsey Anderson was at the bottom of the steps, and we waited together. To our amazement, we saw Colonel Browne striding towards the office with a rolled map in his hand. He ascended the steps on the other side of the high building, and entered General Lan's office by another entrance.

Colonel Thanh, our province chief, later told me that Colonel Browne sailed into General Lan's office and spread the map out in front of him. He then handed him a note and said to the general, in front of all present:

'General Lan, those are the points I would like you to discuss with the FULRO delegates and here's a map showing the area I propose their battalions operate in.'

Colonel Browne had stunned, belittled and embarrassed General Lan in front of his subordinates and the FULRO representatives. Colonel Thanh told me that General Lan had been furious at the behaviour of the more junior American officer, but tried to conceal his anger during the remainder of the discussion. Colonel Browne had left the general's office following his 'advice' to General Lan.

Dorsey and I were oblivious of the incident as we watched the squat, bumptious, little American stride away. Perhaps Colonel Laurence E. Browne, in that action, felt he was appearing in the eyes of all to be the mediator.

When Colonel Thanh later told me of the incident, I could not help but remember the behaviour of another senior American officer, Colonel Freund, during the Montagnard revolt of September 1964.

The conference ended around midday. When everyone had left General Lan's office, he and Colonel Dang thanked me for my assistance in bringing the rebel leaders and the Vietnamese authorities together. General Lan described the second conference as 'quite successful'.

On Thursday 22 July, the unpleasant General Vinh Loc, Commander of the Vietnamese Army's 2nd Corps, flew down from Pleiku to Ban-Me-Thuot. He wanted to assess for himself the credibility of the intentions of the FULRO movement. At the same time, Stu Methven had arrived from Saigon and was staying with me for two days. General Vinh Loc, knowing of Stu's presence in Ban-Me-Thuot, invited him to discussions in General Lan's office at the headquarters of the 23rd Division. Stu asked me to go with him.

General Vinh Loc was the senior of the two Vietnamese generals and, as always, was overbearing and rude. When Stu and I arrived, he launched into a tirade against Americans, whom he accused of interfering in Vietnamese internal affairs. At times, his tirade appeared to be aimed directly at the two of us. On one occasion, General Lan intervened on my behalf, saying I was personally responsible for initiating the discussions between the FULRO representatives and the Vietnamese authorities. He pointed out it was the first direct contact the South Vietnamese Government had with the FUL-RO movement during the ten months since the Montagnard revolt. General Lan went on to say that he, as well as I, had seen the possibility of bringing the FULRO rebels back under South Vietnamese Government control. He said that if I had made a mistake in arranging the recent meetings, then he, as a Vietnamese general, had made a graver mistake in meeting the FULRO delegation. General Lan was very courageous to defend me to his superior officer, particularly in front of his subordinates.

*   *   *

On Friday 23 July, Stu Methven returned to Saigon. As he left he was reserved.

'I think this might be the end of your Truong Son Force, Barry.'

'I don't think so,' I said. I thought it a stupid statement for Methven to make. I had deliberately kept all my dealings with both the FULRO deputation and the Vietnamese completely above board. In no way was our Truong Son Force involved.

'You could see General Vinh Loc wasn't very happy. He's got some influence,' Methven said moodily.

I said: 'Look Stu, I reckon the Truong Son Force has made a good enough name for itself to survive any bullshit like this.'

Methven turned away.

'We'll see', he said, and it was clear he was not convinced at all.

Of the six letters the FULRO delegates had given to me when we first met, five were personally addressed to me and some contained photographs of the writers. Knowing that they contained information of interest to the CIA, I gave those letters to Tom Burke. I asked him to photocopy them for CIA headquarters in Saigon. I told Burke I wanted the original letters and photographs returned to me.

I was foolish to trust him. He sent the originals to Tom Donahue, the head of the Covert Action Branch in Saigon. I later asked Donahue about the missing letters. He denied any knowledge of them. When I told him I knew he had received them, he said the contents were compromising and that they were being held by CIA for handwriting identification. I asked for the photocopies and he refused, saying that, although the letters and photographs were addressed to me personally, they were CIA property. I was rapidly beginning to understand just where I stood with Tom Donahue.

I reported the matter to Brigadier Jackson, my Australian commander and to Colonel Serong, who was still working with the CIA.

It was not to be the last time the CIA would intercept and try to retain letters personally addressed to me.

14 Farewell to the Highlands

That weekend, I received a call from Saigon, asking me to report to the Covert Action Branch in Saigon the following Monday morning. An Air America aircraft had been arranged to fly me down during the week-end.

Months previously, the Covert Action Branch, like the remainder of the CIA, had been moved into the American Embassy building in Saigon. Donahue and Methven were not available when I first arrived, but I ran into Bill Evans, Chief of Programs, Covert Action Branch.

'Tom Donahue and Stu Methven want you out of the highlands, Barry,' he confided.

I was dumbfounded. Stu and I had our differences, and I'd found Donahue a little difficult to get on with. But I had not thought things had gone quite this far.

'Who do they intend replacing me with?' I asked.

'Well, they've got Jack Benefield in mind.'

'Who the hell's he?' I asked.

'A CIA career man,' Evans said guardedly. 'Hasn't been in the country long. He's been trained for operations in South America.'

Then he opened up:

'Methven's talked Donahue into replacing you, Barry,' he said quietly. 'I think the whole thing's stupid. If I were you,

I'd fight against it. Why don't you get Brigadier Jackson to back you?'

Later, I met Wynn Oliver, the deputy chief of the Covert Action Branch. He surprised me by saying the Vietnamese wanted me to leave the highlands. He did not know I already had the true story. I asked to see Tom Donahue, the branch chief, and was later ushered into his office.

Tom Donahue was a shortish man, not pudgy but with a soft body, built and groomed more for the desk than the rigours of field work. In fact I had not seen him in the field. He could have been a Harvard man, and he liked to exude an air of confidence and authority.

'Barry, the Darlac Province officials are beginning to resent your presence,' he said.

That threw me. It was my impression that the province officials were the last people to want me out. My relationship with the province chief, Colonel Thanh, and his staff, had been excellent. My relationships with General Lan and his staff had also been good, particularly after my part in arranging the meetings with the FULRO delegation.

'In what way are the province officials resenting me, Tom?' I asked.

Donahue shuffled a bit, but refused to be specific.

'We just have feedback,' he said.

'From where?'

'From American sources.' Then he said more bluntly, 'Look we've got a fellow called Jack Benefield we want to send up there to replace you.'

I saw no point in arguing, and left.

I reported to Brigadier Jackson, my Australian commander and gave him the news. He seemed surprised at the story that the Vietnamese wanted me out.

'Tom Donahue told me that they felt that two years as a field case officer was more than enough for any man. He told me they felt you deserved a break,' Brigadier Jackson said. 'I told them that you were the best judge of that and that I was going to leave the decision entirely up to you.'

'Well sir,' I said, 'I don't feel as though I need a break. I'm doing fine.'

'I don't know where they got that story about the Vietnamese wanting you out,' the brigadier said. 'I have not heard anything about it. I'm sure I would have by now.'

Then he asked:

'Did they say anything about a replacement for you?'

'They plan on putting a CIA career man in — a bloke called Jack Benefield. I've never met him.'

He jumped. 'Did they tell you that?'

'Yes, sir.'

Brigadier Jackson was looking very annoyed. 'If anyone's going to replace you, I want it to be an Australian officer. If you had decided to take a break, I was going to replace you with Major Don Robertson.'

Brigadier Jackson took me to see His Excellency, Mr H. D. Anderson, the Australian Ambassador. After some discussion, they both advised me that rather than becoming the focus of distrust, it would be in my best personal interests to leave the central highlands. I reluctantly agreed. The Americans said they wanted to retain Warrant Officer John 'Jock' Roy, my assistant, to work under Jack Benefield. Brigadier Jackson was annoyed at that. However, he agreed to leave John in Ban-Me-Thuot for a limited period until the Americans could organize someone to take his place.

During discussions with Donahue and Methven, it was also agreed that I be given time to return to Ban-Me-Thuot to pack my things and say my farewells.

During that conversation, something else came out.

Donahue said: 'You've developed far too much influence with the Montagnard. You've made it very difficult for anyone else to take over from you. You've developed a personality cult in the highlands.'

I neither liked, nor agreed with that.

'Tom, I did no such thing,' I said hotly. 'I know how dangerous a personality cult can be in this type of operation. I would do everything in my power to avoid that happening.'

Evidently, Donahue and Methven appreciated how much

influence I had seemed to have acquired with the Montagnard. Perhaps they were afraid of being unable to match it, using one of their own career officers. My attitude at that time was that I had taken the time and made the effort to get to know the Montagnard and to learn to work well with them. If they classified that as developing a personality cult, then so be it — and damn them!

But was that really what it was all about? Could it have stemmed from my obstinacy in refusing to accept Methven's continual requests for the establishment of counter-terror teams, and the constant urgings for conformity with other Covert Action Branch programs in South Vietnam — programs which I doubted would work better with the Montagnard than my own?

Could it also have had something to do with Ambassador Taylor's fateful remark at the end of the briefing in Ban-Me-Thuot?

'Isn't there an American capable of doing this?'

I arrived back at the house in Ton That Thuyet to learn that during my absence, a security officer from the CIA in Saigon had arrived and removed my files and records from the combination safe. The security section of the CIA knew the combinations of safes used by their field case officers, in case of their death or capture. Tom Donahue later tole me the security officer had found a set of strange code books in my safe. Although they were the type our Truong Son Force used, they were not ours.

Donahue later accused me of possessing those strange code books without authority. He said that they were copies of code books issued to a Vietnamese Army unit. I asked him why in hell I would want to monitor encoded messages of a Vietnamese Army unit, even if I had the radio monitoring facilities to do so. I now believe the code books were planted and that this was an incredibly childlike attempt by the Covert Action Branch to compromise me with the Vietnamese authorities.

Although the CIA security officer confiscated my files and

records, no-one realized I had duplicate copies elsewhere. They still exist in a secure location. I was able to refer to them during the preparation of the comprehensive report Brigadier Jackson later asked me to prepare, and of course I used them in the writing of this book.

Tom Donahue also asked me for my copy of my CIA operational fund accounting records. By that time my fund had amounted to a total of five million Vietnamese piastres (about fifty thousand American dollars) a month — a lot of money in those days. As I had given the CIA's Covert Action Branch all receipts and statements of expenditure on a regular basis during the previous two years, I felt that I was entitled to keep my copies and refused to hand them over. I had temporarily secured those records in the Australian Embassy and they are still in my possession.

Had I surrendered my copies of my accounting records, it would then have been a simple matter to accuse me of misappropriation of CIA operational funds, and I would not have evidence to refute such an accusation. Brigadier Jackson fully supported my retention of those records.

* * *

On Friday 6 August, General Lan presented me with the Vietnamese Cross of Gallantry with Silver Star. Following the official presentation, he asked me to his office. Over coffee, he said:

'You know, Captain Petersen, today when I pinned that decoration on you, I realized how much better it was to deal with you, a soldier like myself, rather than an American civilian from the Central Intelligence Agency.'

He went on to say he was very sorry I was leaving the highlands and that he intended writing a detailed report to the Vietnamese Government in Saigon. He would inform them of my personal efforts in re-uniting the rebel FULRO movement with the South Vietnamese.

He continued, saying that what really upset the Vietnamese more than anything was the interference in their internal politics by the American CIA.

'CIA officers are everywhere,' he said, 'and most Vietnamese military and government officials distrust and hate them.'

He apologized for once having considered me in the same light as American career officers of the CIA.

His frankness astonished me, and I later reported his conversation to both Tom Donahue and Wynn Oliver in Saigon. I was not being vindictive — it was normal procedure for me to relay such information. However, I did feel a certain irony on this occasion. Neither Donahue nor Methven seemed amused, nor did they comment.

Dorsey Anderson later told me that the South Vietnamese Government had banned him from again visiting the Central Highlands. He said he did not know the reason. I now believe the Covert Action Branch was using Dorsey Anderson to maintain contact with the FULRO movement in Cambodia, following the Montagnard revolt. I have often wondered if any of the confiscated letters I gave Tom Burke might have compromised such a CIA liaison, and perhaps the moral support of the FULRO movement conveyed by Dorsey Anderson. I did not have time to read these letters, before leaving them with Tom Burke to photocopy.

I do not know if the American CIA was then aware of the extent of French and Cambodian involvement in the revolt. I did not at that time fully realize it myself.

* * *

I soon met my replacement, Jack Benefield. He briefly looked at the house in Ton That Thuyet, and immediately ordered an electric stove for the Vietnamese cook, and an electric washing machine for the housekeeper from the CIA warehouse in Saigon. I would have enjoyed being a fly on the wall, when Benefield told them that they had to use these machines, instead of their traditional methods of cooking and washing clothes.

I moved the bulk of my things from Ban-Me-Thuot to Saigon, with the intention of returning to Ban-Me-Thuot for a planned two weeks or so of farewells.

* * *

I was to make two further brief trips to Ban-Me-Thuot before I left South Vietnam and another one years later, during my second tour of duty in 1971.

The first of these trips back was to pay outstanding accounts for the program before handing over the operational fund to Jack Benefield. It was during that visit I was told the province chief wished to see me.

Colonel Thanh asked me who the Americans intended sending up to replace me. I told him that it would be Jack Benefield. He then said that he would not mind if another Australian Army officer came but he did not want an American civilian from the CIA. He added that if the Americans insisted on replacing me with Jack Benefield, then he would be permitted to pay day visits only to Ban-Me-Thuot, and to support the Truong Son Force during those visits. He would not be permitted to stay in the province overnight. Colonel Thanh has since told me that this was a directive from his superiors in Saigon.

On my return to Saigon, I also reported that conversation to Tom Donahue and Stu Methven. Tom said, quite emphatically, he could not care less what the province chief had said. But the Vietnamese Government stood its ground, for Benefield never did live in Darlac Province. Instead, he had to live in nearby Dalat in Tuyen Duc Province. He flew across for day-long trips only. His later replacement, Buck Ashby, was subsequently permitted to live in Ban-me-Thuot. But, by that time, a twelve-men Vietnamese Army team had been installed to command, control and administer the Truong Son Force. But more on this subject later.

*   *   *

Another method used to sever my contacts with the Montagnard was the Covert Action Branch's interception of my personal mail sent from Ban-Me-Thuot, including mail from my former assistant, Warrant Officer John Roy and from my Montagnard friends, which John placed inside a large, sealed envelope addressed to me.

I realized this was happening when one day I entered the large room in the American Embassy set aside for the Covert Action Branch's American field case officers. Scattered about, lying open on empty desks, I saw letters addressed personally to me. It was obvious they had been opened and had been read by someone temporarily out of the empty room.

I was not only shocked but bloody annoyed at my find, and I bundled the opened letters up and stalked out of the American Embassy. I thought it would be a waste of time to confront Tom Donahue with my discovery, so I went straight to Brigadier Jackson to report the incident. He was equally annoyed, and said he would speak to CIA Station Chief Jorgensen. Because there were still a few Australians working for the CIA's Covert Action Branch, I didn't want to further strain relationships with the staff. I therefore asked Brigadier Jackson not to mention it. However, I made sure that the other Australians were aware of what had happened.

It took me three days to eventually retrieve what I thought were the full contents of that large sealed envelope. After speaking by telephone to John Roy, I found that there were still others missing and I had to ask Jack Benefield where they were before they were handed over. I'm still not certain I retrieved all of the opened mail.

Some of my Montagnard offsiders visited me in Saigon from time to time. They told me of letters which they had written and sent to me and which I never received. I have no idea how much personal mail the Covert Action Branch intercepted and retained.

Telephone tapping was another form of communication interception between Ban-Me-Thuot and Saigon. We had been given a telephone extension from the American Army advisory group at the Bungalow in Ban-Me-Thuot to our house in Ton That Thuyet. During the last eight to ten months I spent in the highlands, you could generally get through to Saigon — even if it took a few attempts.

Then I noticed subtle changes when I was speaking with John Roy by telephone. Firstly — not so subtle — the extension number had been altered. But he appeared to be guarded in his speech and he indicated that he could not discuss certain matters over the telephone.

A few days later, he arrived in Saigon and told me what had really happened. The American communications officer with the advisory group had warned him he should be careful during his telephone conversations. He said that Colonel Laurence E. Browne, the bumptious little American senior adviser who had embarrassed General Lu Lan during the discussions with the FULRO delegates, had directed that a party line to our extension be installed in his office. He had set up a tape recorder to record conversations as he wished. Colonel Browne was an ex-American Special Forces officer. When he was still with this group they would still have been under the control of the American CIA. I don't know whether he was tapping our telephone conversations on their behalf, or if he was just a curious little man. However, we knew he was eavesdropping.

I never ceased to be surprised at the naïve behaviour of some American senior officials. The observation could also apply to some Australian senior officials.

* * *

Late in August 1965, the President of South Vietnam, General Nguyen Van Thieu, received a personal letter from the self-styled President of the High Plateau of Champa, General Y-Bham Enuol, leader of the FULRO movement. In the letter, Y-Bham appealed to President Thieu for my return to the highlands. The letter gave me credit for bringing together the South Vietnamese Government and the FULRO movement. The CIA gave me a copy of that letter. General Nguyen Van Thieu had sent a copy to the American Ambassador.

Some days later, Wynn Oliver, deputy chief of the Covert Action Branch, told me some senior Vietnamese Government officials had asked the Americans if I was being returned to the highlands and that they had been told I was not. I detected differences of opinion among senior CIA officers. Some CAB officers were supporting me it seemed. Wynn Oliver took

FRONT DE LIBERATION
DES HAUTS PLATEAUX   Zone Liberee, le 9 Aout 1965
DEGA DU CHAMPA

No : <u>346 - FLC</u>.
                    Le President du Front de Liberation des Hauts-
                             Plateaux DEGA CHAM,

                                    a

                       Son Excellence Monsieur le President du
                       Gouvernment de la Republique du Sud
                             VIET - NAM

<u>O B J E T</u> : Demande retenir Monsieur PETERSON.

        En concequences de la reception qu'il a reservee a nos
emissaires Monsieur PETTERSON a subi une regrettable mutation.

        Je confirme qu'il n'a pas d'inconvenients cette question
car il est oblige de recevoir nos agents qui le recherchent dans
son propre bureau.

        Et en plus grace a lui aussi que Votre Gouvernement a pu
rencontrernos representants et que nos affaires vont bientot etre
ameliorees. En nom personnel je vous prie de lui accorder la
toterance et de le laisser poursuivre son travail a Banmethuot.

        Veuillez agreer Exellence, l'assurance de ma tres haute
consideration.

                            Y-BHAM ENUOL.

*Copy of the letter from Y-Bham Enuol to the President
of South Vietnam, asking that I be allowed to continue
my work in the highlands.*

me to dinner one evening. He went to great pains to explain that he personally had little to do with my Truong Son program, and nothing whatsoever to do with my removal from the highlands. He pointed out that, as a career officer in the CIA, he could not publicly support me. He appeared genuinely sincere in his apologies for 'any mistakes which the Covert Action Branch personnel had made'.

Bill Evans, the CAB programs chief, also gave me encouragement. He said that, although he violently disagreed with the decision to replace me, he was in no position to say so. He asked me not to repeat his remarks, as they might jeopardize his career.

I tell these stories some twenty-two years, later, since they are now unlikely to affect these men. I'm quite sure that the CIA chief of station in South Vietnam knew nothing of these internal Covert Action Branch politics.

At this time too, a few journalists began to hear rumours about my experiences with the Montagnard. One journalist anxious to obtain the full story was author Gerald Stone, later to become a prominent television reporter and producer. He almost trapped me one day, while I was enjoying a drink with another journalist and author, Pat Burgess.

Pat and I were sitting on the wide verandah of the Hotel Continental Palace, when Stone walked across to our table. He spoke to Pat about another matter, and Pat deliberately did not introduce us. Pat was aware of the secrecy which still surrounded my work in the highlands and the tensions surrounding my removal. He respected my confidence, as I'm sure Gerald Stone would, had we known each other.

Dorsey Anderson of the Covert Action Branch also tried to divorce himself from the actions of Donahue and Methven. I suspected he had previous direct dealings with the rebel FULRO movement. He told me that Ong Vu Duc Hai, the Minister for Minority Groups and a member of the Prime Minister's Department, wished to meet me. Ong Hai took Dorsey and me to dinner at a North Vietnamese-style restaurant in Saigon.

At one point, while Dorsey was away from the table, Ong

Hai told me that Ong Bui Diem, the head of the Prime Minister's Department, wished to meet me. He told me the meeting was to be kept secret from the Americans, but that Roy Fernandez, the Australian chargé d'affaires in Saigon, was aware of the request, and had agreed.

The meeting with Ong Bui Diem took place at the offices of the Vietnamese Prime Minister, Air Vice-Marshal Ky. I wasn't sure if I was under surveillance at the time and, as the offices were next to the Saigon Zoo, I feigned a visit to the zoo. Cloak-and-dagger stuff, but at the time I considered it necessary. I then slipped through a damaged fence between the zoo and the large shady grounds of the old French-colonial building which housed the prime minister's offices.

Ong Bui Diem started by saying he had heard so much of me, that he wanted to meet me. Our conversation lasted over an hour, during numerous cups of Vietnamese tea. We discussed at length the problems besetting the South Vietnamese Government in the highlands, caught between the Communist offensive on one hand, and the Montagnard autonomy movement on the other.

He asked me what mistakes I thought the Vietnamese and Americans might be making in the highlands. He apologized to me for the attitudes of General Co, the deputy prime minister and of General Vinh Loc, the commander of the Vietnamese Army 2nd Corps. He said both generals were basically anti-European, having served as junior officers under the French.

He also said the Vietnamese Government was not altogether happy with the methods of operations of some Americans in South Vietnam. He said both the president and the prime minister were grateful for what I had done for their country. Ong Diem said that I appeared to have a great depth of understanding of the problems in the highlands, and it was a pity many others did not have a similar perception. He then said that he was very sorry to see me leave South Vietnam. He ended by asking me not to tell the Americans of our meeting. I gained great respect for this man, who was later to become Ambassador for South Vietnam to the United States.

That was one report the American CIA would not receive until perhaps they read this account of it.

* * *

Much later, at the beginning of 1971, General Nguyen Van Thieu, the President of South Vietnam, sent a gift to me with his Minister for Defence who was visiting the Australian Task Force base at Nui Dat in Phuoc Tuy Province. It was a large, beautifully-lacquered cigar box with a thick, gold, presidential seal inside the lid. After the Vietnamese Minister for Defence handed the gift to me, one of his aides quietly whispered to me:

'Take care of it, the seal is solid gold.'

It was as if the president's valuable gift was the Vietnamese Government's way of saying 'Thank you' for what I had done all those years before.

* * *

My intended two weeks of farewells from the central highlands stretched beyond that period. There were many ceremonies and Montagnard sacrifices. Colonel Le Van Thanh, the province chief, gave me a large dinner and so did a number of other province officials and prominent civilians.

It was an exhausting and emotional time. There were so many I had officially to farewell, and even more who wished to say goodbye to me either ceremonially or less formally. I had a round of visits to homes, longhouses or villages to meet the families of some of the Montagnard who worked closely with me — the radio operators, the interpreters, those of the Montagnard commanders with whom I had developed a particular association or friendship.

The main farewell ceremony was held at Dam San base. This was a huge affair that began around nine o'clock one morning and was continued until daybreak of the next day. I remember the occasion clearly, even now.

I arrived for the ceremony with Jut, John Roy and our other offsiders and an Australian Army public relations warrant officer Brigadier Jackson had sent up from Saigon to cover the event. I wore the magnificent traditional Rhade dress given me by the Montagnard some time before. The film he produced was later shown on the Australian Broadcasting Corporation television program 'Weekend Magazine', before I returned to Australia.

About a hundred people were already gathered around the great longhouse which we had built for large gatherings in the Dam San base. It was almost fifty metres long and about fifteen metres wide. Inside it was ten metres high from the earthen floor to the peak of the traditional steeply-sloping Montagnard roof. At ground level, the structure was open on all four sides.

The hall had already been prepared when we arrived and was decorated with palm fronds and wild banana trees. About thirty large rice wine jars were lined down the middle of the huge hall, each tethered to its own elaborately carved and decorated pole. The big buffalo-hide drums — half as tall as the Montagnard who used them — were in place, and a row of bronze gongs lay on a thick teak plank down one side of the hall. Woven sleeping mats had been laid where I was to sit or recline as the central figure of the ceremony.

The sacrifice of the buffalo, a ceremonial procedure with great importance to the Montagard, was held first. The life of the mountain people is dominated by many spirits. These rule the fate of men and animals, govern the harvests and control the elements. The Montagnard believe the spirits must be cultivated and placated through sacrifices. At the lowest level the sacrifice is a chicken, then graduating to a pig, with the first and most important offering being the buffalo. On this occasion there were three buffalo, a number of pigs and dozens of chickens. The Montagnard sacrifice of the buffalo is cruel to Western eyes. The beast is tethered to a pole and a Montagnard elder moves in from behind and hamstrings it. The rear of the poor beast slumps, but its forelegs remain extended. In this way its vulnerable breast is offered, and a second elder approaches with a spear and drives it into the heart. The buffalo drops to its side and dies very quickly. All three buffalo were dispatched in this way.

Huge log fires had been lit. The buffalo were butchered and

much of the blood collected from this was drunk raw as is usual during these ceremonies. The larger pieces of buffalo were buried, unskinned, in the ashes, with the hide acting as a protection for the flesh. Portions of pig were cooked in the same manner as the buffalo meat, although smaller sections, and the chickens, were wrapped in banana leaves to prevent them shrivelling within the ashes.

Although I was familiar with Montagnard ceremonial cooking, I didn't always look forward to these occasions, gastronomically speaking. But in the ceremonial sense I considered it a great honour.

While the meal was being prepared I mingled with the guests, clutching a glass of Vietnamese beer — 'Bia La Rue' — which was cooled as usual by the familiar brown ice bought from the small ice-works in Ban-Me-Thuot. Some of the drama teams were performing, dancing and singing Rhade and Vietnamese songs which provided a colourful and noisy background. The crowd was growing every minute. Eight-man teams of our Truong Son Force were returning on foot or by vehicle from the surrounding countryside, to bathe in the stream and change into their fresh uniforms. Because of operational commitments, it was not possible for all of the Truong Son Force to return for my farewell sacrifice. But by the time the ceremony began, there were between four and five hundred gathered around the great longhouse.

When it was time for the main ceremony, chairs were provided for the dignitaries including John Roy and myself. Y-Liu Buon Ya, the Rhade elder I had groomed as Montagnard commander of the Truong Son Force, made the first speech, then others followed — many of them very touching. I stood at attention as the speeches were read in complete silence. These moments are considered to have great solemnity. In the background, attendants were laying out special portions of the buffalo, including the head of one beast. This was brought to the front of the mat where I was to recline.

The speeches over, I was asked to go to the mats padded with hand-woven Rhade blankets and cushions for my comfort. Another Rhade elder, who performed the ceremonial role of sorcerer, then moved forward and squatted before the large bronze bowl of food set next to the buffalo head. He began to chant incantations before me. This was the expected posture, for it was an indication of status. I felt a little foolish lying there like some Eastern potentate while hundreds of eyes were fixed almost solely upon me. But I had to act in the way my hosts expected, in response to the great courtesy they were extending to me.

The incantation concluded, I sat briefly on a chair. A Montagnard axe-head was placed at my feet and I laid one bare foot upon it. Then blood and rice wine was poured over my foot and a live chicken waved in circles above my head. I have no idea what the symbolism meant save that the ceremony was meant to give me the protection and support of the spirits throughout the remainder of my life.

After that, I returned to my mat and a Rhade woman went to the nearest large wine jar, taking a few sips through the long bamboo straw. She beckoned me forward. I took the straw from her right hand with my right hand, and sat opposite the jar. Then a seemingly endless procession of people moved forward bearing tokens. These were bracelets, lengths of thin brass rods twisted into circles which were then clamped around my right wrist as I continued to ceremonially hold the straw. I later counted two hundred and twenty bracelets and there were about ten necklaces of amber-like beads which the dignitaries had placed around my neck.

It was time for me to drink the rice wine. The gongs rang out. They were beaten in an urgent, rapid-fire rhythm, the persistent but attractive sound punctuated by the booming of buffalo hide drums. I sucked the first of my required portions of rice wine through the bamboo straw. Gradually all the other rice wine jars were broached. The main ceremony was over and the long celebrations that were to continue for many hours had begun.

I had already completed my first and most important task — to say goodbye to members of my Truong Son Force. Just before the ceremony more than three hundred had paraded outside the great longhouse and I had slowly passed along each rank. I had shaken each hand, receiving and returning salutes from each man. It had taken me the best part of an hour, for I paused to speak to many of them. Some had been members of that original hundred-man force I had inherited from the national police two years before. Most were recruits the force had taken, trained and made into soldiers since then. I had experienced battle with many of them, and shared a cause with them.

I was moved to see there were tears in the eyes of many of those soldiers as they said goodbye. But then, I had tears in my eyes too.

I had so many farewells to make in the highlands that I never got around to them all. I tried to return to Ban-Me-Thuot again in an Air America re-supply aircraft but the pilots told me Tom Donahue had strictly forbidden them to carry me.

* * *

If Donahue and Methven had reservations about my continuing effectiveness, the Montagnard did not. Nor did my Australian commander at the time, Brigadier O.D. Jackson. Just before I left Vietnam, he wrote one of the most glowing reports I have received during my army career:

> Captain Petersen's achievements in Vietnam have been outstanding. He has been responsible for the initiation and the building of an extensive para-military, political and civic action program in a critical area of Vietnam. The success of his program is a tribute to his courage, determination, good sense and practical ability. No officer of his age and experience, I am sure, has been faced with more responsible, diverse, difficult and dangerous tasks and handled them with such outstanding success. His work in Vietnam and his unusual environment has been such that it will take a deliberate effort on his part to settle down to a 'normal' military appointment.
>
> Recommended for accelerated promotion.

In late October 1965, I flew out of Saigon for Singapore. That first, memorable chapter of my life with the Montagnard was over.

15

Singapore, Borneo and Unexpected Recognition

Before leaving Saigon, Brigadier Jackson had told me that although I had to leave South Vietnam, I should not immediately return to Australia.

'There are too many people still trying to get a story on you, Barry,' he said. 'Because of the classified nature of your work in the highlands, you should stay out of circulation for a few months until things die down. Where would you like to go?'

At the time, Indonesian 'Confrontation' was in progress and British, Australian, New Zealand and Malaysian military forces were operating in Sabah and Sarawak, resisting Indonesian incursions into those countries. The nation of Malaysia had just been formed.

'I'd like to go to Singapore, sir,' I said.

'I'll see what I can do, Barry,' the brigadier promised.

I got the trip to Singapore and Brigadier Jackson asked me to start writing a comprehensive report on my two years' work with the CIA in Vietnam and to provide him with a copy. I also requested a trip to Borneo if it was at all possible.

I arrived in Singapore in October 1965. I was still officially a member of the Australian Army Training Team Vietnam (AATTV), and under the command of Brigadier Jackson. He had told me to maintain a low profile while in Singapore.

I expected to be quietly received or even ignored. I was

stunned by my reception. I arrived in Singapore to be told that the commander of the Australian Army AUSTARM force in Singapore, Brigadier F. R. Evans, wanted to see me. I wondered what the commander, a brigadier, would want with me, a lowly captain not even under his command. Maybe he wanted to question me about South Vietnam or to re-iterate Brigadier Jackson's instructions to me to lie low while in Singapore.

I entered Brigadier Evans' office. Instead of asking me to sit down or even shake hands with me, he kept me standing at attention and proceeded soundly and very loudly to rebuke me, in front of his operations officer, Major David Wise.

'How long are you going to stay in Singapore?' the brigadier demanded aggressively.

'A few months,' sir.'

'Well, I'm not at all happy about it. I don't want Brigadier Jackson dumping his political outcasts on me.'

I was absolutely thrown. I didn't know what the brigadier had heard about my removal from the highlands and departure from South Vietnam. Perhaps he'd been told that the Vietnamese had expelled me — a story the CIA would have liked to have got around. Brigadier Evans gave me absolutely no opportunity to explain the circumstances of my departure from the highlands of South Vietnam. He just didn't want to listen. His tirade ended with the remark:

'Stay out of my sight. I don't want to even see you around, and I don't want you coming to the officers' mess here at Tanglin.'

Then he curtly dismissed me.

After two years of unusual autonomy I was used to a fair degree of respect and it was a shock to be treated like some recalcitrant junior officer who had wronged or disobeyed the brigadier. What I had done (or not done) had absolutely nothing to do with him, nor any member of his staff.

Despite this initial very unpleasant confrontation, my days in Singapore were pleasant and relatively uneventful — a good chance to unwind after the earlier tensions of South Vietnam. I was accommodated in a British Army officers' mess on the outskirts of Singapore City — sufficiently distant from the heart of military activity, Tanglin Barracks and its officers' mess. I settled down to write the report as Brigadier Jackson had directed.

My next contact with Brigadier Evans was even more uncomfortable. On the recommendation of my former commander, Colonel Serong, I had been awarded the Military Cross, a British gallantry decoration, for my performance during the Montagnard revolt of September 1964. Normally, the recipient of an award or decoration is warned in advance of the public announcement of that award. At the time, all I knew was that Brigadier Evans wanted to see me at his headquarters at Tanglin Barracks.

In part trepidation, part anger, I was again escorted into his office by Major Wise. I was again required to stand to attention. The brigadier thrust at me the message notifying me of the award of the Military Cross, curtly congratulated me, then followed up with another message. It was from my commander, Brigadier Jackson. The message congratulated me on the award of the Military Cross, then went on to say: 'Your trip to Borneo has been arranged. You will be contacted,' — or words to that effect.

It was the latter part of that message which seemed to send Brigadier Evans berserk. His tirade was at shouting level. Through a window, I could see the noise drawing some of his staff to their doors and windows in the adjacent buildings.

'What's this about a trip to Borneo?' he roared. 'Who's sponsoring it?'

'I don't know, sir,' I said. It was true. I really didn't, although I had my suspicions that it might be the British Secret Service (MI6).

'Don't lie to me!' he ranted, shaking with anger. Then turning to Major Wise he demanded a cigarette.

I later learned from members of his staff that when Brigadier Evans was in an uncontrollable rage, he would call for a cigarette.

'Sir,' I reiterated, 'I'm not lying. I really don't know who's sponsoring the trip!'

'You're lying to me! I want to know!'

This sort of thing continued until, still shaking with anger, he told me to get out.

Shaken, I left his office. I was the centre of attention for his staff, most of whom seemed to have heard his outburst. They were still peering at me through doors and windows of the surrounding buildings. I quietly thanked God I didn't belong there.

I immediately went to his legal officer, Major Evan Davies. He, like the remainder of the staff, was aware that I was the brunt of Brigadier Evans' outburst. He laughingly asked me if the Brigadier had demanded a cigarette.

I told Major Davies of my situation, saying I was in no position to tell Brigadier Evans who my sponsors were for the trip to Borneo, even if I had known. Davies then told me he would have a quiet talk with Brigadier Evans.

His advice to Brigadier Evans must have had some effect, because I never again had to appear before him. Major David Wise, on the other hand, appeared unable to contain his curiosity. Although he was aware he should not interfere, I believe that he may have done so later.

It was Major Wise who telephoned me to give me the brief details of my movement to Labuan in Borneo. The information was merely that I was to board a Royal Air Force aircraft, at a certain time, on a certain day, at Changi airbase (the military airbase in Singapore at that time). No questions were asked of me. Headquarters AUSTARM had evidently received those details only from the headquarters of the British Far East Land Forces.

On the due day, I reported to Changi airbase, and sure enough, I found myself on that aircraft's passenger manifest. I still didn't know absolutely who was behind all this.

The airstrip on Labuan Island boasted one small building. It stood on low stumps, was not much more than a shed, and had a verandah on the front side. It was manned by a few members of the British Army Movements Section, only when an aircraft was arriving or departing.

I had no idea who was to meet me. All the other passengers were picked up. As the last vehicle was departing the locked-up building, the driver asked me if he could give me a lift into the town, Victoria. Thanking him, I declined, knowing that I wouldn't know where to go, or who to see, if I did go into Victoria. I decided to wait on the verandah of the locked building, much to the amusement of the occasional indigenous passer-by. As they exchanged brief conversations in Malay with me, they must have wondered why a 'tuan' would wish to sit on the verandah of a locked building at a deserted airstrip. It was like my early days in Darlac Province all over again. Why was I there? What was I doing? What in God's name was expected of me?

Almost an hour later, a young, well-built, blonde Englishman, wearing civilian clothing, drove up. He introduced himself as John Smith. He was an officer of the British Secret Service (MI6). He drove me to the headquarters of the Director of Operations Borneo, where I was introduced to another civilian, the late Guthrie Troupe. Guthrie's appointment was that of Political Adviser to the Director of Operations, Borneo. That was his official cover as head of station for MI6 in Borneo. Years later he transferred to our Australian Secret Intelligence Service, and became the senior training officer for special operations courses. He died of cancer in 1979.

Guthrie asked me what I wanted to see of MI6 operations in Borneo. I asked him how much he would allow me to see.

'We have been told to open the doors completely to you,' he said. 'You're free to see as much as you want to see.'

I was surprised and delighted to receive *carte blanche*. The only proviso was that I was seen to be under the wing of the British 22nd Special Air Service Regiment (22 SAS).

MI6 were sponsoring three major special operations programs in Borneo at that time. All three were training-operation bases, one on an island off the mouth of the Kuching River, one in the Bario Highlands in the north-east of Sarawak, and the third near Sepulot in Sabah. Guerilla-type operations were conducted from those bases, across the border into

Borneo
— Sarawak, Sabah (East Malaysia), Sultanate of Brunei and Indonesian Kalimantan

N

KOTA BELUD
JESSELTON
SANDAKAN

SOUTH CHINA SEA

LABUAN
BRUNEI
SABAH
SEPULOT
TAWAU

Great
Natuna

BARIO
KUBAAN
TARAKAN

SARAWAK

SIBU
KAPIT
Sungai Rejang

BAU KUCHING

INDONESIAN

KALIMANTAN

BALIKPAPAN

Strait

SULAWESI

Bilitung

BANDJERMASIN

Makassar

JAVA SEA

Kilometres
0   100   200   300   400   500

0   100   200   300
Miles

Kalimantan against the Indonesian armed forces. The indigenous members of those special operations groups were all members of various tribal groups in the respective areas.

In the early 1960s, Sarawak and Sabah in British Borneo, and Singapore too, were all British colonies awaiting independence. The British felt that as independent states united they would perhaps stand, but divided they might fall. They therefore proposed the amalgamation of the independent Federation of Malaya with Singapore, Sarawak and Sabah, to form the new state of Malaysia.

But Indonesia's President Sukarno saw the birth of such a large and strong neighbour nation as a threat to the security of Indonesia. He declared 'Konfrontasi' (confrontation we called it) against the proposed amalgamation.

Indonesian armed forces commenced incursions into each state, using commando-type raiding parties. The British, Australian and New Zealand Governments sent armed forces to support those of the new Malaysian nation. Most of the supporting British forces were in Sarawak and Sabah, in Borneo. Although ostensibly not operating into Indonesia, we now know that cross-border operations were conducted by the SAS units of Britain, Australia and New Zealand, and by the British MI6, using indigenous tribespeople of Sarawak and Sabah.

British Army officers, with small, hand-picked special operations teams, commanded and controlled the ethnic minority tribespeople in each guerilla-type force. One exception was the officer commanding the special operations base in Sabah. He was a civilian officer of MI6 — a man called Dick Noone.

Dick Noone was an anthropologist who had come to Malaya in 1939. He had made a study of indigenous tribes, even living with them at times. In January 1941 Dick and his brother Pat, also an anthropologist, were assigned the task of raising the Frontier Patrol, a secret reconnaissance organization. Dick became involved in espionage. He ran eight secret agents among the Malays in southern Siam (Thailand), to gain information on Japanese activities. He also recruited secret agents among the Malays in southern Thailand.

Dick escaped from Singapore during the Japanese invasion and came to Australia. He married a Melbourne girl whom he later divorced. After the Second World War, Dick worked in the Australian Intelligence Department in Melbourne. That department could be regarded as the forerunner of the present Australian Secret Intelligence Service (ASIS).

He returned to Malaya in 1952 to join General Sir Gerald Templer's staff, as Secretary of the Federal Intelligence Committee. He was later appointed head of the Malayan Department of Aborigines (Orang Asli), and given the task of reorganizing it to cope with the Communist emergency.

Dick won the support of General Templer in raising the Senoi Praak — the Orang Asli, para-military organization operating among the indigenous tribes of Malaya, to gain their support against the Communist terrorists.

Dick Noone and I hit it off from the moment we met — and this was unusual. Most people found him bloody hard to get on with. He would much prefer to sit down and chin-wag to a member of some South-East Asian tribe than he would with a fellow Westerner. He had a marked personality barrier in dealing with his own kind. He was a man of secrets who had been involved in clandestine operations for close on thirty years. He didn't waste his breath on those he wasn't interested in and spoke only to those he wanted to. I felt honoured to find I was in the latter category.

I felt I established an instant rapport with Dick because of our similar interest in the peoples of South-East Asia, in anthropology, and in special operations. He was a very heavy smoker and during our many long talks, amid clouds of cigarette smoke, he told me some of his stories. He was intensely interested in learning of my experiences with the Montagnard, and of my admiration for them.

Then, to my amazement he said:

'Yes, I found the Montagnard like that. But I wasn't allowed to deal with them directly, I was saddled with a Vietnamese Special Forces Team.'

'Have you been to Vietnam, Dick?' I asked, because I was very surprised indeed at what he had said.

'Yes,' he said, and then I almost fell off the chair. 'About the same time you were there.'

Then the story came out.

As a British MI6 officer, Dick had taken a special forces team of Malays and tribesmen from Borneo to the central highlands of South Vietnam. He said he worked among the Montagnard in a province to the north of Darlac. The Vietnamese Government had allocated a Vietnamese Army Special Forces 'A' Team to match his own team — along the same lines as they did with the American Special Forces.

Because Dick's team was ethnically Malayo-Polynesian (like the Montagnard tribes in his area) there was virtually no language or cultural barrier. This not only surprised the Vietnamese but also made them very suspicious of the origin of Dick's team members. Animosity between Dick's men and the Vietnamese rapidly developed. Dick told me that the situation became unbearable and he had to request his team's withdrawal from South Vietnam.

This was the first and only indication I had up till then of any British or Malaysian involvement in the war in South Vietnam. During my later attachment to the Malaysian Army in the 1970s, I met a few Malaysian Army officers who had claimed they had served in South Vietnam. With Dick Noone's MI6 background, and the claims of those few Malaysian officers, perhaps there was after all some degree of involvement albeit minor.

After leaving Borneo, I never again saw Dick Noone. He was deeply involved in the search for the legendary American, Jim Thompson, who disappeared in the Cameron Highlands of Malaysia in 1967. Thompson was an ex-Second World War intelligence officer, involved in special operations for the American oss. He was later involved with the American CIA and was the founder of the present Thai silk industry. His home in Bangkok is now a museum.

Because of Dick's unrivalled knowledge of the tribespeople in the jungles around the Cameron Highlands and northern-peninsula Malaysia, the American CIA asked Dick to try to locate the missing Thompson. Dick was a personal and trusted friend of many of the Orang Asli tribesmen in the area, but none of them could help him in his search.

Thompson left behind a beautiful home in Bangkok, a personal fortune and many friends when he disappeared, but there have been stories that he vanished not because of accident or misadventure, but voluntarily. I cannot substantiate these stories. The journalist Richard Hughes wrote later that he had an indication that Dick Noone found out what really happened to Jim Thompson. However, if this is so, Dick Noone took that secret to the grave. He died in 1973 in Bangkok of lung cancer, aged fifty-five. For six years before his death, he was a security adviser with the South East Asian Treaty Organization's counter-subversion and counter-insurgency forces. That remarkable man had died without revealing much of his intriguing life.

* * *

I had asked to see some British special operations in Borneo and was sent to spend a couple of weeks at a place called Kubaan, south of the Bario Highlands, and close to the border with Indonesian Kalimantan. Before leaving Labuan, Guthrie Troupe warned me not to cross the border into Kalimantan under any circumstances. He pointed out the embarrassment I could cause, with my Vietnam history and CIA background, should I be captured or identified in Indonesian territory.

I flew from Labuan to Bario in a Malaysian Air Force Twin Otter aircraft, skilfully piloted by two Malaysian Air Force officers. I say skilfully, because higher into the mountains, which reach up to two thousand metres, we ran into a heavy thunderstorm. As the leaking old aircraft was buffeted about, I occasionally glimpsed rock face and mountainside beside the wing tips. There was no room to turn as we struggled up cloud-filled, narrow valleys, until we broke through the heavy cloud into bright sunshine over the Bario Highlands.

I really had thought we would never make it. My fellow

Borneo
— Ethnic Minority Groups in East Malaysia

passengers were all Gurkha soldiers. Throughout that anxious period, their faces remained expressionless. It was as if they were patiently prepared for death should it come. Gurkhas generally appear impassive in front of strangers — although if aroused, they can become very excited and aggressive.

Bario once consisted of one, very long Kelabit longhouse. When I landed there, it was garrisoned by a British Army Gurkha battalion, which patrolled the border with nearby Indonesian Kalimantan.

I was taken by helicopter from there to Kubaan. The MI6-sponsored special operations group occupied the abandoned Kubaan longhouse, and operated from there across the border, deep into Kalimantan. The officer in command was a special operations-trained British Army infantry major. He had a similarly-trained lieutenant as his second-in-command. The remainder of the British special operations team consisted of approximately six British SAS, infantry and engineer non-commissioned officers plus one Australian sergeant from the Australian Army's 126 Signals Squadron (our Australian special operations communications unit). They had about thirty or thirty-five Kelabits, Muruts, Tagal Muruts, Kenyans, Kayans, Ibans and two Punans (Penans).

I was impressed with the way the British and Australian men lived and ate with their indigenous guerillas. They were very much the one team. I had seen American Special Forces members occasionally eat and drink with the Montagnard — generally their interpreters — but not to the same extent as the British did here. In Borneo, much greater rapport existed between the British and their guerilla troops. It was because of a closer personal relationship, despite the language barrier. Very few of the indigenous guerillas spoke English, so Malay was the working language.

I got quite a kick out of the reaction of the indigenes when I told them stories of the culture and lifestyle of the Montagnard. Because the native tribes of Sarawak and Sabah are ethnically Malayo-Polynesian, as are the Rhade and Jarai of South Vietnam, much of the language and culture is identical

Phuoc Tuy Province — South Vietnam

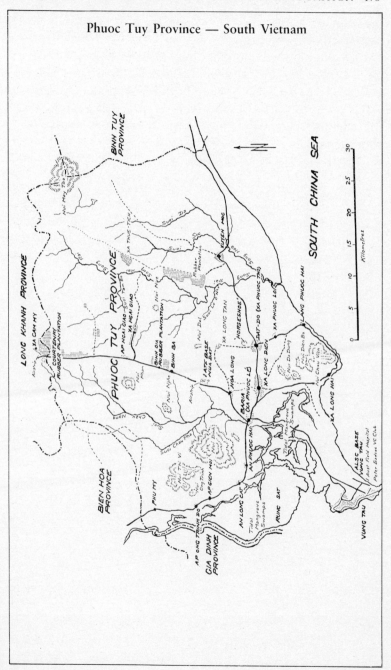

or similar. These indigenes were amazed at their similarity to people who lived geographically so far away from them.

Dick Noone's special operations team of Borneo tribesmen would have no difficulty in assimilating with the Malayo-Polynesian Montagnard of the South Vietnamese Highlands. Deep within Borneo, I found even the rice wine, the jars, and the drinking ceremonies are identical to those used by the Montagnard.

* * *

Close to Christmas 1965, I returned briefly to Labuan, only to find an army message waiting for me. It was from Brigadier Evans' headquarters in Singapore. It said I was to return immediately to Singapore, for onward movement to Australia. No explanation was given, nor could I find out who sent the message.

I was still officially a member of the Australian Army Training Team Vietnam and, therefore, still under command of Brigadier Jackson, not Brigadier Evans. On my arrival in Singapore, I found the signal I had received in Borneo was an interpretation of one sent by Australian Army Headquarters in Canberra, Australia. The message, I later found out, was apparently sent to placate Brigadier Evans and his staff. Evidently he and Major David Wise were still trying to identify the sponsors of my trip to Borneo. The Army Headquarters message in effect stated that, *after* I had completed my tour of Borneo, I *could* be returned to Australia. It clearly did not specify a date for return, but left that entirely up to me.

Evidently somebody in authority on Brigadier Evans' staff had chosen to place their own interpretation on the message from Canberra, presumably to curtail my visit to Borneo. Some months later I met Brigadier Jackson back in Australia. I told him about the messages. He was aware of the Army message from Canberra, and told me why it had been sent. He appeared furious at the misinterpretation. I was, until I returned to Australia, still under his command and not that of Brigadier Evans.

16   Back to Vietnam

I sat at the window of the aircraft as we crossed the delta, approaching Saigon. Below I could see the patchwork of rice paddy-fields, separated by the bunds — earth walls which hold the water in for their flooding. Here and there were copses of trees and coconut palms, a house or two, or a village. It was early 1970. From the air, the country-side looked as tranquil as when I first saw it seven years before, in 1963, though now this war involved a huge American commitment (by 1967, President Lyndon Johnson was to have 525 000 US troops in South Vietnam) and troops from Australia, New Zealand, Thailand, the Philippines and Korea as well.

After my return from Borneo, I had been promoted to major. Based at the Australian Army's Infantry Centre at Ingleburn, just outside Sydney, I was appointed senior instructor in tactics and I had served as an honorary *aide-de-camp* to His Excellency the Governor of New South Wales, Sir Roden Cutler. I was then sent to Fort Bragg, North Carolina, in the United States for further training in psychological operations. Now at last I was returning to Vietnam.

My eye caught a movement below. I could make out three or four military aircraft making a bombing run on a small Vietnamese village — the horrors of war were enacted below us as if we were watching some distant television screen —

flashes and puffs of smoke but no sound. We were flying into a battle zone in absolute comfort aboard a chartered Qantas aircraft to the accompaniment of soft, piped music.

Many of our enemy were entering the same battle zone at the same time. But they had to trek for six or more months from North Vietnam, heavily-laden and under frequent harrassment, although their use of Russian-made trucks and tanks was increasing each year.

The incongruity between the two sides in their approach to the war amazed me. The North Vietnamese troops had their countrymen solidly behind them, faced an indefinite tour of duty in South Vietnam and were imbued with idealistic motivation — almost fanaticism. We were fighting on foreign ground for an uncertain cause, and we knew — or hoped — we would return home at the end of our tour.

Few in our aircraft in fact would have understood the human suffering behind that scene below, enacted to the strains of 'Georgie Girl'. I was a member of the advance party of the 2nd Battalion, the Royal Australian Regiment (2 RAR) and in command of the battalion's C (Charlie) Company — about one hundred and forty Australian soldiers. We were *en route* to Saigon, then to the Australian Task Force operational base at Nui Dat in Phuoc Tuy Province, east of Saigon. About fifteen per cent of the advance party had been to South Vietnam before. For the rest, this was their first look at war.

'Barry, don't get any ideas about getting back to the highlands,' our battalion commanding officer, Lieutenant-Colonel John Church said when we arrived. 'We have a directive that you are to stay away from there.'

The instruction probably came from His Excellency Mr Arthur Malcolm Morris, OBE, Australia's Ambassador to South Vietnam. (Morris had been the desk officer for South-East Asia — the man who had put me through my paces in Canberra in early 1965.)

I might have brooded over the directive, but now I was more concerned with another challenge — that of commanding young Australian soldiers in combat for the next twelve months. I would be trying to bring out the best in them, yet also get as many of them as possible back home alive. It was a task that would keep me mentally and physically stretched. This time I was to play the role of the traditional soldier — a very different job to that which I faced during those two years with the Montagnard.

Before leaving Australia I had briefed my company on what they would find in South Vietnam. I had tried to make my men understand the strains placed on the average Vietnamese peasant they would encounter during our combat operations. I had tried to imbue in them the same consideration I had for those people. The Vietnamese were human beings with problems greater than ours, and they had to be treated with dignity and understanding. It is hard to make young soldiers think like that. But it was important that they try.

Saigon in the Nixon era of early 1970 was greatly different from the Saigon I first saw in 1963. It had traffic jams and smog. American and Vietnamese soldiers and their military transport crowded the streets; the beautiful, shady footpaths and gardens were pock-marked with underground shelters, bunkers and trenches. One small park had even been turned into a display area to show off the captured Russian and Chinese weaponry and equipment — the Russian guns and trucks were a sign that the North Vietnamese were gaining more super-power support and becoming more organized in their steady invasion of the South. Saigon was minus many of its beautiful shady trees — gone to make way for the bunkers and other makeshift installations, or poisoned by pollution and wind drifts of defoliant sprays from aircraft.

The bars and nightclubs, frowned on in the days of the 'Dragon Lady' Madame Ngo Dinh Nhu, were now proliferating, catering to the American soldiers with raucous American music, and bar girls in western-style dresses. It has always amazed me how a beautiful Asian woman can spurn her traditional dress and think for one moment that she looks more attractive painted and dolled-up in crass western guise. Perhaps the girls thought the young American GIs would prefer them that way. I certainly did not. In fact, few Australian soldiers saw Saigon life — their rest and recuperation was taken in Vung Tau. But Vung Tau was quickly trying to copy Saigon.

The war in South Vietnam had 'hotted up'. So, sadly, had the decadence.

The Australian Task Force base at Nui Dat was located on elevated ground mainly in a large rubber plantation about sixty kilometres east of Saigon. Vung Tau, the rest and recreation spot for the Australians about twenty-five kilometres to the south, was once Cap Saint Jacques, formerly a fashionable seaside resort for the earlier Saigon-dwelling French. The area set aside for Charlie Company in Nui Dat base appeared pretty basic to me. The shared officers' and sergeants mess looked good. A lot of effort had been put into it. But the quantity and quality of the facilities for the soldiers were inadequate as far as I was concerned.

By the time the remainder of our battalion arrived, I was aware that we could expect to be absent from the Nui Dat base, on combat operations, for approximately four or so weeks at a time. On these operations troops 'rough it', often wet with either perspiration or rain, sometimes very short of drinking water, and they have to go without bathing for days or even weeks at a time. They are required to carry an average of fifty-three kilograms of equipment and ammunition. Their rations are limited to tinned or dried food, with no fresh food or vegetables. They are required to communicate with one another at all times, by silent signals or by whispering. They are constantly under strain, anticipating a fire-fight with the enemy at any moment or accidentally triggering a mine or booby trap. I considered it therefore essential that they be provided with as much comfort as possible back in a support base. Sometimes it is difficult to convince some of those officers and troops who stay permanently in the support bases ('pogos' as the fighting troops call them) of this. Their (rather weak) argument is that such relative comforts are a waste on the fighting soldiers, as they only get to use them for very short durations between their operations!

I was quietly annoyed at the living conditions of Delta

Company 6 RAR, back in Nui Dat base. Some soldiers had to live four to a tent approximately eighteen square metres in area. Half of that area was lower than one and a quarter metres high. Due to the tent's sloping roof standing room with four men in a tent was very limited indeed. There were insufficient toilet seats — ten only, for a full company strength of approximately one hundred and forty men — not enough if there was an outbreak of diarrhoea. There were too few showers and none had hot water.

But the pogos living permanently in Nui Dat base had time and the facilities to set themselves up with roomy accommodation and hot showers. Hot water could be provided using a forty-four gallon drum, with a dripping fuel system.

So I immediately submitted a requisition for extra toilets, tentage, and sandbags for protection around the walls of the extra tents. I wanted them provided before the arrival of the rest of Charlie Company. I was annoyed at the opposition of the garrison engineer's staff to drilling extra holes for the additional toilet seats I had requested. To support my requisition I virtually had to threaten them with a complaint to the senior medical officer, about the existing limited toilet facilities. During my Army service, I generally found that those with little or no combat experience, were the least sympathetic or helpful to the average fighting soldier.

Then, as soon as the remainder of Charlie Company arrived by sea, I tasked Captain Harry Haneveld, my second-in-command to beg, borrow or steal anything he needed for the troops. Harry and 'Tassie' Cocker, our company quartermaster sergeant and Captain Phil Hayden, Harry's replacement, managed to achieve what I thought were the best living conditions in the battalion lines. They, together with Warrant-Officer 'Jules' Baville and Company Sergeant-Major 'Kiwi' Gibbons, must have got sick to death of my constant nagging.

Re-supply of rations during operations was generally every seven days. Harry, and later Phil, would hitch a ride on the re-supply helicopters. They were interested in our operations and were probably bored stiff at supplying details of what improvements they had made back at base to me, their grumpy old company commander.

*　*　*

Our periods of operations were to last from four to six weeks each, with a period of about a week between each to rest, re-equip and re-train. Our search-and-clear areas covered large tracts of land encompassing open countryside, paddyfields, rubber plantations, jungle, mangrove swamp, mountains, squatters' huts, hamlets and villages. Our job was to find and engage the enemy — mainly Viet Cong National Liberation Front with some North Vietnamese Army units. The Vietnamese words 'Viet Cong' literally mean 'Vietnamese Communists'. They were basically of South Vietnamese origin generally bolstered by some North Vietnamese 'political' cadre. Many Viet Cong leaders had received extensive military training and political indoctrination in North Vietnam from 1954 to 1962.

The Geneva Accord of early 1954 had partitioned Vietnam at the 17th parallel (17 degrees latitude north). A period of 300 days had been decreed to enable those who did not wish to live on either side to move to the side of their choice. During this time, about one hundred thousand people moved from South Vietnam to the North, and about one million moved from the North to the South. Most of those who moved northward were young Vietnamese and Montagnard. They began returning to the South as fully-trained Communist cadre from 1962 onwards. I knew of some of them during my earlier period in the highlands. Many of those who moved from the North to the South were Catholic, and many were ex-Viet-Minh nationalists who had fought for national independence against the French colonialists. Now they were fighting on the side of the Government of South Vietnam against the Communists — Viet Cong or North Vietnamese.

We were to fight both Viet Cong and North Vietnamese Army units during the next twelve months. Many of them had made the long journey from North Vietnam down the Ho Chi Minh trails into South Vietnam. Many of these incursion trails ran through Darlac Province.

* * *

Charlie Company's first day out was stinking hot and humid. We moved through a vast area of scrubby country and tall, itchy lalang (giant grass) and darkness was upon us before we were able to move from scrub into jungle. We had located a well-worn path, clearly used by the Vietnamese from nearby villages to fetch wood from the forest edge.

I knew from my earlier experience in South Vietnam that the Viet Cong always made use of paths to move about quickly. Then they would protect themselves from us using mines or booby-traps, cunningly placed so that only the unaware could trigger them. However, as long as the likely places for these mines and traps were observed or avoided, paths were generally safe to walk along.

I decided we would establish a night base astride this particular path and set up an ambush. Innocent Vietnamese villagers were subject to well-promulgated night curfews, and knew that they could be shot if they strayed outside their villages after 5 pm or before 6 am.

About 9 pm, all hell broke loose. Two Viet Cong political-cadre officers had walked into the ambush and were killed. Sergeant Van, our Vietnamese Army interpreter, identified the bodies as those of officers, and gave us an outline translation of the documents they carried. We buried them the following morning.

In the days that followed, each platoon searched for more signs of the enemy, but they had been alerted by the night ambush and were avoiding contact with us. Above one underground bunker system we found a freshly laundered shirt and a pair of socks still wet and hanging on a clothes line. The bunker system had been abandoned only minutes before. The enemy we were facing were part of the North Vietnamese D 67 Engineer Battalion. We knew, from the documents captured that first night that they had a large stock of mines and explosives.

Soon after, late one afternoon when we were establishing our defensive position for the night, I heard a noise. Distant explosions and gunfire could be heard each day, and they were normal background noise, generally ignored. This late afternoon explosion was different. I had a feeling that it related to us. It came from the area patrolled by Lieutenant Colin Purcell's 8 Platoon.

I called 8 Platoon by radio to ask if they had just had a 'mine incident' — an accidentally-detonated enemy mine or booby trap. The quicker I could find out, the quicker we could call for medical evacuation helicopters if necessary.

Minutes which seemed like hours passed before I received a reply to my repeated question. Suddenly a breathless and obviously anxious young radio operator's voice came back.

'Three, this is three-two — mine incident!' he shouted.

'Three-two, this is Sunray, call-sign three. Tell me what happened,' I said.

'Three, I'll fetch Sunray,' (meaning his platoon commander, Lieutenant Purcell) he replied.

'No,' I replied emphatically, 'your Sunray is busy. Tell me if you have any casualties.' I knew Colin Purcell would be flat-out sorting out the situation. To call him back to the radio would only interfere with his work. I was hoping to extract reasonably accurate information from the young radio operator. Minutes later I had it: two dead and three wounded. Company Sergeant Major 'Kiwi' Gibbons radioed for casualty evacuation helicopters before darkness fell.

To try to link up with 8 Platoon that night would have invited further casualties through enemy mines and booby traps. I assured Colin by radio that we would join them as soon as possible the following morning. Sergeant Bob McKeown, Colin's platoon sergeant and deputy, was a casualty — wounded through the throat. Bob had already been wounded during an earlier tour of duty in South Vietnam.

When we reached 8 Platoon the following day, my observation confirmed the brief story given to me by Colin Purcell the previous night. The forward scout had found an abandoned enemy underground bunker system with a well-used path on the other side of it. His section commander had gone forward to observe, and then called forward the section machine gunner with his deputy. He signalled the machine gunner to take up a good fire position on the other side of the path, so that he could move his section out onto the path. The machine gunner had silently crossed the path with his young deputy, and then crawled forward to a position behind a fallen tree lying across the path and rested his heavy machine-gun on it. It was enough pressure to detonate a hidden mine, which instantly blew away the bottom half of his body, and also killed his young offsider. Shrapnel from the mine wounded the other three.

The horrific incident shattered the morale of 8 Platoon. I saw a dejected group of about twenty-three men and the discarded, heavily bloodstained and damaged personal equipment of the dead and wounded. They had suffered a dreadful shock because they had lost their mates. It needed a real effort on their part to recover their confidence.

I again stressed the need for self-discipline in using paths and I told Colin to prepare his platoon for a patrol down the same path. I told Lieutenant Ian 'Chips' Rafferty, commander of 9 Platoon, to establish a defensive position and to look after 8 Platoon's heavy packs. I then took a reluctant and dejected 8 Platoon on a patrol down the same path where the tragedy had occurred.

I instructed them to walk down the centre of the path, and not to stray to the sides. The enemy rarely laid mines in the middle — they used the paths themselves and knew that other uninformed Viet Cong units and innocent villagers also did so. By walking down the middle, by not stepping on heaps of leaves or debris, not pressing on or lifting trees which had fallen across the path, not taking short-cuts in a bend and by not moving off to the side to a more inviting spot, one stood a good chance of never triggering a mine or booby trap. All too often tired, lazy or unthinking Australian or American troops became careless and ignored these precepts.

While we were absent from the mine incident site, another buried mine was located on the edge of the path, only metres from where the other one had exploded. We had walked within centimetres of it, but by carefully walking down the centre of the path, we had avoided detonating it. The confidence of 8 Platoon was restored by the time we returned from the patrol.

*   *   *

The New Zealand company of our integrated Australian/New Zealand battalion had successfully ambushed elements of a Viet Cong re-supply force west of Vietnamese Land Development Centre, Xa Ngai Giao, in the north of Phuoc Tuy Province. A captured Viet Cong officer had revealed under interrogation that his unit's base was located in the northwest of the province. Our CO, Colonel Church, directed me to take Charlie Company to search for the base. We both believed the captured enemy officer could have been lying, but we could not ignore the information. Charlie Company set off on the five kilometre trek into the area of the reported base.

We moved as swiftly as possible through the jungle, bamboo forests and savannah country, taking care not to be ambushed. 'Swiftly' under those conditions was as fast as a forward scout could move. He would take a few paces, listening and searching for any movement or sign of the enemy. He was always under strain because of the constant threat of ambush or mines. His second scout and the remainder of the lead seven or eight-man section, under similar pressure, covered and watched his every move and signal.

Further back down the line the tension decreased. The stop-start-stop-start movement could be tedious to the heavily laden troops to the rear, and boredom could set in. At my age, I felt the weight of my equipment much more than my younger men. That didn't seem to deter my batman from loading me up with my share of Charlie Company's extra ammunition, grenades and mines.

My years of experience at searching for signs of the enemy stood me in good stead. During one of the 'stop-and-wait' periods, I bent over and shrugged my heavy pack up off my tired back, onto my shoulders. Still doubled over, I looked carefully for anything unusual in the surrounding vegetation. I had little else to do but wait for the next few slow paces. It was then I saw in the undergrowth the elusive signs of human movement.

The area had been badly marked by the tracks and diggings of wild pigs. No human footprints were visible, but there were the unmistakable signs that humans had recently moved through the area. The way the longer grass and weeds had been swept indicated that a group of humans had recently moved across the direction of our path.

I radioed the lead platoon commander asking if any of his men had seen the strange track. Negative. I ordered a break of ten minutes and recalled the platoon commander, Lieutenant Geoff Bradd, with his lead scouts and section commanders. When Geoff's two forward scouts saw what I showed them, they smugly said,

'They're only pig tracks, sir.'

'Pig tracks — my bum,' I replied.

I told the lead platoon commander to send two of his sections, minus their heavy packs, one back along the line of swept long grass, and the other in the other direction, following it. Each was given a radio and they set off, while the remainder of the company established a better defensive position and waited.

The section following the track reported heavier and quite definite recent human footprints and markings. I reported our find by radio to Colonel Church. He agreed that Charlie Company should investigate.

Our follow-up took three days and three nights. The enemy group appeared to be progressively growing larger. When I first noticed the marks in the long grass, I had estimated they had been made by about five persons. The size of the abandoned enemy camp we found on the third morning indicated the group we were following had increased to about fifty.

Late each afternoon we would lose the enemy trail, generally just before crossing a stream. Each morning, a search of the area would locate their overnight camp on the other side. They were cleverly backtracking, dispersing, then re-forming, some two hundred metres on the other side of the streams.

I had asked Colonel Church to keep all aircraft and artil-

lery fire away from us, and had postponed our ration re-
supply, in order to retain the element of surprise. We were
exactly twenty-four hours behind the enemy group.

There were signs they had a female group with them,
possibly a mortar crew. We found a few small empty scent
bottles, and indications of separate sleeping arrangements.
Their trail led us on hands and knees through hundreds of
metres of thick, thorny, bamboo forest, through which they
had made a small tunnel. If the enemy females were the
mortar crew, then their stamina was amazing. They would
have been carrying heavy mortar parts while on their hands
and knees. We much larger and stronger Australians had
enough difficulty with our heavy packs.

On the third afternoon, the tracks ended abruptly at the
base of a large tree. Darkness was approaching and heavy
rain was beginning to fall. We quietly established a base for
the night.

I knew that we would have to locate the enemy within the
next twenty-four hours as we needed more rations. Despite
our shortage of food, the spirits of Charlie Company were
high that night. We were obviously on to something quite
big, and the whole battalion, aware of our findings, was also
anticipating a success.

That night, as I lay on my bedding on the ground, I
wondered what lay ahead. The overnight enemy camp we
had discovered that morning indicated the enemy strength at
about fifty people. Our's was not much larger at eighty-two
men. I did not know it then, but at that time, we were based
about two hundred metres from the hitherto-elusive permanent enemy defensive position of underground bunkers and
fighting trenches known as Chau Duc District Headquarters.
It was set on higher ground in swampy country, on the other
side of the main stream. As we were to find later, enemy
strength was in fact about one hundred and thirty. They
outnumbered us by almost fifty, and were well dug-in in their
defensive position.

Early the next morning, we began our careful search of the
banks of the stream and the swamp on the other side. Sud-

denly the surrounding quietness was shattered by heavy gunfire close by. Moments later, further gunfire erupted from a different location. Two of Charlie Company's reconnaissance patrols had clashed with enemy patrols. I immediately called for helicopter gunships and my artillery forward observer, Lieutenant David McPherson, had artillery fire support standing by. Colonel Church, in his Sioux helicopter, quickly headed towards us.

The clashes with our patrols were enough warning for the remainder of the enemy force. Instead of remaining in their well-defended bunker system to fight us from there, they fled in all directions. Some were shot from the helicopter gunships overhead, and others were killed or wounded by our supporting artillery fire. Bedlam prevailed as patrols from Charlie Company tried to follow up fleeing enemy groups, while I coordinated the artillery and helicopter gunship fire support from company headquarters. I also asked Colonel Church for the battalion's tracking team with their tracker dogs to be flown in to us by helicopters.

Once the tracker team had arrived, I placed it under the command of Lieutenant Colin Purcell, and sent him, with his 8 Platoon, to follow up one large group of the fleeing enemy. That group had crossed the deep, muddy stream using a log bridge, concealed just below the surface of the water. By mid-afternoon, 8 Platoon had caught up with them. They had zig-zagged across a large clearing to the forest on the other side — a trick often used by the enemy. Tracker dogs follow the scent trail, and if troops follow them too closely, then they can end up exposed in the clearing, which the enemy then uses as a killing zone.

The enemy group consisted of the district chief, plus his well-armed protection unit. They were already digging a new defensive position inside the forest edge whence they could observe and ambush their zig-zag trail across the open clearing. They opened fire on 8 Platoon and the tracker team, inflicting casualties.

Lieutenant Colin Purcell called for artillery and helicopter gunship fire on the enemy position, and their likely withdrawal routes, but before they could move in on the position, the enemy withdrew taking their dead and wounded with them.

A check of the abandoned position revealed considerable blood throughout the area, but no bodies. Some days later, we were told that a monitored enemy radio transmission had reported a loss of fifteen of their men during that last skirmish.

Although we never did find out exactly how many Viet Cong died, mass graves later found, plus intelligence summaries, indicated that the enemy may have lost as many as thirty-two dead. A large number of survivors, some wounded, surrendered, one or two at a time, during the weeks which followed. We inflicted a major blow on the Chau Duc district headquarters that day and it did not re-form while our battalion served in South Vietnam.

* * *

A couple of months after commencing combat operations, I damaged the tendons around my right elbow during one of our skirmishes. I must have partially torn them from the bone. The result was severe tendinitis, or 'tennis elbow', as it is sometimes called. It is an inflammation of the damaged tendons, resulting in constant, acute pain. A jungle vine, just lightly brushing against my affected elbow, could cause agony, almost bringing tears to my eyes.

I found that I had to carry my rifle by lifting it with the left arm, and resting it across my ammunition pouches. Then I had to take care not to brush my right elbow against vines or saplings. My batman had to help me to put on and take off my heavy back-pack. It made my life impossible. Carrying a rifle on combat operations now seemed a waste of time to me, as I couldn't have used it properly anyway.

During one break between operations, I discussed the problem with our battalion medical officer, Captain Roger Thatcher. He referred me to an orthopaedic surgeon at the Australian Field Hospital at Vung Tau. The surgeon's recommendation was that I return to Australia for corrective surgery. He didn't wish to perform the operation in South Vietnam.

In no way did I want to leave Charlie Company and return to Australia. I told the surgeon so. His next recommendation was regular injections of the anti-inflammatory drug cortisone. After about two days of sheer agony and little sleep, the cortisone began to work and all pain suddenly disappeared. We held the tendinitis at bay with regular cortisone injections every six to eight weeks. But it was not to be the end of my physical problems which later became a matter of great concern and ultimately affected my army career.

17

Charlie Company and Another Sad Farewell

Australian Army Engineers were rebuilding the road through Phuoc Tuy Province, north into Long Khanh Province. The French-owned Courtenay Rubber Plantation stood astride this road. There was an Australian fire support base on a knoll on the northern side of the plantation which housed the engineers by night and supported operations in the area. Infantry companies took turns in occupying the base and in patrolling the area in and around the plantation. Viet Cong and North Vietnamese units used the South Vietnamese villages in the area for the supply of food, equipment and intelligence so we were kept pretty busy. During Charlie Company's operations, our patrols and ambushes achieved considerable success.

I guessed that one major enemy unit was operating from a base to the west of the province, possibly near a creek system up there. I asked Colonel Church if Charlie Company could conduct an operation in that area and he agreed. Some months later the opportunity came. I chose to concentrate on three creek junctions.

The battalion headquarters arranged for Charlie Company to be lifted by helicopters to a bombed-out area near the creek system. Diversionary helicopter landings were arranged to confuse any enemy. We landed on our site amid an artillery smoke screen. An approach march through jungle for a few thousand metres took us to the first of the creek junctions.

As we approached the suspect areas in turn, I deployed Charlie Company around each before we closed in. The first two junctions revealed nothing. But around the third there were signs of the enemy. We found tracks, bird and fish traps, and stumps of trees which had been selectively cut down to construct underground bunkers and other defences.

My company headquarters, with its support section, was to act as part of the blocking force surrounding the third creek junction. I selected our position purely because there was a hole in the canopy of the forest above. This enabled us to hoist our radio antennae up through it. I had the platoons on our side of the creek leave their heavy packs, camouflaged in low heaps, before moving into position.

To 8 Platoon fell the task of clearing from the north, towards our blocking force. As they were moving into position, they found a well-worn track leading south into the creek junction. This was surely an enemy defensive bunker system.

8 Platoon carefully began to close in on the creek junction, expecting to locate enemy sentries at any moment. In the hot, still afternoon, everything was silent at company headquarters, except for the occasional soft radio transmission. I even had time to quietly chastise a young member of the support section, whom I thought was daydreaming instead of watching for enemy movement.

'I *am* watching, sir,' he replied indignantly — which he was later able to prove.

There was little likelihood that any enemy would come our way as there had been no tracks. I had positioned the company headquarters so as to gain the best radio communications to battalion headquarters, to our artillery and mortar support and to my three platoons and their ambushes.

Suddenly gunfire erupted, shattering the relative peace of the jungle. An enemy patrol, returning to the base bunker system along the track found earlier had accidentally run into the rear of 8 Platoon. The Platoon was prepared and surprised the Viet Cong, killing two.

The shots had warned the enemy in the bunkers. They dispersed in all directions, scattering like dried peas dropped on the floor. 8 Platoon left the bodies where they were and, at a quicker pace, closed in on the bunker system. Firing again broke out. This time it was to the east. Some fleeing Viet Cong had run into the blocking force on the other side of the creek.

Suddenly, the soldier I had earlier chastised showed us just how alert he really was. Clicking his fingers to attract our attention, he placed his hand to his ear — the silent signal meaning that he had heard movement. Then he gave the thumbs-down sign — enemy identified.

I was listening to a radio message from one of my platoons. Our radio operators seized their rifles and quickly and quietly, slid into firing positions on their stomachs. To avoid all further noise, I took the handsets of my two principal radios, then quietly whispered a message over both simultaneously:

'All stations, this is Sunray three. This callsign is about to have contact with the enemy. Stay off the air.'

I then clamped the two handsets to each ear, to deaden any transmission from other stations. Dave McPherson, my artillery forward observer, did likewise. We lay waiting in the dappled sunlight.

Then I saw them, only two at first. They were pushing through the undergrowth and about to enter the clearing. To move even slightly would have attracted their attention and their fire.

The two leading men should have seen us, although we were lying very still. They seemed to be looking directly at me and I suddenly saw a third one behind them.

'Fire, you buggers! Fire now before they do!' I desperately, telepathically, tried to tell my men.

Everything seemed to be happening too slowly. The Viet Cong were coming closer and closer. The lead man was no more than four to five metres from me. Our rifles were beside us, but to reach for them would have meant releasing the radio handsets from our ears. The enemy would have heard other radio transmissions and seen our slightest movement, turning us into instant targets. We were very, very still as they came closer.

'Fire now!' I prayed.

All hell broke loose as our men opened fire. The lead three Viet Cong returned fire but minutes later dropped to the ground, dead. There was a further brisk exchange, then silence — the rest of the group had retreated. We could shout to one another, radio transmissions recommenced. It was all over.

A company headquarters is rarely involved in direct confrontation with the enemy. The platoon troops look upon us as pogos (those unlikely to ever be in direct contact with the enemy, like base troops). The further back from the enemy, the greater the pogo you are. We were the cause of much mirth in Charlie Company. Fancy our pogo company headquarters having its very own combat action with the enemy — and suffering no casualties, to boot!

In fact, the only 'casualties' were the heaps of packs belonging to two of the platoons. Although they were camouflaged, in the heat of the fight the enemy had mistaken their bulky, dark shapes for men. Many had bullet holes in them, to the dismay of their owners.

The bunker system appeared to support an enemy hospital. We found a bloodstained operating table and surgical instruments but no beds or casualties except those we caused. We also found that the enemy were able to drill narrow air vents down to underground tunnel systems, sometimes up to twelve metres below ground level.

These air vents were only five centimetres or so across, but were drilled down to tremendous depths. The Viet Cong would use a long length of bamboo, with a series of v-shapes cut into the bottom segment thus creating a circle of long sharp teeth. They would wet the ground where they wished to drill, then they would jab the circle of bamboo teeth into the earth. The bottom segment of bamboo would gradually fill with damp earth which then had to be cleaned out. The process was painstakingly repeated. When the air vent became too deep for the length of bamboo, they would extend it by tying the home-made drill to a sapling. Digging such deep air vents obviously required great patience, a quality for which the Vietnamese are noted. The vents were generally cunningly concealed, and even locating one did not necessarily lead to the discovery of a tunnel entrance.

In this case, I suspected that the Viet Cong wounded were below ground in a tunnel system. *En route* to the area a few days previously, I had located a vent, just off the track that we were using to approach the creek system. We tried to explore that tunnel system. We couldn't see down it with flashlights, but using burning plastic explosive tied with wire on the end of a long cord, we were able to light up a tunnel four or five metres below ground level. We managed to bounce the burning plastic explosive around on the tunnel floor, into and down another air vent, to yet another tunnel, much further down.

But we searched in vain for the tunnel entrances. We tried sending up a spotter aircraft while we dropped coloured smoke grenades down the air vent — we hoped some of the coloured smoke from the grenades would emerge from the concealed entrances. No luck. So I called in an engineer tunnel clearance team to continue looking. They never did find them.

If we tried to dig down to the tunnels using the air vent as a guide, the vent would merely block up. Such an excavation was beyond our resources. Some tunnels located in Phuoc Tuy Province by the Special Air Service (SAS) patrols revealed large caches of weapons and equipment after the SAS were lucky enough to locate the tunnel entrances.

*   *   *

I tried to ingrain into Charlie Company the quality of flexibility. The company motto was 'Stay Loose.' Our flexibility and ability to act quickly was severely tested from time to time in South Vietnam. One such occasion was when we were detached to our sister battalion, 7 RAR.

We were on search and clear operations at the time and my company headquarters was travelling with one of my platoons. It was night and we were in a temporary night defensive position in very heavy jungle. You couldn't see your hand in front of your face in that darkness. I was woken by the company headquarters duty radio operator with a message. Together, we lay under a hot nylon shelter to conceal our flashlights and, covered in a lather of perspiration, decoded the message.

With effect from 10 am the following morning, Charlie Company would be under the command of the CO 7 RAR. We would be lifted by a flight of Iroquois helicopters, from a cleared fire trail in our own area of operations, across to a 'hot insertion' in 7 RAR's area. A hot insertion was the term used for a mass helicopter landing of combat troops into an area expected to be occupied by resisting enemy. The landing is supported by helicopter gunships and artillery fire and is controlled generally by the commander — in this case myself — from a light Sioux helicopter overhead.

Lieutenant-Colonel Ron Grey, the CO, required me for a briefing and reconnaissance well before 10 am. It was after midnight by the time we decoded the message. I had to wake the company sergeant-major, brief him, then radio my three platoon commanders. At 4 am I set off with the support section, through thick jungle in total darkness. We were still a few hundred metres from the designated clearing, when Colonel Grey's small Sioux helicopter arrived overhead to pick me up. I left my support section to wait until the remainder of Charlie Company arrived from different directions later in the morning. The fire trail would provide a degree of security for the isolated support section as they waited. Fire trails were wide cleared, jigsaw-like trails cut through the heavy jungle, dividing the vast area into segments. They were generally cut in prohibited areas to make aerial sighting of the enemy much easier. Unidentified persons moving on or across a fire trail became likely targets of armed aircraft, as most inland fire trails had a twenty-four-hour curfew on them and all Vietnamese knew that.

The company would later be lifted in a fleet of Iroquois helicopters from there, linking up with me in my helicopter over the target area at 10 am. If all went well, following preliminary artillery shelling of the target area Charlie Company would land in waves, to avoid exposing too many men and helicopters to possible enemy ambush.

So I was taken to Colonel Grey's headquarters where he greeted me with a hot mug of coffee and told me to use his shower and razor to clean up. He directed his RSM, Reg Bandy, to get me a brand new set of clothing. I protested, knowing how I would appear when I rejoined my hot, sweaty and dirty Charlie Company on the ground. I would be the brunt of ribbing from my men for being so clean and sweet-smelling. But Colonel Grey insisted that I clean up thoroughly, despite the consequences.

Following breakfast and the briefing, he sent me off — again in his helicopter — to reconnoitre the area for Charlie Company's operations later in the morning. There was evidence of a great deal of North Vietnamese and Viet Cong activity in 7 RAR's area, evidence too, of the enemy's use of elephants to carry their heavy weapons and equipment. The gallant, but rather foolhardy young helicopter pilot insisted on hovering only feet above fresh elephant dung. He wanted to show me the steam rising from it. I was more interested in watching the surrounding jungle for enemy snipers. On one occasion, my own CO, Colonel John Church, had been shot down in his Sioux helicopter by the enemy, and he and his pilot had both been wounded before they were rescued. I did not feel like tempting fate.

The hot insertion went well, and on time. Nice and clean and dressed in new uniform, I received my deserved ribbing from my soldiers. I was a very proud company commander. Charlie Company showed that it could stay loose.

*   *   *

Charlie Company was moved across into 7 RAR's area of operations to react to a 'special agent' report. These sensitive reports stemmed from information supplied by radio transmission-monitoring units which scanned radio frequencies used by the enemy. We were then given enemy locations, together with the time of their latest radio transmission. This was the 'special agent' report. Reaction had to be swift, because well-disciplined enemy groups would either move away soon after transmitting, or would transmit from a location away from their permanent defensive bunker systems.

In the 7 RAR area, we were to try to locate an enemy position whose transmission had been overheard in the area around a stream called the Tam Bo. We were moved into the area by armoured personnel carriers bouncing across the terrain. We left our transport before crossing the Song Rai (Rai River), where we based up for the night.

By midday the following day, we had reached the general area of the 'special agent' report. I then gave each of my three platoons their area of search responsibility.

In the mid-afternoon, a patrol from 8 Platoon reported sighting an enemy sentry guarding a track up a spurline. He must have been a particularly slack sentry as he obviously hadn't detected our patrol. I told Lieutenant Colin Purcell, 8 Platoon commander, to leave a group to watch the sentry and to try to reconnoitre the enemy position.

I then recalled 7 and 9 Platoons, with instructions to join me then we would link up with 8 Platoon. Lieutenant Ian Rafferty's 9 Platoon reached my company headquarters first when 7 Platoon was still quite some way off. The afternoon was wearing on. If the enemy detected us, they might escape. With elements of my company headquarters and radio communications, we quickly moved on with 9 Platoon to join 8 Platoon in the area of the enemy sentry.

Before we could link up with 8 Platoon, firing erupted. One of 8 Platoon's reconnaissance patrols had been observed by another enemy sentry who opened fire on them. We had lost the element of surprise and 7 Platoon was still some distance away.

Quickly, company headquarters with 9 Platoon linked up with 8 Platoon below the enemy position. After a briefing on the extent of the enemy bunker system, I decided to launch a two-platoon company attack.

As we fought our way up the slope towards the bunker system, Lieutenant David McPherson, my artillery forward observer, controlled the artillery fire on the rear of the enemy position to cut off any enemy escape. We also had helicopter gunship support. It would have been about 4 pm.

As company commander, I positioned myself with my radio operators, artillery forward observer, mortar fire controller and support section, between, and slightly to the rear of the leading troops of the two assault platoons.

Suddenly heavier enemy fire was concentrated on the troops just to my right front. I could see a young machine gunner and his offsider leaping, rolling and crawling, from one protective log or ditch to another to avoid being hit by enemy fire. In doing so, those two were unconsciously moving backwards towards me. Above the din of fire and explosions, I shouted out at them:

'Hey, you blokes, the war's that way!' emphatically jabbing my forefinger in the direction of the enemy. They both looked across at me with broad grins and immediately leapt forward again towards the enemy.

They were both National Service conscripts whom I found to be just as good and dependable as any regular army professional. I wondered what their thoughts were when I shouted at them. Probably — 'Jeez, we're back as far as that old bastard!'

Unfortunately, the enemy concentrate their fire in the direction of any shouting, because they interpret that as shouted orders from commanders. They are generally correct. Having shouted at those two lads, I suddenly attracted a hail of enemy fire and exploding anti-tank projectiles. Such fire has the effect of stripping the trees and undergrowth of leaves and twigs and of spraying small stones and dirt over everyone. It also has the effect of shutting you up and making you dive for cover. I tasted blood in my mouth. Was I wounded in the mouth, or had I just bitten my tongue in the excitement? Some months later, two small pieces of shrapnel worked their way down through the bottom of my tongue. Until then, I hadn't realized they were there.

Small wounds of that nature are commonplace in combat. You receive cuts, scratches, punctures and abrasions, most gained diving, rolling, crawling and running through thick undergrowth and thorny bamboo. Only after the excitement of a combat engagement, do you have time to take stock of yourself. Some of the many small punctures in the skin, initially considered as thorn punctures, may turn out days later to be small shrapnel wounds.

Often our medical officers became upset when days elapsed before we reported these wounds. It was hard to convince them that the injured soldiers didn't initially recognize them as the results of enemy fire. And you didn't evacuate anyone with cuts, abrasions or small flesh punctures as casualties under normal circumstances.

After Charlie Company had taken the enemy bunker system, we found we had attacked the headquarters of the Viet Cong D445 Regiment. These Viet Cong troops were not well-disciplined. Their position was filthy. They had left their radio antennae still erected when they fled and rubbish was lying everywhere. The following morning, communications experts were flown in to us to note the configuration of the enemy radio antennae and to glean information from them.

* * *

As an infantry officer, I had commanded a platoon of Australian soldiers in Malaya during two years of operations against the Communist terrorists. My experience commanding a company of Diggers against the Viet Cong in South Vietnam only confirmed my high opinion of our fighting men.

Traditionally, the Australian Digger, particularly the front line soldier, is easy to command if treated with respect and dignity. He has a strong sense of comradeship and a personal need to do the right thing by his mates. This attribute helps to create a sense of self-discipline. He won't let his side down.

Enlistment in Australia's regular army is very competitive and the general physical and intellectual calibre of young Diggers is high, especially in the absence of a major war. The National Servicemen of the 1960s and 1970s were selected from a broad spectrum of Australia's young men. They were subject to a ballot which was based on their date of birth and not their social or employment status. Those chosen then had to undergo a stringent psychological and medical selection procedure and lengthy, thorough training before being committed to a combat theatre of operations. With these young Regular Army and National Service Diggers, any commander had a potentially first-class group of soldiers — a group which could only be defective by poor leadership and bad administration — and unfortunately that did occasionally occur.

The average Australian soldier seems to have a basic respect for the local people and their lifestyle and situation. Fortunately the Australian Digger respects fair play and will give the other bloke a fair go. He likes children and having fun with them. I found a distinct absence of malice among my troops towards either the Malayans or the Vietnamese. In Charlie Company I had Diggers who liked their cigarettes or beer but I could never classify any of them as addicts. I watched for any use of other drugs but never found any and I have since been pleasantly surprised to learn from some of my ex-troops that very few, if any, would even have tried smoking marijuana in South Vietnam. Perhaps peer pressure among the front-line or combat Digger had something to do with it.

On a recent visit to Hanoi, I heard Lieutenant-General Hoang Phuong, a senior officer of the People's Army of Vietnam and a former enemy, pay the Australian Digger of great compliment in words to this effect:

As enemies, we considered the Australians very good soldiers. They were well-trained and well-disciplined. Their combat tactics were very good, particularly their ambush techniques which we had difficulty in countering.

Your Australian advisers [members of the Australian Army Training Team Vietnam] were skilled in jungle warfare and in counter-guerilla operations.

An Australian commander, providing he retains a sense of humour and properly cares for his men, couldn't wish for better soldiers. I could write of numerous instances of loyalty, endurance, courage, comradeship and consideration for others, but this book is not about the Australian Digger. That is a separate story.

* * *

Early in 1971, Colonel Church warned me I had been selected, together with other American and New Zealand Army servicemen, to lecture at the Vietnamese Armed Forces Command and General Staff College in Dalat in Tuyen Duc Province, in the central highlands. One of the American lecturers was Colonel David Hackworth, said to be the most decorated American officer alive at that time. He now lives in Brisbane and is married to an Australian girl.

Colonel Church wanted me back in Nui Dat by the Monday night, immediately after I had given my talks, because the Vietnamese Minister for Defence was to visit us to present gallantry awards to Australians. I was to be awarded a second Vietnamese Cross of Gallantry with Silver Star. (I had already been awarded one during my earlier tour in South Vietnam in 1965.) Colonel Church had sought and gained special permission for me to wear it. The Australian Government has never approved the wearing of Vietnamese or American decorations awarded to Australian servicemen for acts of gallantry or service.

The Army Aviation aircraft to take us back to base arrived in Dalat on the Monday morning while I was still lecturing. But it wasn't until late afternoon that a break appeared in the cloud cover over the airstrip to allow a take-off. The American senior adviser — a lieutenant-colonel — volunteered to drive the two young pilots, the battalion intelligence officer

and myself to the airstrip. I sat in the front with the colonel
while the three younger officers sat in the back.

We were rounding a bend in the mountain road with a
high embankment on one side and a cliff on the other. A
Vietnamese Army truck came round the corner at high speed
and drifted into our traffic lane. We had nowhere to go — it
was a head-on collision. The American colonel and I were
thrown against the dashboard hitting our heads against the
windscreen. The front bench seat, with the weight of three
husky young officers behind it, snapped off its mounting.
Their combined weight forced the colonel and I harder into
the windscreen and dashboard. I regained consciousness
stretched out on the front seat, fighting for breath and surrounded by concerned onlookers. The colonel was in even
worse shape, as he had been pushed into the steering wheel,
breaking it with his impact.

The American medical dispensary in Dalat examined us
and wanted to fly both of us to the American Military Hospital at Phan Rang on the coast. I had received injuries to my
spine, my left shoulder and collarbone, my right arm and I
had a fine fracture of the lower left side of my jaw. I was sick
and sore but I declined the American effort to evacuate me to
Phan Rang. Once in the hands of the American medical
evacuation system, it could take months to get out of it, and I
was soon due to return with the battalion to Australia. I
chose to stay in Dalat overnight and returned with the other
three to Nui Dat base early the following morning.

When I arrived, the parade was over and the Vietnamese
Minister for Defence had departed. I was handed my decoration, still in its box, as I entered our officers' mess.

Still present was His Excellency Mr A. M. Morris, the Australian Ambassador, and also Major General D. B. Dunstan,
the Commander of the Australian Forces in South Vietnam. I
stood in my bloodstained clothes, managing to sip a gin and
tonic. After being re-introduced to the ambassador, I overheard him say to General Dunstan that he wanted to borrow
me to return to the central highlands in order to collect some
intelligence for the Australian Government.

I could hardly believe my ears. This was the same man who early in 1965 headed the 'inquisition' at the Australian Department of External Affairs in Canberra. I also believed that he was behind the directive banning me from visiting the central highlands during my second tour of duty in South Vietnam.

I was called over and asked if I would be prepared to return to the highlands. Would I! I would seize on any excuse to re-visit my old friends. Our regimental medical officer, Major Brian Todd, had other ideas. He wanted me hospitalized for about a week before I went anywhere. After quietly sneaking a few more gin and tonics, I was whisked off to the Australian Field Hospital in Vung Tau.

I find hospitalization boring, despite the comfort, friendliness, good food and the chance to sleep in clean linen. However, I didn't languish for long. A few days later, General Dunstan arrived at the hospital after flying by helicopter from Saigon to see me.

'Barry, when will you be able to do that job for the ambassador?' the general asked.

I sat in bed, one arm in a sling.

'Anytime, sir,' I replied.

General Dunstan appeared doubtful. I certainly did not appear to be in any shape to go hunting intelligence in the central highlands.

'I don't want you to go alone,' he said. He asked how I planned to conduct the trip. I said I would pretend to be on leave, merely visiting my old friends in the highlands. General Dunstan warned me to be careful and wished me good luck.

Colonel Church didn't agree that I should take an officer or senior NCO with me. He pointed out that if anything went wrong, he would lose two senior members of his battalion. He suggested I select one of my more capable soldiers, so I chose my batman, Private Graham Nelson. Graham was a National Serviceman, an officer of the Rural Bank in civilian life, a footballer and quite capable of looking after himself, and hopefully me too if necessary. But he was not impressed with the idea of wandering around the central highlands without his rifle. All Australian soldiers, especially those in the infantry, are trained never to be more than two metres away from their weapons, either in training or on combat service. Graham would be hundreds of kilometres away from his.

Whether or not to carry arms is a big decision, when operating out of combat alone or in pairs. If captured, or even questioned by Viet Cong or a North Vietnamese patrol, the chance of survival is probably better if you are unarmed. Death or interrogation is not then a certainty. The enemy might think you are stupid but you have a better chance of staying alive. 'Rambo' might be able to defeat an enemy patrol, but two armed Australians have little chance of doing so in a fire fight with a large enemy patrol. I felt we could rely on the loyalty and local knowledge of my Montagnard friends to prevent our capture.

*   *   *

The Ban-Me-Thuot town airstrip was dustier and busier than ever. The far sides of the airstrip were crowded with row upon row of sandbagged American tentage. American units were in Ban-Me-Thuot in force.

The highland town seemed to be full of American and Vietnamese soldiers. Some of the masonry buildings still showed the scars of the 1968 Tet Offensive when the Viet Cong attacked the town. Madame Ly's Hotel Darlac bar blared loud American music and all the bar girls were strangers to me. They were not the simple provincial girls I had met when I first arrived in Ban-Me-Thuot in 1963. These women wore western dress, were loud-mouthed and appeared quite rapacious.

I looked up some earlier business friends in the town and was given an enthusiastic welcome. We borrowed a vehicle from one of them and then visited the surrounding Montagnard villages. I was aware that the Vietnamese Sûreté had us under surveillance within forty-five minutes of our arrival on the airstrip. But they couldn't keep it up once we left the safety of the town.

Life in the countryside around Ban-Me-Thuot reflected the changes that had overtaken many areas of the highlands. In 1970, General Ngo Dzu, the Vietnamese 2nd Corps commander, had launched a massive resettlement of Montagnard from those parts considered to be 'insecure'. An estimated 40 000 people from more than one hundred villages had been moved to more easily-controlled camps.

The Montagnard had been forced to leave everything behind and their longhouses had been burned as they were moved out aboard American or Vietnamese helicopters or trucks. They had been taken to barbed-wire compounds with little or no shelter. Some villagers had kilometres to walk to fetch water. Food and medical treatment were in short supply and many of the Montagnard were suffering from malnutrition. There were reports that the Viet Cong had moved in to the abandoned villages and were farming the rice paddy fields.

Buon Enao was again the quiet Montagnard village I had first known in 1963. There was no sign of the Truong Son school or the hospital. Vietnamese and Montagnard Regional Force troops appeared to occupy Dam San base and it was in a bad state of disrepair. There was no sign of the Truong Son Force as it had once existed. By the middle of 1972, Dam San base actually became a Montagnard refugee centre.

The only indication I had of ever being in Darlac Province was the overwhelming welcome I received from my few business friends in Ban-Me-Thuot, and from my many Montagnard friends in the outlying villages. As usual, their hospitality was accompanied by the opening of a jar of rice wine and the sacrifice of a chicken or two. The Montagnard were much poorer. The resettlement had cost them their longhouses, their fields, their livestock and many of the personal possessions that had been classified as wealth — rice-wine jars, gongs and buffalo-hide drums. They were now totally dependent on the Vietnamese administration for material support. Many had defected to the FULRO movement.

American Army advisers took three days to learn of our presence. Lieutenant-Colonel Wayne R. Smith, the US Army adviser to the province chief, seemed very annoyed when he and another of his officers confronted me in Ban-Me-Thuot one afternoon. He asked what I was doing there, so I gave him the story of being on leave and visiting old friends. The Americans in the highlands acted as if South Vietnam was their country; their responsibility and theirs alone. Without appearing rude, I told the colonel that I was an Australian major and that I had my Australian commander's permission to be where I was and that I felt this was all I needed. We were left alone after that.

My subsequent report reflected the situation I found: that of division, disillusionment and even despair among the Montagnard. There were few redeeming features I could include. I have no idea what the Australian Embassy thought of that report or what action, if any, was taken because of it.

My return to Darlac Province was a bitter pill for me. I had seen many positive things happen during my time in the highlands and the security provided by my Truong Son Force was not the least of these. The Truong Son Force had been able to protect their own people from the Viet Cong very effectively. But in 1971, protection had degenerated into a procedure where villagers were uprooted from their own villages and put behind barbed wire fences. A defensive position had been adopted around Ban-Me-Thuot and those newly-established 'refugee' settlements.

My return to the highlands was one of my last duties during that second tour of duty in South Vietnam. It was one of the saddest I had to perform. Soon after, I left South Vietnam for the last time.

18

Malaysian Experiences

It was mid-winter in June 1971 when I arrived in Canberra to a home posting. There were no living quarters for officers serving at Army Headquarters. Officers either lived at a hostel, with all its restrictions, or in accommodation designed for public servants. As a major in the army, I was entitled to a bed-sitter. It consisted of a single room with a very small closet-sized bathroom, and similar sized kitchen, attached. It was totally unfurnished. The rent was quite nominal, and so it should have been.

From a relatively high-ranking army officer, having commanded over one thousand Montagnard guerillas, and later about one hundred and forty Australians in combat operations, I suddenly found myself living alone in an empty, concrete room on the second floor of a drab, cold building in Canberra. My neighbours were nameless, faceless, grey people, who preferred to stay that way. Quite a let-down.

Being a single man, I was not entitled to removal or storage of furniture or household effects if I was moved around. If I wanted to furnish my bare room I did so out of my own pocket.

Canberra is a well laid-out city — a showplace on the surface, but dull and full of inbred, narrow-minded, unimaginative, Australians — successive generations of public servants who, unlike their armed forces counterparts, never have to move from the city during their lifetime. There is little exposure to the realities of life outside Canberra.

I was still suffering from my injuries in South Vietnam. The cold winter was almost crippling me. At times, I had trouble in getting in and out of my car and even carrying my brief-case. The medical officer prescribed physiotherapy, but I could feel the development of osteoarthritis in my injured joints and spine. I realized it would only be a matter of time in any cool climate, and I would be permanently crippled with that degenerative disease.

My appointment made me responsible for equipment for the infantry corps in the Australian Army. I could influence — to a degree — selection of equipment, scales of equipment and allocation of stocks of equipment within the corps. I found myself having to attend conferences and meetings to argue the infantryman's point of view. I had many arguments with narrow-minded, shallow-thinking, inexperienced officers and public servants. I have always been told I suffer fools poorly and that I should listen more to the points of view of others, regardless of their ability or experience — but life is far too short to waste on such people.

I occasionally had to brave the cocktail circuit in Canberra. One evening I was invited to the Swedish Embassy. I took along a doctor friend of mine, Julia Potter. Soon after we arrived, I felt a light tap on my arm. I found Finn Bergstrand, the Swedish First Secretary, at my side. With him was a short, solidly-built man.

'Barry,' he said, 'I would like you to meet the Soviet Chargé d'Affaires, Mr Smirnov.'

Then turning to the thickset man with him, he said,

'Mr Smirnov, I would like to introduce Major Petersen and his friend, Dr Potter.'

'Ah! Major Petersen,' Mr Smirnov said, jovially, 'You had a very interesting tour of duty in South Vietnam.'

It was 1972 and therefore natural for Mr Smirnov to assume that, as an Australian Army major, I would probably have served in South Vietnam.

Without thinking, I asked: 'To which tour are you refer-ring, sir?'

'To your first tour, when you were with the Montagnard tribes,' he replied.

Had I heard him correctly? How did he know I had served with the Montagnard in South Vietnam? How would he have found out? Did he also know I had been attached to the CIA?

I managed to mumble something then tried to change the subject. But the thought that the Soviets had information on me, and that seven years after I had worked with the Montagnard they would still be interested in me, sent a chill down my spine.

It was not to be the only brush I had with Russians.

*   *   *

Late in 1972, I was lent for two years as an instructor to the Malaysian Army. I had all the required qualifications for the job: I had seen army service in that country, was a graduate of the Australian Army Staff College, was single and could speak the Malay language.

The Director of Infantry, Colonel Alec V. Preece, had not wanted me to leave. He had argued that my promotion to the rank of lieutenant-colonel would become due during my absence, and that I could not expect promotion until my return to Australia. Personally I could not have cared less. I had just wanted to go. Army Headquarters in Canberra held no interest for me and the boredom of public service life had been getting me down. I longed for the Malaysia I loved — its warm climate and people — and a new challenge in my army career.

The appointment was with LATEDA (Sekolah Latehan Tentera Darat), literally translated — 'School of Training of the Land Army'. LATEDA was located about five kilometres south of Port Dickson on the west coast of the Malaysian Peninsula. I became an instructor on the staff duties wing (Chawangan Turgus Turus) — the forerunner of the present Malaysian Army Command and General Staff College.

Life at LATEDA was very pleasant indeed. I liked the work, loved the people and revelled in the hot tropical climate.

Initially, I had great trouble in securing suitable accommodation but was finally given approval to rent an old two-storeyed colonial-style wood and masonry house at Port Dickson — the only suitable accommodation available near the college. It was called 'Beaumaris Bungalow' and it stood in very large grounds surrounded by a chain-wire fence with a beach-frontage overlooking the Malacca Straits. There were old empty mansions either side of it — week-end villas, used a few times a year by their owners, rich Chinese 'Towkays' from Kuala Lumpur.

There was a lot of waste space at 'Beaumaris Bungalow', and the building was far from secure. Access from the house to the beach was through a locked gate in the high, vine-covered fence. From the main road you entered through an overgrown rubber plantation then a gate at the rear of the large grounds. A garage stood just inside the gate and both were out of sight on higher ground, some eighty metres up the driveway from the house.

I gradually got to know some of the British expatriates, most of whom had taken Malaysian citizenship. One was old 'Perky' Perkins, a wealthy bachelor who lived in a large house he had built on the heights of Cape Richado overlooking the Malacca Straits.

'Perky' told me one day the Russian Ambassador from Singapore had asked to buy his house on Cape Richado. The ambassador had evidently told 'Perky' that the Soviet Government wanted it as a recreation resort for the staff of the Soviet embassies in both Kuala Lumpur and Singapore. The house overlooked the deep water channel of the Malacca Straits which passes below the lighthouse and cliffs of Cape Richado. 'Perky' observed that had the Russians managed to get hold of his house, they could have observed the decks of the ships of the United States Sixth Fleet, as they passed to or from the Pacific and Indian Oceans. In addition, the Russians could have used sophisticated monitoring equipment and thus possibly eavesdroped on the American naval radio transmissions.

'Perky' had been well aware at that time of the Russian policy of staffing all overseas establishments only with Russians in order to retain total security. Had the Russians bought the house it would have been almost impossible for the Malaysian authorities to find out just what activities were taking place there. 'Perky' refused the Soviet Ambassador's offer.

Some months later an unusual incident occurred at Beaumaris Bungalow. It was a Sunday, and I had given the day off to both Mokhtar my part-time gardener and Fedila my housekeeper. I was busy in an upstairs room marking students' exercises, when I heard a soft noise downstairs.

I ran down the steps to see two heavily-built men walking out of the house — across the verandah — down the steps — then up the driveway. One was Chinese and the other, to me, was obviously Russian.

I called to the departing men, asking them what they wanted. Initially they did not reply, so I made a more insistent request. They refused to look at me as they kept walking up my driveway. I then threatened to report their trespass to the police. Finally the Russian, still avoiding looking at me, called out with a heavy accent:

'We look for Perkin! We look for Perkin!'

I had painted 'Major Petersen, Australia' under the words 'Beaumaris Bungalow' on a sign outside the main entrance to the bungalow's large grounds. They couldn't have missed seeing it and would have known that an Australian major lived there. Their ambassador from Singapore certainly knew where old Mr Perkins lived. To say they were looking for his residence was just an outright lie.

As the pair disappeared towards the main entrance, I grabbed a shirt. (Driving without a shirt in Malaysia was then an offence.) I wanted to follow them and properly identify them. I knew that Russians from both their Singapore and Kuala Lumpur Embassies stayed at one or another of two motels at Port Dickson — the Si Rusa Inn or the Pantai Motel. I would check both places.

They hadn't stayed at the Si Rusa Inn, but the Pantai Motel confirmed they had just checked out. The Russian had given his address as care of the Soviet Embassy in Singapore.

I reported the incident to the Malaysian Police Special

Branch. They suggested my visitors might have bugged my house. When they offered to check Beaumaris Bungalow, I readily accepted. They later told me they had found nothing. But I knew I had to be careful of what I said in the house in future.

That was the first strange incident at Beaumaris Bungalow. The second was far more disturbing.

*   *   *

In early April 1975, the Communist terrorists had simultaneously fired rockets into five Malaysian military camps. Two of the camps, Siginting and Sabatang Karah, were quite close to Beaumaris Bungalow. The previous week, the Malaysian Army had suffered twelve dead, and more than thirty wounded, by Communist terrorist mines and booby traps, smuggled into Malaysia through Thailand from Vietnam.

At 9.20 in the evening on Friday 11 April 1975, when I was alone in Beaumaris Bungalow, the phone rang. A voice with a slightly Indian accent asked if I was Major Petersen. The caller then said:

'Would you wait a moment please? Haji Ariff from Tanah Merah would like to speak with you.'

The English of the next speaker was so good that I could not identify the accent. His voice was soft yet firm as he said:

'Major Petersen, I'm calling you because you can help us.'

I told my caller I was having difficulty hearing him and asked him to repeat his statement. He did so, adding the words:

'...We are prepared to pay you for your help — twenty thousand dollars for the information you can provide.'

I was astounded. I asked him to repeat his name.

'Never mind that,' he said, even more firmly. 'We want you to help us and we will pay you handsomely.'

'What sort of information do you want?' I asked.

'Military information,' he replied.

I laughed and said, 'I'm an army officer. Surely you don't seriously expect me to give you any military information!'

He said, his voice very hard:

'If you provide the information we want, you will receive twenty thousand dollars in cash. If you don't, then you will die.'

I felt a tingling running up my spine.

'Who *are* you?' I asked, already half-knowing.

'Our people were responsible for the rocket attacks on the Malaysian Army bases and the recent successes against the security forces near the Thai border,' the voice said. 'Major Petersen, we have been watching you for some time. Our men have photographs of you and we know your car. We know all about you and your movements. We know that you are alone in your house this week-end.' Then he added, speaking more firmly than ever, 'Even now, we are watching your house.'

My telephone was on the upstairs open verandah and, in case I was indeed under observation, I slid off the chair and lay on the floor for safety. I did not like the thought of being watched from the darkness outside. Initially I had thought this highly melodramatic call was a hoax, but now I was beginning to take it more seriously. Perspiration dampened the palms of my hands.

I asked him what sort of military information he wanted.

'We want details of the security patrols and ambushes around the Port Dickson Garrison, the locations of all the ammunition bunkers, and the number of troops in the garrison,' he said in a more friendly tone.

'I'm a foreign officer,' I hedged, 'I don't have access to that sort of information.'

'You can get it for us,' was the reply.

He wanted the information by the following afternoon — Saturday 12 April 1975. I was to drive my car to the bus stop in Port Dickson at 2.00 pm and somebody would get into my car, probably a girl. That person would then guide me to the meeting place where I would receive cash in return for information. Haji Ariff again made it clear that I would die if I did not cooperate.

'Don't try to telephone the police or anyone in Port Dickson Garrison,' he said before hanging up. 'We will know if you try.'

I had to assume the house was being watched, and that I would probably be intercepted if I tried to drive through the abandoned overgrown rubber plantation to the main road. My telephone number was unlisted — yet my callers knew it.

I had to take a chance on my telephone being tapped. I had no choice but to report the conversation — hoax or not. I tried to telephone the duty personnel at the Australian High Commission in Kuala Lumpur. All were away, or at parties. The telephone answering machine at the High Commission gave me an emergency number. Nobody answered. I then tried the armed forces advisers' telephone numbers — in vain.

I eventually succeeded in contacting the wife of the Australian High Commissioner. She said she would get the message to the security officer that night. He was also attending a party and I was later told he had tried to return my telephone call a number of times, without success. I received no other telephone calls that night, and certainly none from anyone in the Australian High Commission for the remainder of that week-end.

After this frustrating saga, I decided to take things into my own hands. I telephoned a trusted and close Chinese doctor friend of mine, Major Ching Kim Lian, and in veiled speech related the telephone conversation to him. I asked him to notify the Port Dickson Garrison commander, Colonel Mohammed Ariff, and my own commandant, Colonel Victor Stevenson. Both reacted immediately. Colonel Ariff, using a scrambled telephone call, contacted the Chief Police Officer for the State of Negri Sembilan, and passed the details of the telephone call on to him.

I couldn't sleep for the rest of the night. I could hear a motor scooter patrolling the dirt tracks through the old rubber plantation until dawn. Was it the Malaysian Police Special Branch already on the job, watching my isolated house? As I found out the following day, that guess was wrong.

The following morning I drove to the Port Dickson Garrison. *En route*, I kept checking my car's rear vision mirror to see if I was being followed. I went with Colonel Stevenson to see Colonel Mohammed Ariff. Colonel Ariff told me that the state's chief police officer, Superintendent Nicholas, would like me to keep the meeting with the terrorists. Did I want a pistol for my personal protection? I have always believed that to be armed in the sort of situation when you are well outnumbered is inviting trouble — possibly worse. I declined the weapon.

My contact for my briefing was to be in the Port Dickson Club at 1.30 pm that Saturday afternoon. I walked up to the bar, greeting an Indian acquaintance as I did so. He said, 'Hello Barry, let me buy you a beer.'

'No, thank you,' I replied, 'I'm waiting for someone.'

'Yes, me. You're here to meet me,' my companion said. I had never realized he was a senior officer in the police special branch. We both broke up with laughter.

The briefing, held over a couple of beers, involved a small group of assorted races. One member was a grubby-looking taxi driver. I had noticed his battered old taxi parked outside the Port Dickson Club — a very unusual sight. The car park was exclusively for members and their guests and taxis only delivered or collected people under the awning at the main entrance.

I was to drive into Port Dickson proper to the appointed rendezvous, and park opposite the taxi stand. The taxi driver would position his car close to me. My Indian contact would play the part of an impatient passenger, sitting in the front seat of the old taxi, facing me in my parked car. We could watch each other's signals.

I was told to roll under my car should shooting commence at any stage, and I was to stay there until it was over. My car was relatively new and I feared for it, envisioning bullet holes in the powder-blue, gleaming bodywork.

I was told that more than sixty special branch agents had been mobilized for that operation, yet I could not identify more than five. My Indian acquaintance obviously held a fairly senior appointment, and he told me that Superintendent Nicholas had even had some men recalled from their leave and week-end stand-down to take part in the operation. Until I saw the seriousness of the special branch operation, I thought the whole thing might still have been a joke.

It was almost 2.00 pm and my contact said, 'Well Barry, you'd better get going if you're going to be on time.' The small group was still half-way through their drinks.

'Hey, I hope that you're going to keep me under observation the whole time,' I anxiously requested.

'Our agents will be watching you all the time,' I was assured.

As I left the Port Dickson Club, they still appeared to be enjoying their drinks at the table. I wasn't too sure I had done the right thing by agreeing to go through with the meeting. Maybe those special branch agents were less interested in me than I had thought.

Worried, I drove towards Port Dickson township, frequently glancing in my car's rear-vision mirror, hoping in vain for a glimpse of the battered taxi following my car. As I slowly pulled into the prearranged parking position, I looked across at the taxi stand. My special branch taxi was already in position with my Indian acquaintance sitting in the front seat, looking at me. They must have been right behind me but out of sight, and taken the short cut to the taxi stand.

We waited and waited, frequently exchanging glances. All to no avail and after some time, the trap was abandoned. During our subsequent debrief, again at an isolated table in the Port Dickson Club, I was told the first meeting arranged by the Communist terrorist organization was probably to test my credibility. From now on, all telephone calls to Beaumaris Bungalow would be monitored and constant surveillance would be maintained on me and the house.

However, despite these precautions, Colonels Ariff and Stevenson were still anxious. The last thing they wanted was the murder of an Australian officer on loan to their army. It would display a lack of ability to protect foreign nationals. In any case, I only had another few weeks left at the Port Dickson Garrison before leaving for Australia. Colonel

Stevenson suggested it might be safer for me to move out of the Port Dickson area as soon as possible.

Until I did, I had some rather fit looking young men camping on the beach in front of Beaumaris Bungalow. It was very obvious that the Malaysian Police Special Branch wanted me to leave Malaysia alive.

* * *

Despite these alarms, life in Malaysia was good. My general health was excellent, with a distinct absence of osteoarthritis. The warm weather of tropics, rain or shine, clearly suited my health and arthritic condition.

I decided to reveal my physical limitations to the military secretary at Australian Army Headquarters in Canberra. He was the officer responsible for officer career planning and future postings. I had been keeping my health problems to myself rather than jeopardize my army career. I finally accepted the fact I could never again serve in the cold climates of Australia, without becoming an arthritic cripple.

I wrote to the military secretary revealing my deteriorating physical disability and requested a posting to Queensland on my return to Australia, in May 1975. With some consideration, he posted me as a lientenant-colonel to the headquarters of the 1st Military District (Queensland) at Victoria Barracks, Brisbane. I was very pleased with that.

* * *

In April 1975 the Communist forces were finally taking over in South Vietnam. The central highlands and Ban-Me-Thuot fell. In Cambodia, the Communist Khmer Rouge had besieged Phnom Penh. On 12 April, the American Embassy was evacuated by American Marine Corps helicopters and, on 17 April 1975, the Khmer Rouge entered Phnom Penh. The selective genocide in Cambodia commenced as the Khmer Rouge moved the total population out of the city.

On 30 April 1975, the city of Saigon fell to the North Vietnamese. In Malaysia that night, I wept. It was as if I had lost part of my life. A people who had become dear to me during previous years were, in a sense, lost. Until Saigon fell, the impact of the fall of Ban-Me-Thuot didn't really hit me. I felt so helpless, unable to save the Montagnard who had been so close and loyal to me, and those Vietnamese who had left North Vietnam in 1954 because they did not want to live under a Communist government. With the fall of Saigon there was no longer any choice.

My heart ached.

A little later, after a few days in Kuala Lumpur and a few more in Singapore, I left by air for Brisbane, Australia — a very sad man.

19

More of the Montagnard

For years after I had left Vietnam up until the fall of South Vietnam, I had kept up correspondence with my close Montagnard friends in the highlands. And I was kept abreast of later developments by refugees and reports.

After my removal from the highlands in August 1965, members of the Truong Son Force began to desert to the FULRO movement in Cambodia — soon to be called Kampuchea. Jack Benefield's brief day visits to Ban-Me-Thuot rendered him ineffective. The Vietnamese authorities nominated a team of twelve of their own army officers to administer the Truong Son Force. Warrant Officer John Roy, my former Australian assistant, was withdrawn from Darlac Province in November 1965 and re-posted somewhere else in Vietnam.

At the end of 1965, four months after taking over from me, Jack Benefield was replaced by another CIA officer, Buck Ashby, who, until mid-February 1966, was also forbidden to live in Darlac Province. After this date he was based in Ban-Me-Thuot — the Vietnamese authorities considered him no threat to their own control.

In December 1965, the second FULRO revolt occurred in the highlands. The Montagnard were angry and frustrated at government procrastination in granting the promises made by General Nguyen Huu Co in 1964. No blood was shed the first day, but later thirty-five Vietnamese, both military and civilian, were killed at the Phu Thien District headquarters, north-west of Ban-Me-Thuot. General Vinh Loc, the arrogant officer I so disliked, had four of the rebel Montagnard leaders executed publicly, and fifteen others jailed.

In January 1966, because intelligence reports indicated enemy presence, the Montagnard villages of Buon Ea Mur and Buon Kram were bombed by American jet fighters. A number of villagers were killed and many wounded. A school and nineteen longhouses were destroyed and others damaged. The Montagnard began asking why the Americans were betraying them.

Early in 1966 the principally Montagnard Mobile Strike Force was formed in the highlands. Organized in companies of between 150 and 200 men, they established twenty-two camps along the Laotian and Cambodian borders. A number of Australian Army Training Team members together with American Special Forces operated with the MIKE Force companies. I was told that the use of my name among the Montagnard helped in recruiting volunteers from Darlac Province for the program.

But by the end of February 1966, the whole concept of the Truong Son Force had become a defensive one. The force was used to occupy a line of Montagnard villages around Ban-Me-Thuot — a far cry from the earlier and aggressive operations against the Viet Cong.

*   *   *

The war in South Vietnam appeared to be a political miscalculation on the part of both the North Vietnamese and America. The planners in Hanoi seem to have reasoned that the South Vietnamese could not indefinitely hold out against the Viet Cong, supported by regular North Vietnamese Army troops, both armed with a continual supply of weapons, equipment and medical supplies from Communist bloc countries — particularly the Soviet Union. They seemed to believe that the United States would restrict their involvement to support of the South Vietnamese with money, plentiful supplies, advisers, CIA special operations and airstrikes within South Vietnam and against those parts of the Ho Chi Minh Trails in Laos and Cambodia only. They reasoned quite correctly that a prolonged American effort of this nature would eventually wear down the patience of the American public. They were obviously aware that the extensive media coverage of increasing American casualties in such a prolonged conflict would increasingly anger the American voters. Their own North Vietnamese population on the other hand were unaware of the mounting casualties among their own People's Army of Vietnam conscripts.

Late in 1968 the Communists increased their attacks on principally American targets in South Vietnam. In February 1969 alone they killed 1140 US soldiers.

On 20 January 1969, Richard Milhous Nixon became the thirty-seventh president of the United States. He had inherited Lyndon Johnson's 'undeclared presidential war'. Nixon resolved to end the conflict. His plan to reduce American involvement was the American three-phase program of 'Vietnamization' — to upgrade South Vietnamese ground forces, to develop South Vietnamese combat support capabilities and to gradually reduce American presence in South Vietnam to that of a military advisory mission.

In June 1969, the Communists announced the creation of the Provisional Revolutionary Government in South Vietnam — an ostensibly nationalist government-in-waiting. It was quickly recognized by fifteen Communist-bloc nations and allies as the legitimate government of South Vietnam. North Vietnam improved its army and its logistic support with massive assistance from the Soviet Union.

Vietnamization left the South Vietnamese in no doubt that American and other allied troops would be withdrawn from their country. During 1969, Nixon announced US troop withdrawals of 25 000 in June, another 25 000 in September and a further 50 000 in December 1969, and, in line with the American troop withdrawals, her allies, including Australia, reduced their combat troop commitment. Allied troop withdrawals clearly appeased the protestors at home. The South

Vietnamese were to be left to fend for themselves against an increasingly strong North Vietnamese army.

In an article which appeared in the Ho Chi Minh City newspaper *Saigon Gia Phong* in 1982, the CIA is accused of attempting in 1974 and 1975 to arm and prepare the Montagnard forces as a resistance group in the highlands. The CIA were apparently carrying on what I had initiated with the Truong Son Force ten years before. Perhaps they left it a bit late to act on my contingency plan.

At 2 am on Monday 10 March 1975, the Communist People's Army of Vietnam (the North Vietnamese Army) began their attack on Ban-Me-Thuot and the town fell to them on Wednesday 12 March.

*　　*　　*

As the highlands fell to the advancing North Vietnamese Army, Ban-Me-Thuot was evacuated by the South Vietnamese administration and the armed forces. They retreated east along Highway 21 towards the coast. The North Vietnamese General Trin Dung wrote in his book *Great Spring*: 'We annihilated them as they fled'. Of the estimated 250 000 escaping from the highlands, only about a third made it to the coast. The South Vietnamese were also harassed by bands of Montagnard, who attacked them in order to capture their weapons and other equipment. The Montagnard had nowhere to go. The mountains were their home and they would continue to fight for them.

By early 1976, it was evident that any autonomy the Viet Cong and the North Vietnamese had offered the Montagnard in the event of a Communist takeover was merely a ploy to win their support against the South Vietnamese Government. In June 1975, the Ministry for the Development of Ethnic Minorities, established under the South Vietnamese Government, was abolished under the new Communist regime, and the leaders told to return to their homes in the highlands. As each returned to their own area they were taken into custody and sent to 're-education' camps. The minister himself, Nay Luett, was sent to Dam San camp, my old Truong Son base which the Communists had turned into a concentration camp for selected detainees. There, he was held in solitary confinement until his family were told he had committed suicide.

Of those who were close to me in those early days, I have learned something from my friend Jut, now living in the USA and the recipient of smuggled letters from friends in Vietnam and news from refugees. Some died fighting the North Vietnamese. Some are held prisoner still — Y-Tin, one of our interpreters, has been a prisoner in a 're-education' camp near Hanoi for twelve years. H'Pam and her family are still alive. Her husband was imprisoned for 're-education' for a short period. They joined the Communist Party in order to survive.

During the years following the fall of South Vietnam, resistance groups continued to flourish. One of these is reported to be in the delta region of the country. The other, and more influential one, was in the highlands. It was, and maybe still is, the Montagnard-supported Front for the Liberation of the High Plateau (FLHP). It is the successor of the FULRO movement and is still often referred to by this name. Many former members of the Truong Son Force were members of it. At one time it was reported to number 20 000 armed Dega. ('Dega' means 'sons of the mountains' and refers to the Montagnard of the central highlands of Vietnam, eastern Kampuchea and southern Laos.) In November 1979, one of my former offsiders, Y-Ghok Nie Krieng, was promoted to the rank of brigadier-general and reported to be appointed prime minister of the FLHP. Officials of the present Vietnamese Government still refer to the FLHP as 'the FULRO bandits'.

Initially, the FLHP had had some success in its operations against the Communist SRVN forces in the highlands. A refugee, Thien Quang, stated that in April 1978 FLHP units occupied the highland town of Cheo Reo and later clashed with Communist units including the SRVN Third Army Division in the area south of Ban-Me-Thuot. Surprisingly, they are also reported to have collaborated with the Communist Khmer Rouge in their fight against the Communist People's Army of Vietnam forces occupying Kampuchea. This latter information was provided by another refugee, Ieng Sary, a

Khmer Rouge leader, when he was interviewed in 1979 by a journalist for the *Far Eastern Economic Review*. He said that during February and March 1979, the FLHP killed some two hundred SRVN troops in the Ban-Me-Thuot, Pleiku and Kontum areas. The clandestine radio station 'The Voice of Democratic Kampuchea' described FLHP attacks against SRVN government posts and convoys in Lam Dong, Dac Lac (formerly Darlac and Quang Duc) and Gia Lai-Cong Tum (formerly Kontum, Pleiku, Phu Bon and west Binh Dinh) provinces during the 1979–1980 period. The sites of these actions were pinpointed and there were claims of many Communist troops 'put out of action' and the capture of numerous weapons. On 18 October 1980, John Burgess in his article 'Right-Wing Rebels Aided by China Worry Laotians, Vietnamese' in the *Washington Post* described Chinese military aid — 'with Chinese weapons also flowing to Khmer Rouge and Khmer Serei forces fighting the Vietnamese in Kampuchea, and probably to anti-Communist Montagnard insurgents in Vietnam's central highlands as well, Peking appears to be nurturing in all three countries of Indochina a front against domination by Hanoi'.

However, in recent years, the FLHP has suffered severe setbacks, as the present Socialist Republic of Vietnam attempts to repress them.

According to a 1982 *Saigon Gia Phong* newspaper article, in August 1980 secret agents of the present Vietnamese government trapped some of the key officials of the resistance FLHP, including its deputy prime minister, Ya Duk. They used the blue-headed, foreign-made letter paper of the Bac Ai organization (the Catholic Caritas charity organization) to trap the FLHP leaders. A letter, typed in French and smuggled to the FLHP, offered to put the FLHP in contact with friendly ASEAN and Western governments, enabling them to gain support for the Dega resistance movement. At four o'clock on the morning of 13 August 1980, SRVN secret agents trapped ten FLHP officials south of the town of Duc Trong with the first forged letter. Interrogations of the captives followed, resulting in further forged letters, signatures, and photographs taken of a 'happy' Ya Duk and other FLHP officials on the beach and in hotels in Danang. Using double agents, these forgeries were then sent into the FLHP jungle bases to dupe then trap more FLHP officials. These skilful SRVN operations succeeded in depleting the Montagnard resistance movement of much of its command structure. The report does not say what happened to the FLHP captives. I think it is likely they are at best in prison, if not already executed.

The same article also tells that early in 1978 the Chinese Communist Government sent one of their secret intelligence agents, who introduced himself as Lieutenant-Colonel Ba Don, to establish contact with the Montagnard FLHP. Colonel Ba Don is reported to have been about fifty at the time, and able to speak Vietnamese with a Cantonese accent. In March 1978 he is reported to have met Ya Duk near Tin waterfall behind the palace in Dalat. He is said to have advised the Montagnard FULRO (FLHP) to move their headquarters into north-east Kampuchea, then still controlled by the Pol Pot regime. The Chinese would then provide Chinese military attachés and counsellors to the FLHP headquarters. He also apparently said the Chinese Government offered to set up a radio broadcasting station for the FLHP in north-east Kampuchea. He further suggested the Montagnard provide suitable young men and women for training in southern China.

The alignment of the present Vietnamese Government with the Soviet Union gives added credence to this relatively recent report. The development of the Russian Naval Pacific Fleet base at Cam Ranh Bay in Vietnam could only have agitated Beijing.

* * *

A 'debrief' in 1986 of a refugee and former member of the FLHP, Kra Jan Mai, revealed a Vietnamese massacre of young rebels in Darlac Province and east Kampuchea in 1981. This was reported in *Asiaweek*, of 7 December 1986. On 18 March 1981, fifteen hundred young members of the guerilla FLHP were spotted by the Vietnamese, west of Ban-Me-Thuot. The present Vietnamese Army relentlessly followed them and, during the period 20 March to about 23 April 1981, near the Kampuchean village of Orlov, just across the border from Darlac Province, used infantry, tanks, heavy artillery, aircraft and heliborne troops to systematically slaughter them. Kra Jan Mai, one of the few survivors, who was then just fifteen years of age, said:

'We were just running and dying, running and dying.'

The SRVN Armed Forces didn't take prisoners.

On 23 January 1980, the clandestine 'Voice of Democratic Kampuchea' broadcast a Dega-FULRO (FLHP) letter. It accused the Hanoi regime of 'massacre against our people behind closed doors' and it claimed that since 1975, some 150 000 Montagnard highlanders had perished and many had been jailed. Young highlanders were being pressed into military service 'to fight in Kampuchea, Laos and at the Sino-Vietnamese border'. It continued: 'Villagers are subject to corvée labour for construction of military roads into Cambodia and Laos, for construction of military installations and to act as bearers for transporting military goods'. The letter ended with an appeal to all in the world 'who cherish freedom and justice' for help. It was signed, 'Anuk N'Gram, Prime Minister of the Dega-FULRO Government'.

*   *   *

Life for the remaining Montagnard in the Socialist Republic of Vietnam, is undoubtedly tenuous. Escape across Kampuchea to Thailand is perhaps even more risky because of the continued existence of Communist Khmer Rouge forces and of Vietnamese Army patrols from the Socialist Republic of Vietnam operating in Kampuchea. But one group at least made a successful attempt.

In 1985, Brigadier Y-Ghok Nie and other FLHP leaders led two hundred Dega FLHP members from the highlands of Vietnam across Kampuchea and into Prachin Buri Province in eastern Thailand. They aimed to seek support from the West for their resistance against the Socialist Republic of Vietnam. An Australian film crew headed by Kyle Hadley accidentally stumbled upon the refugees in a camp at Site 2, near the border with Kampuchea. (Site 2 is occasionally shelled by Vietnamese artillery from Kampuchea.)

On learning that Kyle was an Australian, Y-Ghok gave him a letter addressed to me and asked him to try to find me — which he did on his return to Australia.

I decided to try to help my friend. In order to sponsor Y-Ghok and his family into Australia, I wrote and asked him for particulars of his immediate family. I followed up with a further letter. I received no reply. I also wrote to Mr Ben M. Scheelings, the Second Secretary for Immigration in our Australian Embassy in Bangkok, seeking his help. He replied saying: 'We here understand that the Montagnards are not available for resettlement in Australia as they have been accepted by the US and will be moved there shortly'.

I again wrote to Y-Ghok after I heard that he and the others had been moved to a refugee holding camp in the Philippines. Again receiving no reply, I wrote to him on 21 July, sending one letter direct to him, and a copy of it to him through my old friend Y-Jut, living in the United States. To my surprise Y-Ghok received the copy I sent through Jut. It seemed as if any mail posted from Australia was being intercepted.

I began to wonder if my former employers, the CIA, were deliberately preventing me from contacting Brigadier Y-Ghok Nie. I knew they had agents working in the refugee camps, so they were certainly in the position to block my mail — a, they had done in Saigon, back in 1965. If such interception did occur, I can only assume it was designed to prevent my learning any new intelligence on the resistance movement in the SRVN — information which could be provided by my close friend, Y-Ghok.

On 24 November 1986, the group, including Y-Ghok Nie, arrived in North Carolina in the USA. I had failed in my attempt to get them to Australia. The American Army Special Warfare School is at Fort Bragg, close to where Y-Ghok and the other Montagnard refugees have been resettled. Langley, the headquarters of the CIA, is located in the State of Virginia, just north. Perhaps this information is quite coincidental —

or perhaps their sponsors are retired Special Forces members, living in North Carolina.

In a letter I received from Y-Nen Nie, one of the two hundred Dega led by Y-Ghok when they escaped from Vietnam, he spoke of continuing Dega resistance movement against the present government of the Socialist Republic of Vietnam.

His letter continued: '...However, you are well-known leader toward Dega people, you are father of Dega people, for your name and body are always imagine to Dega people on highland of Dega'.

Although I have settled down to semi-retirement, it should be clear to the reader that my experience with the Montagnard of South Vietnam left an indelible mark on my life. Some day, I would like to write more of the tribulations of those very fine, brave, almost forgotten people.

20 Of Jut and Other Matters

I have not discussed the fate of Y-Jut Buon To, my interpreter, friend and 'younger brother' who had played such an important role during my first memorable stay in Vietnam. Jut had been my constant companion during those first two years in the highlands. He had been my principal helper, guide and trusted adviser in so many matters relating to the Montagnard. I came to rely on him greatly and could not have achieved nearly as much without him.

I had not seen Jut since my departure from Ban-Me-Thuot in 1965, although I had received information about his career. He had married Rec, the daughter of Y-Djap Kpor, the commander of the first hundred men I had inherited from the National Police in my early days in Ban-Me-Thuot. Soon after my departure from Ban-Me-Thuot, Jut had left the highlands to undertake further education in Saigon. He had done well in the following years and had graduated from Saigon University. He and Rec had raised a family and subsequently he was appointed Superintendent to the Directorate of Ethnic Minorities in the Second Military Region. In this position, he was to help many of the Montagnard attend universities and gain degrees themselves.

It was mid-1975 — almost ten years after the completion of my first Vietnam tour — that I received a letter from Jut. I was in Queensland — a lieutenant-colonel and head of the

Personnel Branch of the Australian Army's First Military District Headquarters in Brisbane. I was still plagued with the problems of osteoarthritis and was even then contemplating an early retirement from the Army.

Jut's letter had been posted in the United States thirteen weeks before, and had been redirected by the Australian High Commission in Kuala Lumpur from Malaysia where I had recently completed a two-year posting. He wrote of his escape from South Vietnam early in 1975. He had been stationed at Nha Trang on the coast of South Vietnam where the Second Military Region had been headquartered following its enforced move from Pleiku in the central highlands because of the encroachment of the Communist North. Jut and his young family had come under intense rocket, mortar and artillery fire at Nha Trang — hundreds of civilians had been killed at that time. On 1 April 1975, Jut and his family had been flown out of Nha Trang by the CIA to Saigon. Just before the fall of the capital, Mr David Devin of the CIA had arranged for the evacuation of the family via the Philippines to the United States.

Jut was one of the lucky ones — he had escaped to America, but he said that he was not happy there. He appealed to me for help to have himself and his family join me in Australia.

So I submitted an application to the Australian Department of Immigration to sponsor Jut and his young family into Australia. With the application, I included a guarantee to provide them with accommodation and to support Jut until he could gain employment.

I was rudely told by one of the peons in the department that I did not stand a chance, and that I was wasting my time. Prime Minister Gough Whitlam eventually had the final say and that petty bureaucrat was correct — a government had to fall before I succeeded.

I sought help from a number of politicians at the time, and also from Denis Warner, the well-known Australian author, foreign correspondent and journalist. I had known Denis in

South Vietnam, and he knew of my work with the Montagnard. His article on my frustrated efforts to get Jut and his family into Australia received nation-wide publicity during the October of 1975.

I found myself beseiged by newspaper journalists and television interviewers and I appeared on the evening television current affairs programs. In America, the Australian Broadcasting Corporation's New York correspondent, Ray Martin (later of '60 Minutes' and 'The Ray Martin Show') spent some days with Jut and his family in Seattle. He wrote from New York in January 1976:

'Jut continues to be an inspiration. A marvellous bloke. I can understand your long-standing affection for him. (I can add that he thinks of nothing but you... 'Barry Petersen' seems to be the solid pillar of his faith in mankind. That's a heavy personal image to live up to. I don't envy you.)'

I felt that heavy responsibility too, and was hoping to live up to it. But despite the media pressure to allow Jut and his family to enter Australia, Prime Minister Gough Whitlam was adamant. One of his private secretaries, who shall remain nameless, telephoned me and told me that Mr Whitlam had removed the power of decision from some of his ministers — among them was Senator McClelland, the Minister for Labor and Immigration.

Then, about a week after the election of the new Liberal/ National Party Government, I received a telephone call from the Department of Immigration. My sponsorship application had been approved. Their attitude had completely changed and they could not have been more helpful.

*   *   *

In order to accommodate Jut, his wife Rec and their four young children, my sister Coralie and I bought an old apartment block in Brisbane. I moved out of my army accommodation into one of the flats and Coralie and I began to renovate the others. I worked every free evening and with the help of family, friends and relatives we made them quite attractive. Brigadier Ian Murray Hunter, a retired Army officer and chairman of a number of companies, kindly offered to employ Jut on his arrival in Brisbane.

As a result of the Australia-wide publicity, donations of money, clothing and household items began arriving. We had already provided most of the furniture and the remainder of the household items for the flat. The place began to look like a branch of the Saint Vincent de Paul Society. I found myself snowed under with letters offering assistance and moral support. There were so many I was simply unable to answer them all and felt quite bad about it.

Jut and his family were to arrive from San Francisco on Sunday 7 March 1976. We all went to Eagle Farm airport to meet them. The media was there waiting to record the reunion. But we waited in vain. Jut and his family had not even boarded the aircraft in San Francisco. On the following Monday morning, I telephoned the Department of Immigration in Canberra and they checked with San Francisco. Apparently the family had been unable to travel. Rec had suffered a nervous collapse.

A French Jesuit priest expelled from Vietnam by the new Communist Government, had contacted the family in Seattle. He had told Rec some terrible news. Her father and all the remaining members of her family — even babies — had been executed by the new Vietnamese Government. Y-Djap Kpor, her father, had been a friend of mine, and also an officer of the South Vietnamese Police Sûreté.

It was a devastating blow to Rec and the young family.

The publicity generated in Australia reached the US and sympathetic Americans offered help. One couple bought a small house for them and Jut was offered a job. With American assistance flowing in to the family, new-found American friends and the security now offered to them, Jut decided to remain in America after his wife recovered rather than risk another unsettling period for his family.

Jut himself later learned of the deaths of his younger brother, Y-Phon, and of his mother. They were the last surviving members of his family. An Italian woman whose late husband had owned a coffee plantation north of Ban-Me-Thuot was in a 're-education' camp with Jut's mother. Madame Santelli had spent six months as a prisoner of the new Communist regime — in fact until she signed over to them the deeds to her coffee plantation. She was then repatriated to Italy. From there she wrote to Jut in May 1976 to tell him that his mother had been executed by a firing squad.

Jut's children would never have grandparents nor uncles nor aunts. Those who managed to survive the war had now been killed.

* * *

I was very disappointed about Jut's decision to remain in the United States, but quite understood the situation. I had money and a house full of household items and clothing to dispose of. I resolved to help other refugees — the 'boat people' — from South Vietnam.

I contacted religious orders and the Migrant Hostel at Wacol, west of Brisbane. The Vietnamese refugees at Wacol were eager to get out of hostel and to become independent and self-supporting. Many were prepared to work for a week or two without pay to prove their worth to a prospective employer. I know that the majority arrived in Australia with nothing but what they stood up in.

* * *

I found most of the Vietnamese refugees to be intensely anti-Communist. They hated what the Communists had done to them and their country. And they told me the identity of paid Vietnamese left-wing or Communist agents carrying out intelligence operations among the refugee community. Some of these agents were students at Australian education institutions when South Vietnam fell to the Communist North. They were apparently paid a retainer of one hundred Australian dollars a week by the Embassy of the Socialist Republic of Vietnam in Canberra. I passed these reports on to our Australian Security Intelligence Organization.

* * *

The South Vietnamese refugees also told me of horrific punishments carried out by the new government.

A former South Vietnamese policeman received his 'political re-education' sharing a 200-litre drum with a colleague. Even though the Vietnamese are small, it is hard to imagine how two men could be squeezed like sardines into a drum approximately 87 centimetres high and 57 wide, with a lid and weight placed on top. It was impossible either to sit or to stand and cramps quickly resulted. They were allowed out for twenty minutes each day to eat their small ration of rice and to defecate. The normal sentence in these conditions was eighteen months.

One ex-policeman told me that after such treatment it took him three months to learn to stand up and to walk properly again before he could escape from Vietnam.

A private soldier of the South Vietnamese Army's Special Forces was automatically sentenced to three months imprisonment in a Conex (a metal container used in shipping cargo). One Conex was the prison for thirty soldiers. A Conex normally has no ventilation and certainly no windows. Crammed like sardines they were unable to sit or to lie down, and they also were only let out for twenty minutes each day.

None of the ex-police or army refugees could tell me what happened to their officers. They were simply taken away and not seen again. All intelligence officers or agents were allegedly excuted with all their families down to the smallest infant.

* * *

While still stationed in Brisbane, I was also the president of the local Australian Army Training Team Vietnam Association. I felt strongly that as many of the South Vietnamese refugees fought alongside us in South Vietnam and as they were now becoming Australian citizens, they should march with us on Anzac Day. After all, I have often seen Frenchmen, veterans of Indo-China and Algeria, marching on Anzac Day parades and they have not fought alongside Australian nor New Zealand troops since the Second World War.

So in April 1976, I suggested to my fellow AATTV Association Members that the Vietnamese march with us and they agreed. The RSL in Brisbane disagreed. I 'leaked' the plan to the media which immediately sprang to our support. On Anzac Day 1976, South Vietnamese ex-servicemen marched alongside the AATTV Contingent in Brisbane, Queensland. It is now quite commonplace for the Vietnamese ex-servicemen to march in Anzac Day parades throughout Australia.

21   Reflections

I often reflect on the years of my first tour of duty in South Vietnam. Indeed, they are rarely out of my mind and I am constantly reminded of my experiences as I learn more and more of the fate of those mountain people. Of the tens of thousands of Vietnamese refugees who have fled the Socialist Republic of Vietnam (SRVN) since April 1975, very few have been Montagnard. For they are trapped in the highlands of Indo-China surrounded by vigilant patrolling armed forces of the SRVN who have also occupied Kampuchea to the west. The gauntlet they would run to escape is terrifying in a region where life is still considered so cheap.

I recall those early days in 1963 when Bryan Mills first took me into that exotic part of the world. I was a keen, fit, young army captain looking forward to the adventure and challenges which lay ahead. Little did I know what I would face. My only previous experience outside Australia had been my two years in operations against the Communist terrorists in Malaya. Like the highlands of Vietnam it was a country of deep jungle, high mountains and fast-flowing rivers and streams with their rapids and waterfalls. But we were operating among the primitive Orang Asli of West Malaysia, a race of small stature — almost pigmies — armed with blow-pipes with poisoned darts. I think I expected a similar situation among the Montagnard. Instead, I found a very proud, independent, intelligent and resourceful race of people, quite un-like the Orang Asli of Malaysia or even the Vietnamese themselves.

When Bryan Mills flew out of Ban-Me-Thuot that second day, I had felt alone. Where would I start? What was really expected of me by my CIA masters?

I found many answers during the next two years. I faced an assortment of situations — the overkill techniques and exces-ses of our American allies; the intrigue and tension of politics and espionage; the betrayals; the poisonings and combat with our Truong Son Force. I grew to understand and often share the aspirations, the joy, the disappointments and the heart-break of the people — Vietnamese as well as Montagnard. They became a real part of my life and I probably became a small part of theirs. I never thought of returning home to Australia. After the first year passed, I was often asked when I would be leaving them to return to my country. I honestly didn't know, nor did it concern me. I was deriving complete satisfaction living and working with those people.

I look back on that experience and the subsequent occurr-ences as a profound lesson — one I frequently wish I could share with others. We went into South Vietnam to help that nation — despite her faults — to retain her independence. To some outside observers, particularly those furthest from the problem, the occasional excesses (particularly those of our American allies) were frequently misconstrued. There were some foreigners, as my story relates, who tried to influence the leaders of that nation. Most of us however, did our utmost to stay out of internal, local politics. We could see the instances of corruption, but which society is devoid of those?

On reflection, I still believe that we should have been a presence in South Vietnam, but I don't believe that the allied powers should have sent combat troops into that country.

When he set about reorganizing the South Vietnamese Army in 1956, US Army General Samuel T. Williams did so along conventional army lines. He expected South Vietnam to face a conventional conflict with North Vietnam, as South Korea had done in its war with the North and Communist

China. This sort of army was unsuitable to eradicate the Communist insurgents. Had North Vietnam then entered South Vietnam with conventional forces, South-East Asian Treaty Organization forces could have legally participated. And had we increased our advisory effort rather than committing troops to the field, although it would have placed a strain on our respective regular volunteer armies, it might have attracted less adverse public criticism at home. South Vietnam needed outside assistance to resist a determined insurgent. We — Australia, New Zealand, America, Thailand, the Philippines and Korea — allowed ourselves to be convinced by the American Joint Chiefs of Staff that conventional combat troops would solve the problem. When this failed, then the next solution was to increase the number of combat troops. The Communists knew that this would ultimately become an unpopular political decision in our own countries.

I wish I'd had the benefit of hindsight when asked back in 1965 what I thought of Australia sending combat units to South Vietnam. An adverse reply from me might have been noted — although of course the decision had already been made. America wanted the support of allied combat troops in South Vietnam and it was politically expedient for our leaders to comply at that time.

South Vietnam did not fall to the Communist North because America and her allied troops lost the war on the battlefield. After all, there were none of those combat troops left in South Vietnam in 1975. South Vietnam fell because our respective political leaders had to withdraw our heavy military commitment to avoid political censure.

The Americans participated in the war in South Vietnam on a massive scale. And our political leaders assured the South Vietnamese that we would support them until the insurgency was defeated. When it looked like costing votes at home we abandoned our crusade, thereby leaving the South Vietnamese at the mercy of a greatly enlarged and strengthened North Vietnamese Army, heavily supported by the Soviet Union which now has its largest naval base in the Pacific Ocean in Cam Ranh Bay (the previous us naval base).

I was serving with the Malaysian Army at the time South Vietnam fell to the Communist North and I know that our credibility and reliability has been seriously damaged in the eyes of other South-East Asian nations whose future sovereignty might be threatened.

I believe it is naïve to say that the occupation of another sovereign nation is not our concern. If every nation adopted that attitude, then we might all eventually come under the domination of a more aggressive and powerful nation. If a stand is taken, then it should be maintained at all costs. The position which we abandoned in South Vietnam has in part cost us our reputation for reliability. And it has cost the people of South Vietnam their freedom.

*　*　*

Postscript

In late August and early September 1987, I was able to visit Hanoi, capital of the Socialist Republic of Vietnam (SRVN). I found a desperately poor nation, in need of humanitarian and economic assistance as the result of lengthy wars — against the Japanese in the 1940s, the French in the 1950s and more recently, the Americans and allied forces.

Despite their plight, the people (including soldiers and police) were cheerful, outgoing and friendly. The old hardline leaders we once knew had been replaced by younger, progressive and more moderate men and women who seemed eager to forget the conflicts of the past.

While I was there, a very lengthy Central Committee meeting took place. I believe that out of that meeting came the announcement that the SRVN were to release over 6000 political detainees held since the war in 're-education' camps. Y-Tin Hwing and other of my Montagnard friends were among those prisoners. The SRVN invited a group of Australians, including myself, to witness the release.

It is my sincere hope that this gesture will lead to a reconciliation between the Vietnamese and those still-disident minorities, including the Montagnard, who have suffered so much in the past.

Index